Second Workshop on Human-Informed Translation and Interpreting Technology (HiT-IT 2019)

Varna, Bulgaria
5-6 September 2019

ISBN: 978-1-7138-0299-0

Printed from e-media with permission by:

Curran Associates, Inc.
57 Morehouse Lane
Red Hook, NY 12571

Some format issues inherent in the e-media version may also appear in this print version.

Copyright© (2019) by the Association for Computational Linguistics
All rights reserved.

Printed with permission by Curran Associates, Inc. (2020)

For permission requests, please contact the Association for Computational Linguistics
at the address below.

Association for Computational Linguistics
209 N. Eighth Street
Stroudsburg, Pennsylvania 18360

Phone: 1-570-476-8006
Fax: 1-570-476-0860

acl@aclweb.org

Additional copies of this publication are available from:

Curran Associates, Inc.
57 Morehouse Lane
Red Hook, NY 12571 USA
Phone: 845-758-0400
Fax: 845-758-2633
Email: curran@proceedings.com
Web: www.proceedings.com

Second Workshop on Human-Informed Translation and Interpreting Technology (HiT-IT 2019)

Proceedings of the Workshop

September 5 - 6,
2019 Varna, Bulgaria

Proceedings of the Second Workshop
Human-Informed Translation and Interpreting Technology
associated with RANLP 2019
Varna, Bulgaria
5 - 6 September 2019
ISSN 2683-0078

Designed and Printed by INCOMA Ltd.
Shoumen, BULGARIA

Preface

The Second Workshop on Human-Informed Translation and Interpreting Technology (HiT-IT 2019) took place in Varna, Bulgaria and spanned over two days (5-6 September 2019), as a post-RANLP 2019 conference event. This is a continuation of the one-day workshop HiT-IT 2017 (`http://rgcl.wlv.ac.uk/hit-it/`) organised in conjunction with RANLP 2017. Both workshops proved very popular attracting the highest number of participants across all the RANLP workshops organised in their respective years.

In addition to academic submissions, this year's workshop also welcomed submissions from industry (translation agencies or companies developing translation and interpreting technologies) and practitioners (translators and interpreters). This was to reflect the fact that the HiT-IT events seek to act as a meeting points for researchers working in translation and interpreting technologies, practicing technology-minded translators and interpreters, companies and freelancers providing services in translation and interpreting as well as companies developing tools for translators and interpreters, including researchers and developers of machine translation engines.

Translation Technology (TT) has the core objectives of speeding up and easing the translation process, and of assisting human translators. The emerging field of Interpreting Technology also seeks to support the work of interpreters. TT relies heavily on methods developed in the field of Natural Language Processing (NLP) and Computational Linguistics (CL). Typical examples are Computer-Assisted Translation (CAT) tools, electronic dictionaries, concordancers, spell-checkers, terminological databases, terminology extraction tools, translation memories, partial machine translation of template documents, speech recognition systems for automatic subtitling, to name just a few. However, quite often these tools do not address the actual needs and quality required by translation and interpreting professionals.

Natural Language Processing and Machine Translation (MT) make use of the knowledge and expertise of professional translators and interpreters in order to build and improve models for automatic translation or for developing more advanced CAT tools. This includes using parallel aligned human translations and speech interpretation corpora for machine learning, human evaluation of machine translation outputs and human annotations, or by trying to learn from humans, in order to fine-tune their algorithms. However, NLP and MT researchers rarely meet in person with professional translators and interpreters to learn from their expertise and points of view.

By organising HiT-IT, we aimed to provide a discussion forum for professionals working on or with translation and interpreting technologies (including machine translation), in order to find ways to make machine translation output closer to human quality. These discussions also focused on ensuring that CAT tools are being developed in a way that will ease and speed-up translation and interpreting practitioners' job.

This year HiT-IT 2019 featured a large Programme Committee, consisting of well-known experts coming from industry, universities, and active practitioners. The nationalities and affiliations of PC members covered almost all continents and included: Europe (Belgium, Bulgaria, Czech Republic, Denmark, France, Germany, Greece, Hungary, Ireland, Italy, Portugal, Spain, Switzerland, UK), Australia, South America (Argentina, Brazil), Asia (Hong Kong, Japan, Jordan, Qatar), Africa (South Africa).

HiT-IT 2019 attracted a variety of participants with various backgrounds, including: machine translation development specialists, practicing translators and interpreters, owners and representatives of translation agencies from Bulgaria and from overseas, developers of tools and resources for translators and interpreters (including of translation memories), researchers working on the evaluation of machine translation, and computer-assisted translation tools, including automatic translation of subtitles, researchers, applying Natural Language Processing techniques on human translation and interpreting, as well as TT students. This year HiT-IT invited submissions on theoretical ideas, practical applications, and position papers promoting new ideas, challenging the current status of the fields and proposing how to take them forward.

The topics of submissions included:

User needs:

- interpreting and translation tools: user needs and user requirements

- incorporating human knowledge into translation and interpreting technology

- what existing tools for translators (including subtitlers) and interpreters do not offer

- user requirements for electronic resources for translators and interpreters

- translation and interpreting workflows in larger organisations and the tools employed for translation and interpreting

Existing methods and resources:

- latest developments in translation and interpreting technology

- electronic resources for translators and interpreters

- annotation of corpora for translation and interpreting technology

- crowdsourcing techniques for creating resources for translation and interpreting

- latest advances in pre-editing and post-editing of machine translation

- human-informed (semi-)automatic generation of interlingual subtitles

- technology for subtitling

Evaluation:

- (human) evaluation of translation and interpreting technology

- crowdsourcing techniques for evaluating translation and interpreting

- evaluation of discourse and other linguistic phenomena in (machine) translation and interpreting

- evaluation of existing resources for translators and interpreters

- human evaluation of neural machine translation

Other:

- position papers discussing how machine translation should be improved to incorporate the expertise of translators and interpreters

- translation and interpreting technologies' impact on the market

- comparison between human and machine translation

- changes in the translators and interpreters' professions in the new technology era especially as a result of the latest developments in Neural Machine Translation

HiT-IT 2019 featured four invited talks and one special presentation. Yves Champollion from WordFast gave two presentations: the "Rosetta Stone Decipherment" and "MT Acceptance Among Translators: Are We Nearing the Tipping Point". Dr Vilelmini Sosoni from the Ionian University, Greece, gave a talk on "Translators and Technology: Dancing a Tango Nuevo". Dr Carla Parra Escartín, the Director of Linguistic Services at Unbabel Portugal gave a talk on "The story of how academic and industrial research meet to put humans in the loop of Artificial Intelligence".

Professor Dr Ruslan Mitkov, director of the Research Institute in Information and Language Processing and Head of the Research Group in Computational Linguistics at the University of Wolverhampton, UK gave a special presentation on "The world's first Erasmus Mundus Masters programme in technology for translation and interpreting and the new generation of translators and interpreters".

The authors came from a large number of countries: Algeria, Austria, Belgium, Bulgaria, Brazil, Egypt, France, Greece, Hong Kong, Portugal, Qatar, Russia, Spain and Switzerland. The HIT-IT 2019 presentations attracted a lot of interest and generated active discussions between listeners and presenters. The discussed topics included: human and machine evaluation of machine translation; using NLP, automatic tools and techniques to study and extract meaningful patterns from interpreting, human translation, and manual post-editing of machine translation; new tools and resources for translators and interpreters; learning from practitioners in order to make speech machine translation closer to human quality; human evaluation of CAT tools, including subtitling technologies; translators and translation agencies experiences in adopting and improving the usage of CAT tools; analysis of translation technologies performance in translating wordplay.

The HiT-IT organisers would like to thank the authors for submitting their articles to the HiT-IT Workshop, the expert members of the large Programme Committee for providing exhaustive reviews, and the RANLP 2019 conference, which hosted HiT-IT 2019. We would also like to thank the other members of the organising committee: Souhila Djabri (University of Alicante, Spain), Rocío Caro (University of Wolverhampton, UK) and Encarnación Núñez (University of Malaga, Spain) for their great assistance with HIT-IT organisation.

Irina Temnikova, Constantin Orăsan, Gloria Corpas Pastor, and Ruslan Mitkov (the HIT-IT 2019 workshop chairs)

Workshop Chairs

Irina Temnikova (Bulgarian Academy of Sciences, Bulgaria)
Constantin Orasan (University of Wolverhampton, UK)
Gloria Corpas Pastor (University of Malaga, Spain)
Ruslan Mitkov (University of Wolverhampton, UK)

Members of the Organising Committee

Souhila Djabri (University of Alicante, Spain)
Rocío Caro (University of Wolverhampton, UK)
Encarnación Núñez (University of Malaga, Spain)

Program Committee:

Anja Rütten (Conference Interpreter, Member of AIIC, Germany)
Anna Zaretskaya (TransPerfect, Spain)
Bart Defrancq (Ghent University, Belgium)
Carla Parra (Unbabel, Portugal)
Claudia Angelelli (Heriot-Watt University, UK)
Claudio Bendazzoli (Università Degli Studi di Torino, Italy)
Claudio Fantinuoli (Johannes Gutenberg-Universität Mainz/Germersheim, Germany)
David Orrego-Carmona (Aston University, UK)
Dicken Minta (Televic, UK)
Dragos Ciobanu (University of Leeds, UK)
Eleanor Cornelius (University of Johannesburg, South Africa)
Eleni Zisi (EL-Translations, Greece)
Eva Dolezalova (MemSource, Czech Republic)
Federico Gaspari (ADAPT Centre, Ireland)
Filip Šanca (Memsource, Czech Republic)
Gabriela Gonzales (E-Trad, Argentina)
Haris Ghinos (ELIT Language Services, Greece)
Hendrik J. Kockaert (Hamad bin Khalifa University, Qatar)
Janice Jun Pan (Hong Kong Baptist University, Hong Kong)
Johanna Monti ("L'Orientale" University of Naples, Italy)
Joss Goldsmith (AIIC Interpreter, Geneve)
Joss Moorkens (Dublin City University, Ireland)
Juanjo Averallilo (HERMES Traducciones, Spain)
Kim Ludvigsen (Interprefy, Switzerland)
Lieve Macken (University of Ghent, Belgium)
Maja Popovic (ADAPT, DCU, Ireland)
Manuel Herrandez (Pangeanic, Spain)
Marcello Federico (Amazon, USA)
Maria Kunilovskaya (University of Wolverhampton, UK)
María Mercedes Enríquez Aranda (University of Malaga, Spain)
Maria Stambolieva (New Bulgarian University, Sofia)
Maria Stasimioti (Ionian University, Greece)
Mark Shuttleworth (Hong Kong Baptist University, Hong Kong)
Masaru Yamada (Kansai University, Japan)
Mercedes Garcia Martinez (Pangeanic, Spain)

Michael Carl (Copenhagen Business School, Denmark)
Michael Ustaszewski (Universität Innsbruck, Austria)
Mina Ilieva (Mitra Translations, Bulgaria)
Nannan Liu (The University of Hong Kong, Hong Kong)
Nieves Jiménez Carra (University of Malaga, Spain)
Omar Atari (University of Petra, Jordan)
Peter Reynolds (MemoQ, Hungary)
Pieter Demuytere (Televic, Belgium)
Pierrette Bouillon (University of Geneva, Switzerland)
Preslav Nakov (Qatar Computing Research Institute, HBKU, Qatar)
Raisa McNab (Sandberg Translation Partners Ltd, UK)
Rozane Rebechi (University Rio Grande do Sur, Brazil)
Sabrina Baldo (University of Evry Val d'Essonne, France)
Santanu Pal (Saarland University, Germany)
Sara Moze (University of Wolverhampton, UK)
Sharon O'Brien (Dublin City University, Ireland)
Sheila Castilho (ADAPT Centre, Ireland)
Silvia Bernadini (University of Bologna, Italy)
Sin-Wai Chan (Chinese University of Hong Kong, Hong Kong)
Stephen Doherty (The University of New South Wales, Australia)
Veronique Hoste (Ghent University, Belgium)
Verónica Pérez Guarnieri (Colegio de Traductores, Argentina)
Vilelmini Sosoni (Ionian University, Greece)
Yota Georgakopoulou (Athena Consultancy, Greece)
Yves Champollion (Wordfast, US/France)

Invited Speakers:

- Yves Champollion (WordFast, US/France): Talk 1: *MT Acceptance Among Translators: Are We Nearing the Tipping Point*, Talk 2: *Rosetta Stone Decipherment*

- Vilelmini Sosoni (Ionian University, Greece): *Translators and Technology: Dancing a Tango Nuevo*

- Carla Parra Escartín (Unbabel, Portugal): *The story of how academic and industrial research meet to put humans in the loop of Artificial Intelligence*

- Special presentation: Ruslan Mitkov (University of Wolverhampton, United Kingdom): *The world's first Erasmus Mundus Master's programme in technology for translation and interpreting*

Table of Contents

Research papers

Users papers

Comparison between Automatic and Human Subtitling:

A Case Study with *Game of Thrones*

Sabrina Baldo de Brébisson
University of Evry Val d'Essonne/Paris-Saclay
91000 Evry, France
sabrina.debrebisson@univ-evry.fr

Abstract

In this article, I would like to share my experiences with the software *DeepL* and the comparison analysis I have made with human subtitling offered by the DVD version of the corpus I have chosen as the topic of my study – the eight Seasons of *Game of Thrones*. The idea is to study if the version proposed by an automatic translation program could be used as a first draft for the professional subtitler. It is expected that the latter would work on the form of the subtitles, that is to say mainly on their length, in a second step.

1 Introduction

Internet research has revealed the existence of many free software applications that produce subtitles for videos including *Time Adjuster; VisualSubSync; Subtitle Workshop; Subtitle Creator; Aegisub Advanced Subtitle Editor; DivXLand Media Subtitler; WinSubMux; Subtitle Editor* and *AHD Subtitles Maker and SubEdit Player*.

These programs offer many features such as extracting files from a video, editing these files, viewing subtitles of a video, inserting subtitles into a video, synchronizing subtitles with images, and searching for existing subtitle files on the Internet. *YouTube* provides something more by the use of two tools: *Google Voice* and *Google Translate*. It offers automatic translations using automatic transcriptions (voice recognition). Also, it can provide automatic translations using human transcriptions (source scripts).

Furthermore, research on post-editing in translation is becoming more and more extensive. It focuses on the question of the quality/time ratio in the translation activity (O'Brien, 2014).

But what about interlingual subtitling, machine translation and post-editing? Why is research bringing together these three points which is almost non-existent?

It is true that the specific constraints of subtitling make it a very special form of translation. It is also referred to as "adaptation" because the adapter/subtitle translator must *adapt* to the existence of the image as well as to the space-time parameter. It is therefore not surprising that subtitling research focuses on the form of this type of translation and its polysemiotic context.

Recent decades have seen the increasing use of machine translation by professionals, the nature of whose work has gradually been transformed. In France, the very sophisticated software program *DeepL* has become a popular tool, but how effective is it when applied to the translation of subtitles with their very specific formal constraints?

In what follows, I will compare the automatic translation of subtitles for a television series with the one carried out by human translators. I will focus on the quality of an automatic translation, regardless of formal restrictions. The idea is to evaluate whether the version proposed by the automatic translation program could be used as a first draft by a subtitler. The latter would then concentrate on the formal aspects of the subtitles in a polysemiotic environment.

2 Choice of the Corpus

I have chosen as my corpus the eight Seasons of the American television series *Game of Thrones*, directed by David Benioff and Daniel Brett Weiss and broadcast on HBO from 2011 to 2019. This fantasy drama is an adaptation of the novel *A Game of Thrones,* from the fantasy series *A Song of Ice and Fire* written by the American author George R. R. Martin and published in 1996.

Temnikova, I, Orăsan, C., Corpas Pastor, G., and Mitkov, R. (eds.) (2019) *Proceedings of the 2nd Workshop on Human-Informed Translation and Interpreting Technology (HiT-IT 2019)*, Varna, Bulgaria, September 5 - 6, pages 1–10.
https://doi.org/10.26615/issn.2683-0078.2019_001

According to the 2016 edition of the Guinness Book of Records (Lexpress.fr, 2015), *Game of Thrones* is the most widely distributed series in the world, with no less than 171 countries. It holds the record for global diffusion and plot twists. Its popularity has led to a large amount of data available on the Internet, including the entire English script of the eight Seasons (more than 800,000 words) and the French subtitles from the DVDs of the eight Seasons.

The nature of the dialogues in *Game of Thrones* are interesting from a *linguistic* point of view for several reasons. First, the vocabulary is relatively extensive, rich and varied. There is frequent us of specialized words specific to the Middle Ages, which makes it possible to analyze the processing of a specialized glossary (rather than a general one) by the machine translation system. Then, the themes of social hierarchy, political and power relations being widely explored, the translation of the personal pronoun *you* into *tu* or *vous* is particularly important. It was an opportunity to analyze this recurrent problem in English to French translation. Finally, the dialogues contain relatively long and complex syntactical elements, which puts the system's ability to handle non-canonic sentences and literary style to the test.

3 Research on Subtitling

The term "adaptation" was chosen to refer to the translation of subtitles because it is subject to specific spatial and temporal constraints. The professional adapter must adapt their translation using specific techniques in order to produce bare, general and sometimes unfair subtitles (Baldo, 2009). The adapter is therefore required to express an idea in a limited number of words – depending on the time and space at his/her disposal - and deliberately discard certain semantic information from the source script.

It is therefore not surprising that academic research in subtitling focuses on its polysemiotic nature and its purpose: the comfort of the viewer (Orero, 2008). Some researchers argue for the use of creative subtitles to overcome traditional constraints, made possible with advances in digital technology (Nornes, 2007; Diaz, 2007; Baldo, 2019).

4 Automatic Translation of Subtitles with *Google*

There is a gap between university research in France on automatic subtitling translation, which is very rare, and the large number of computer programs that offer automatic subtitling services on the Internet, such as the ubiquitous YouTube. YouTube provides us with the opportunity to do automatic captioning for videos thanks to the coupling of two systems: *Google Voice* and *Google Translate*. The subtitles which are first generated by voice recognition technology (*Google Voice*) are then automatically translated by the machine translation tool (*Google Translate*).

My research so far in the field of automatic subtitling has focused on the use of the automatic subtitling tool provided by Google on YouTube, entitled *"Is automatic subtitling a new technology that professional adapters can use?"* (Baldo, 2015). The latter was the continuation of a study entitled *"Automatic subtitling: a technological innovation that can be used by professional adapters?"* that I presented at the University of Rennes 2 (France) during the Symposium "Optimizing the place of the human in translation: facing the technological challenge" in 2013.

My research was based on a comparative analysis between human translations done by a professional adapter and the automatic translation provided by Google. In other words, I studied the quality of vocal recognition *and* machine translation proposed by the program, thanks to a comparative analysis with the work of a professional adapter. My purpose was to discover whether this technology was potentially helpful for a professional adapter or not.

I limited my research to a qualitative study of speech recognition (automatic transcription), automatic translations using automatic transcriptions (voice recognition) and automatic translations using human transcriptions (source scripts). The use of both of these tools, *Google Voice* and *Google Translate* proved to be chaotic, unmanageable and therefore unusable by a professional adapter:

—   The automatic transcription quality using speech recognition provided an unusable track. Speech recognition remains a complex multidisciplinary domain (involving cognitive science, neuroscience, computer science, mathematics, signage, phonetics and linguistics). The results can be highly variable from one video to another and they depend on many parameters, from the quality of speaker enunciation to the sonic environment, not to mention the recording quality of the medium itself;

– The quality of a machine translation from an automatic transcription: pure madness. Without a doubt, a machine translation system cannot produce meaningful text from text which is senseless;

– The quality of a machine translation from a human transcript: sweet madness since in the context of adaptation, the automatic translation would probably not be acceptable as it cannot provide subtitle-length segments. It would be hard to read on the screen.

The conclusion of my work, valid for the corpus of my study, was that Google's automatic subtitling system in 2015 was an unsuitable technology for professional adapters. Using it was a technological feat: the final quality was unusable (with or without Google Voice), even when the machine translation was acceptable. On the rare occasions when machine translation was acceptable, it did not meet the *sui generis* requirements of adaptation

5 Automatic Translation of Subtitles with *DeepL*

DeepL, as an online machine translation service of *DeepL* GmbH, was launched in 2017 by the Linguee team, authors of the world's largest dictionary since 2010. The dictionary is based on a program that detects bilingual sites, which are collected in the *Linguee* database. Afterwards, an automatic learning algorithm judges the quality of the translations of words, phrases or sentences and sorts them. *DeepL* uses Convolutional Neural Networks which are part of automatic learning (CNN or ConvNet) and that are built on the Linguee database.

The service offers seventy-two combinations from nine languages (Dutch, English, French, German, Italian, Polish, Portuguese, Russian and Spanish,) the quality of the combinations likely quite variable, depending on the combination. According to one study (Coldewey, Lardinois, 2017), *DeepL* is more nuanced and more precise, with similar speed, to its competitors *Google Translation*, *Microsoft Translation* and *Facebook*.

My analysis has focused on the *linguistic* quality of the machine translation offered by *DeepL* from English into French, as regards subtitles.

5.1 Analysis

My analysis focused on a sample of 5,000 words per Season, which makes a total corpus of 40,000 words. I developed the assurance quality grid in two main steps. First, by considering other existing professional grids, such as the one from Lisa software (Localization Industry Standards Association) and the one created by my colleagues of the University of Rennes 2 (Toudic & al.: 2014), then in parallel with the corpus analysis phase. In the end, the grid I will present is adapted to the analysis of subtitles produced by *DeepL's* system as a first draft for the adapter.

I have identified five categories to illustrate the errors identified in *DeepL* translation followed by my comments. *DeepL*'s mistakes are presented in bold print. Lastly, I have added the human subtitled translation for comparison.

Category 1: Grammar; Spelling; Typography
This first category includes grammatical, spelling and typographical errors (including punctuation). In short, these are errors that can be attributed to the program, in the sense that they are correctable, such as a wrong conjugated verb or a capital letter that is not reproduced.

Example 1 Season 1	Go on, Tommy, **shear** him good.
Human translation	Allez, Tommy, **tonds**-le.
Machine Translation (*DeepL*)	Vas-y, Tommy, **tonde**-le bien.
Machine Translation: Incorrect conjugation	
Example 2 Season 1	I hear he's a drunken little lecher, **prone** to all manner of perversions.
Human translation	C'est un coureur alcoolique **porté** sur la perversion
Machine Translation	J'ai entendu dire que c'est un petit alcoolique, **sujette** à toutes sortes de perversions.
MT: French adjective with wrong gender	

Table 1: Grammatical error.

It should be noted that *no* misspelled words were found in the translation provided by *DeepL* of my study corpus

S6	And without an heir, well let's hope the **maesters** are right and Lady Walda's carrying a boy.
HT	Sans héritier, eh bien... Espérons que les **mestres** disent vrai et que lady Walda porte un fils.
MT	Et sans héritier, espérons que les **maitres** ont raison et que Lady Walda porte un garçon.
MT: Spelling (missing accent.) **"Maître" with accent is more common than "maitre" without accent. The latter is rare but not considered as a complete error since the 1990 Spelling Reform in France.**	

Table 2: Spelling error.

S2	King Joffrey is a **Baratheon**, Your Grace.
HT	Le roi Joffrey est un **Baratheon**.
MT	Le roi Joffrey est un **baratheon**, Votre Grâce
MT: Absence de majuscule	

Table 3: Typography error.

Category 2: Style

I borrowed the name of the second category – Style – from my colleagues at the University of Rennes 2 (Toudic & al.: 2014).

The Style category is divided into five sub-categories: inappropriate lexicon, terminology, phraseology, language register and finally non-fluidity. It accounts for all the clumsy writing, approximations or even inaccuracies in the translation of a word or a group of words, whether or not they are specialized.

S1	Is it true they **lie** with their horses?
HT	Est-ce vrai qu'ils **dorment** avec leurs chevaux ?
MT	C'est vrai qu'ils **mentent** avec leurs chevaux ?
MT: Nonsense due to the polysemiotic verb "lie".	
S2	I had two **cups of wine**
HT	J'ai bu deux **coupes**.
MT	J'ai bu deux **tasses de vin**.
MT: Wrong collocation	
S2	Or do you want to trade gossip like a couple of **fishwives**?
HT	Ou veux-tu échanger des ragots ?
MT	Ou tu veux échanger des ragots comme deux **femmes-poissons** ?
MT: Lexical calque (instead of "poissonnières" for fishmongers.) Good translation by *DeepL* when "fishwife" is in the singular.	

Table 4: Inappropriate lexicon.

S3	Small council meetings.
HT	Réunion avec le Conseil restreint.
MT	**Réunions des petits conseils**
MT: Terminological calque	

Table 5: Inappropriate terminology.

Ex 1 S3	It's not easy for girls like us **to dig our way out**.
HT	C'est pas évident pour nous autres **de bien s'en tirer**.
MT	Ce n'est pas facile pour des filles comme nous **de creuser pour s'en sortir**.
Ex 2 S6	Your Grace, when **I was ready to drink myself into a small coffin**, Lord Varys told me about a queen.
HT	Majesté. **J'étais sur le point de me noyer dans l'alcool** quand Varys m'a parlé d'une reine.
MT	Votre Grâce, quand **j'étais prêt à boire dans un petit cercueil**, Lord Varys m'a parlé d'une reine.
MT: Phraseological calque	

Table 6: Inappropriate phraseology.

The series is known for its different language levels. Brienne of Tarth uses a much more formal register than The Hound, who doesn't hesitate to swear.

S1	And you, you're Ned Stark's **bastard**, aren't you?
HT	Et toi, tu es le **bâtard** de Ned Stark.
MT	Et toi, tu es le **salaud** de Ned Stark, n'est-ce pas ?
Literal vs. figurative meaning **Formal vs. informal**	

Table 7: Inappropriate language register.

S4	For 40 years I've tried to teach you. If you haven't learned by now, **you never will**.
HT	40 années passées à t'éduquer. **Tu es irrécupérable**.
MT	Pendant 40 ans, j'ai essayé de t'apprendre. Si tu n'as pas encore appris, **tu ne l'apprendras jamais**.
MT: Badly expressed because of the ellipse	

Table 8: Non-fluidity.

Category 3: Morphosyntax

This category includes only one type of error, that of a morphosyntactic nature including syntactic calque.

S1	Whatever Jon Arryn knew or didn't know, **it died with him.**
HT	Ce que Jon Arryn savait est mort avec lui.
MT	Ce que Jon Arryn savait ou ne savait pas, **il est mort avec lui.**
MT: Morphological calque	
S2	When Eddard Stark learned the truth, **he told only me.**
HT	Ned Stark **n'avait alerté que moi.**
MT	Quand Eddard Stark a appris la vérité, **il n'a dit que moi.**
MT: Syntactic calque	

Table 9: Morphosyntactic error.

Category 4: Localization

This category is probably the most interesting for a translation scientist as it deals with the most difficult cases in translation. Indeed, (briefly explain what localization is). One wonders how the system could operate to provide a correct translation. The category contains all the translations that seem unsuitable due to the context (i.e. temporal, social one) or to the linguistics itself of the target language.

S1	We've been **riding** for a month, my love.
HT	Le voyage a été long.
MT	Ça fait un mois qu'on **roule**, mon amour.
Temporal context. MT: Anachronism.	
S2	And when those affections become common knowledge, well, that is an awkward situation indeed, especially in a **prominent family**.
HT	Lorsque ces liens sont révélés au public, la situation devient délicate, en effet. Surtout dans les **grandes familles**.
MT	Et quand ces affections deviennent de notoriété publique, eh bien, c'est une situation délicate, surtout dans une **famille nombreuse**.
Social context. **The family in question is the Lannisters'. "Prominent family" is to be taken in the social sense of "grande famille" in French and not "famille nombreuse" (large family).**	

Table 10: Non-adaptation to the context

By "non-adaptation to the linguistics of the target language", I refer to all the cases that present difficulties due to differences in linguistic matters. For example, the female or male gender of French determiners, adjectives or names, the translation of the pronoun *you* by the pronouns *tu* or *vous* or the translations of modal auxiliaries.

S1	All these years, and I still feel like **an outsider** when I come here.
HT	Depuis toutes ces années, je me sens toujours **étrangère** en ces lieux.
MT	Toutes ces années, et je me sens toujours comme **un étranger** quand je viens ici.
MT: French noun translated with wrong gender	
S4	- Do you like women? - When **they** look like her, my lord. - **This one** will do nicely.
HT	- Tu aimes les femmes ? - Quand **elles** lui ressemblent, oui. - **Elle** devrait faire l'affaire.
MT	- Vous aimez les femmes ? - Quand **ils** lui ressemblent, mon seigneur. - **Celui-ci** fera très bien l'affaire.
MT: French pronoun translated with wrong gender	
S6	She was fearless. There was nothing she **wouldn't do.**
HT	Elle était intrépide. Elle ne **reculait** devant rien.
MT	Elle n'avait peur de rien. Il n'y avait rien qu'elle ne **ferait** pas.
MT: wrong tense **Modal auxiliaries: habit value (past tense) vs. conditional value**	

Table 11: Non-adaptation to the linguistics of the target language

Category 5: Omission or Addition of Information

This fifth category is essential in a study on subtitling. Indeed, an omission of information in subtitling is rarely considered an error, unless it affects the viewer's understanding of the film. I have included in this sub-category the untranslated parts as as a form of omission.

S3	The **Unsullied** have stood here for a day and a night with no food or water.
HT	Les **Immaculés** sont plantés là depuis un jour et une nuit.
MT	Les **Unsullied** sont restés ici un jour et une nuit sans nourriture ni eau.
MT: Non-translated	

Table 12: Omission.

The addition, on the other hand, is not part of the practice for obvious reasons of spatiotemporal constraints.

S3	One brother inside his army will be worth **1,000** fighting against it.
HT	Un homme infiltré dans son armée vaudra **1 000 hommes** le combattant.
MT	Un frère à l'intérieur de son armée vaudra **mille dollars** en combattant contre elle.
MT: Addition of incorrect information. Erroneous meaning due to an ellipse: "dollars" has been added instead of "men."	

Table 13: Addition

5.2 Results: Comparison between *DeepL* and Human Translation of Subtitles

DeepL Quantitative Analysis

The analysis I did on *DeepL* was significant for the corpus that was used. It found that the French version provided by the program could be used *a priori* as a draft. Indeed, only an average of 1.18% of errors was found. Also, the number of errors per category varied: 45.9% of style errors; 36% of localization errors; 13% morphosyntactic errors; 5% of grammatical, spelling and typography errors and only 0.1% of omission/addition errors.

Several conclusions can be drawn from this. The most common errors concern stylistic clumsiness involving a poor choice of the lexicon and expressions. The Localization category represents more than a third of all errors, the ones that are due to a failure to consider the context (i.e. feminine sex of the character, of the pronouns and of determiners). Morphosyntactic and grammatical errors are few and spelling errors are non-existent. The least represented category is the omission/addition category, with a very low percentage. However, this deserves more attention as it raises, among other things, the question of non-translation, including the non-translation of proper names. This point proved to be delicate because it is quite subjective (Delavaud: 2014).

The saga is extremely rich in names, nicknames, houses, places, castles, cities, villages, rivers, lakes, regions, islands.... If I had counted the occurrences of non-translated proper names by the program, the percentage of errors in this category would have been higher. But this would have required a full study on a very complex point. The adapters of the series acknowledged that they had mainly relied on the literary translation of Jean Sola and Patrick Marcel of the fantasy novel series *A Song of Ice and Fire* (Pacheco: 2017). This is not without reminding us of the massive translation work done by Jean-François Ménard (Mariaule: 2019) on *Harry Potter*, which could be used

as a model for the adapters of the French subtitled version of the *Game of Thrones* series.

Here are some examples illustrating the fact that the translation of proper names by *DeepL* has been very variable: from non-translation to translation, including partial translation.

S6	**Castle Black** is his.
HT	Il règne sur **Châteaunoir**.
MT	**Castle Black** est à lui
MT: Not translated	
S4	A vulture grasping a baby in its talons, **House Blackmont**.
HT	Un vautour agrippant un bébé, **maison Noirmont**.
MT	Un vautour tenant un bébé dans ses serres, **Maison Blackmont**.
Partially translated (*House* by *Maison*)	
S4	**The Halfhand** believed our only chance to stop Mance was to get a man inside his army.
HT	**Le Mimain** pensait arrêter Mance en infiltrant son armée.
MT	**La Demi Main** croyait que notre seule chance d'arrêter Mance était d'avoir un homme à l'intérieur de son armée.
MT: Translated litteraly	

Table 14: Proper names

Besides, I couldn't consider the translation of *you* by the French pronouns *tu* or *vous* in my quantitative analysis of *DeepL* translation. First of all, because there is, like the translation of proper names, a great deal of subjectivity. Secondly, the task is a complex one given the many characters and their multiple and complex relationships. In order to better manage this point, the adapters have created what they call a Bible, which is a very detailed table listing the characters and their use of *vous* or *tu* in addressing this or that character (Pacheco: 2017).

More broadly, I was confronted with several problems:

– the repetition of erroneous occurrences. I opted to count them only once, but they are problematic ;

– it was not always easy to determine the appropriate category for errors that sometimes covered different fields. The error mentioned above in "you're Ned Stark's bastard" translated by *DeepL* into "Tu es le **salaud** de Ned Stark" is from an Inappropriate language register but could also have been identified as a lexical translation error;

– the non-homogeneity of *DeepL*'s translations (sometimes correct, sometimes not, sometimes different depending on the sentences).

S1	What is it? **Mountain lion?** There are no **mountain lions** in these woods.
HT	Qu'est-ce que c'est ? Un **puma** ? Il n'y **en** a pas dans ces bois.
MT	Qu'est-ce que c'est ? Le **lion des montagnes** ? Il n'y a pas de **pumas** dans ces bois.
MT: "Lion des montagnes" is a calque but might be acceptable in a fantasy context.	

Table 15: Non-homogeneity

Lastly, the percentage of errors obtained in my corpus is only indicative but we can assume that given the very low rate of errors that was obtained, *DeepL* could be used as a draft.

DeepL Better than Human Translation?

In choosing to work from DVDs, I assumed I was avoiding the amateurish quality of subtitling associated with, for example, Netflix. The quality of its translation of French subtitles has been subject to controversy and accused of being amateurish (Wachthausen: 2019). So, I chose to rely on the French subtitles of the DVD box set of the series because I assumed that they would be of a more professional quality. However, I have identified a number of errors that are so gross that it cannot be assumed that the subtitles have been reviewed by a professional human being. Here are some examples:

Ex. 1, S1, Episode 1	They were meant to have **them**.
HT	Ils **leurs** sont destinés →**leur**
MT	Ils étaient censés **les** avoir.
HT: Grammar error **MT: Correct grammar**	
Ex. 2 S2, E3	This bastard**'s been meddling** where he shouldn't.
HT	Ce bâtard **à fourré** son nez où il n'aurait pas dû. → **a**
MT	Ce salaud **s'est immiscé** là où il ne devrait pas.
HT: Grammatical and typographical error **(confusion between the preposition *à* to and the auxiliary *avoir*.)** **MT: Proper translation**	
Ex. 3 S1, E3	You never **fall**.
HT	Tu ne **tombe** jamais.→ **tombes**
MT	Tu ne **tombes** jamais.

Ex. 4 S1, E4	What did I buy you for?
HT	Pourquoi **t'ais**-je achetée ? → **t'ai-je**
MT	Pourquoi **t'ai**-je acheté ?
Ex. 5, S2, E3	He **ran off** before anyone could split.
HT	Il s'est **enfuit** en une clin d'œil. → **s'est enfui**
MT	Il **s'est enfui** avant que quelqu'un puisse partir.
HT: Conjugation error **MT: Correct conjugation**	

Table 16: Grammar error.

Ex 1 S1, E3	She must take his side even when he's **wrong**.
HT	Elle doit le défendre même s'il a **tord**. → **tort**
MT	Elle doit prendre son parti même quand il a **tort**.
Ex 2 S2, E3	You didn't win my father's **support** or his army on charm alone.
HT	Tu n'as pas gagné le **soutient** et l'armée de mon père uniquement par ton charme. → **soutien**
MT	Tu n'as pas gagné le **soutien** de mon père ou de son armée par le seul charme.
Ex 3 S2, E3	Your **enemies** aren't happy about us. They want to tear us apart.
HT	Notre union déplaît à tes **ennemies**. Ils veulent nous séparer. → **ennemis**
MT	Vos **ennemis** ne sont pas contents de nous. Ils veulent nous séparer.
HT: Spelling mistake **MT: Correct spelling**	

Table 17: Spelling mistake

S1,E2	It's **time** we reviewed the accounts.
HT	Il est **tant** de revoir les comptes. → **temps**
MT	Il est **temps** de revoir les comptes.
HT: nonsense because of a major grammatical/lexical error (homonymic confusion between the adverb *tant* and the name *temps*) **MT: Correct translation**	

Table 18: Inappropriate lexicon

What is interesting to note here is that all translations offered by *DeepL* are correct. This does not mean that *DeepL* is a better translator than the human being. Nevertheless, what can be highlighted here is that the typology of errors that we have found in our corpus is very different in human translation and in machine translation.

The human errors identified are typical of those found in writings by people who have poor command of French spelling, grammar and typography. However, I have found relatively few such errors (5%) with *DeepL*.

Even in case of a pun (Brisset & al.: 2019), which generally poses a difficulty in translation, *DeepL* is surprisingly successful:

S1	- Why they call you **Littlefinger**? - When I was a child, I was very small, and I come from a **little** spit of land called the **Fingers**, so you see, it's an exceedingly clever nickname.
HT	- Pourquoi le surnom de **Littlefinger** ? - Enfant, j'étais très **petit (little)**, et je viens d'une terre appelée **Doigts (Fingers)**…, c'est un surnom très malin.
MT	- Pourquoi on t'appelle **Littlefinger** ? - Quand j'étais enfant, j'étais très **petit**, et je viens d'un petit bout de terre appelé les **Fingers**, alors vous voyez, c'est un surnom extrêmement intelligent.
HT: Explanatory translation **MT: Acceptable translation**	

Table 19: Pun

The adapter chose to propose an explanatory subtitle, which deconstructs the play on words. This is what I called, the "note-on" (Baldo: 2019, p. 345) by analogy with the word "pop-on". The note refers to a type of subtitle that includes a translator's note. It is becoming more and more common, especially in the case of wordplay or complex translations. As for *DeepL*, the automatic software goes beyond explanations and submits an acceptable and fluent translation, relying on a minimum of English knowledge on the part of the viewer for his/her understanding of the pun.

DeepL's Limits When Applied to Subtitling

Some of the errors found in the *DeepL* version could not have been avoided. For instance, in a case of syntactic ambiguity:

S3	The girl likes you. You like **her back**, Snow?
HT	La fille t'apprécie. C'est réciproque ?
MT	La fille t'aime bien. Tu aimes **son dos**, Snow ?
HT: Correct translation **MT: Correct translation but wrong context**	

Table 20: Syntactic ambiguity

Or in the case of an ellipsis that creates a misinterpretation:

S6	Martell **raped** and **murdered**, and you did nothing. Oberyn Martell **butchered**, and you did nothing.
HT	Elia Martell **a été violée** et **tuée**. Vous n'avez rien fait. Oberyn Martell **a été massacré**. Vous n'avez rien fait.
MT	Elia Martell **a violé** et **assassiné**, et vous n'avez rien fait. Oberyn Martell **a massacré**, et vous n'avez rien fait.
HT: Correct semantical translation **MT: Correct syntactic translation vs. incorrect semantical translation.**	

Table 21: Ellipse of the auxiliary *be*

Above all, *DeepL*'s output is limited in the second phase of the adapter's work: the one that consists in reducing the length of the subtitle. This is not surprising since *DeepL* was not developed for this purpose. Here is an example that shows the adapter's work of synthesizing:

S7	With their help, the Mad King's daughter has ferried an army of savages to our shores, mindless Unsullied soldiers who will destroy your castles **and your holdfasts**, Dothraki heathens who will burn your villages to the ground, rape **and enslave your women**, and butcher your children **without a second thought**.
HT	Avec leur aide, la fille du roi fou a conduit des sauvages à nos portes. Des Immaculés écervelés qui détruiront vos châteaux. Des brutes dothraks qui brûleront vos villages, violeront vos femmes et égorgeront vos enfants.
MT	Avec leur aide, la fille du Roi Fou a transporté une armée de sauvages sur nos rives, des soldats sans scrupules qui détruiront vos châteaux **et vos possessions**, des païens Dothraki qui brûleront vos villages, violeront **et réduiront vos femmes en esclavage**, et abattront vos enfants **sans hésiter**.
HT: Use of omission and short synonyms. 36 words and 221 characters including spaces **MT: Full translation. 48 words and 295 characters including spaces**	

Table 22: Synthesizing

During this second phase of rewriting, the adapter must conform to a number of standards that I cannot develop here in detail (Baldo, 2009)

6   Conclusion

In France, today, we can no longer ignore the use
of *DeepL* in the field of translation. There is no
longer any shame associated with the use of an automatic translation program and translation agencies now offer machine translation services with
post-editing. Whereas a few years ago this was a
taboo subject among agencies, today *DeepL* is part
of the reality of professional translation practice, at
least with regard to the English-French combination of languages. The real question is no longer
whether or not to use *DeepL*, but how to manage
this new market reality.

The objective of this research has been to establish whether *DeepL's* automatic translations are a
pure utopia or if they can be used by professional
adapters. My study has attempted to answer the following question: Can automatic subtitling be of a
sufficiently high quality to be used primarily by the
human subtitler? I would answer that this is a possible option. The error rate seems low enough to
save the translator time. The next step of this research on automatic subtitling practice could be to
compare the time adapters spend translating with
and without *DeepL*.

However, the integration of an automatic translation program into the adaptation process is a major
issue, that of the image of a profession already ex-
posed to criticism. This also explains why few subtitlers admit to using fansubbing translations as a
draft for their professional ones.

References

Abé Mark NORNES. 2007. *Translating Global Cinema*,
Minneapolis, University of Minnesota Press.

Daniel Toudic, Katell Hernandez Morin, Fabienne Mo-
reau, Franck Barbin & Gaëlle Phuez. 2014. Du con-
texte didactique aux pratiques professionnelles : pro-
position d'une grille multicritères pour l'évaluation
de la qualité en traduction spécialisée.
http://journals.openedition.org/ilcea/2517

David Benioff, Daniel Brett Weiss (dir.). Game of
Thrones. 2017. 34 DVD.

DeepL
https://www.DeepL.com/translator

Devin Coldewey, Frederic Lardinois. 2017. DeepL
schools other online translators with clever machine
learning.
https://techcrunch.com/2017/08/29/DeepL-schools-
other-online-translators-with-clever-machine-learn-
ing/

Frédérique Brisset, Audrey Coussy, Ronard Jenn, Julie
Loison-Charles (éds.). 2019. *Du jeu dans la langue.
Traduire le jeu de mots*, Collection « Traductologie »,
Presses du Septentrion, Lille.

Game of Thrones Episode Scripts
https://www.springfieldspringfield.co.uk/epi-
sode_scripts.php?tv-show=game-of-thrones

George R. R. Martin. 1996. *A Song of Ice and Fire*,
Bantam Book.

Jadine Labbé Pacheco. 2017. Game of Thrones : Blan-
dine a vu les épisodes avant vous.
https://www.nouvelobs.com/rue89/rue89-nos-vies-
connectees/20170731.OBS2783/game-of-thrones-
blandine-a-vu-les-episodes-avant-vous.html

Jean-Luc Wachthausen. 2019. Pourquoi les sous-titres
de Netflix frisent l'amateurisme.
https://www.lepoint.fr/pop-culture/series/pourquoi-
les-sous-titres-de-netflix-frisent-l-amateurisme-06-
05-2019-2310985_2957.php

Jorge Diaz Cintas. 2007. Back to the Future in Subtitling [en ligne]. In *MuTra Conference Proceedings*.
http://euroconferences.info/proceedings/2005_Pro-
ceedings/2005_DiazCintas_Jorge.pdf

Lexpress.fr. 2015. Game of Thrones entre dans le livre
des records.
https://www.lexpress.fr/culture/tele/game-of-
thrones-entre-dans-le-livre-des-re-
cords_1712204.htm

Lisa (The Localization Industry Standards Association) QA
http://dssresources.com/news/1558.php

Mickaël Mariaule. 2019. Harry Potter : la traduction
française des noms propres. In *L'intraduisible. Les
méandres de la traduction*. Sabrina Baldo de Brébisson et Stephanie Genty (éds.). Artois Presses Université, Arras, pages 361-373.

Pilar Orero. 2008. Le format des sous-titres : les mille
et une possibilités. In *La traduction audiovisuelle*.
Jean-Marc Lavaur & Adriana Serban (eds.),
Bruxelles, De Boeck, pages 55-65.

Sabrina Baldo de Brébison. 2019. La note à l'image :
un méandre insolite plutôt qu'insoluble. In *L'intraduisible. Les méandres de la traduction*. Sabrina
Baldo de Brébisson et Stephanie Genty (éds.). Artois

Presses Université, Arras, pages 335-59.

Sabrina Baldo de Brébisson. 2017. « Venture into the untranslatable: A tribute to the subtitler explorer, a hero with a thousand faces », in Élisabeth Navarro et Jean-Michel Benayoun (éds.), Langues, diversité et stratégies interculturelles, Michel Houdiard Éditeur, Paris, pages 302-322.

Sabrina Baldo de Brébisson. 2015. Is automatic subtitling a new technology that professional adapters can use? In *La main de Thôt*, n°3, Miscellanées, Traduction et mémoire, mis à jour le : 08/03/2018. http://revues.univ-tlse2.fr/lamaindethot/index.php?id=517.

Sabrina Baldo de Brébisson. 2009. Traduction et Adaptation : Analyse comparative. In *Traductologie et enseignement de traduction à l'Université*. Michel Ballard (ed.). Artois, Presses Université Arras, pages 157-167.

Sharon O'Brien, Laura Winther Balling, Michael Carl, Michel Simard, and Lucia Specia. 2014. *PostEditing of Machine Translation: Processes and Applications*. Cambridge Scholars Publishing, Newcastle upon Tyne.

Thibault Delavaud. 2014. La traduction de Game of Thrones est-elle si mauvaise. http://thibaultdelavaud.unblog.fr/2014/04/28/la-traduction-de-game-of-thrones-est-elle-si-mauvaise/comment-page-1/#comment-758

Wondershare. 2019. Créer des sous-titres à vos vidéos : 10 meilleurs logiciels sous-titrage gratuits

https://filmora.wondershare.com/fr/astuces-montage-video/creer-des-soustitres.html?gclid=Cj0KCQjwhdTqBRDNARIsABsOl9_g_Amy-ZVhNWhnPNOFO75TtgMBu67YRey6oat_sq_LG mGUh0zuFOA8aArIwEALw_wcB

Parallel Corpus of Croatian-Italian Administrative Texts

Marija Brkic Bakaric
Department of Informatics
University of Rijeka
Croatia

mbrkic@uniri.hr

Ivana Lalli Pacelat
Faculty of Interdisciplinary, Italian and Cultural Studies
Juraj Dobrila University of Pula
Croatia
ilalli@unipu.hr

Abstract

Parallel corpora constitute a unique resource for providing assistance to human translators. The selection and preparation of the parallel corpora also conditions the quality of the resulting MT engine. Since Croatian is a national language and Italian is officially recognized as a minority language in seven cities and twelve municipalities of Istria County, a large amount of parallel texts is produced on a daily basis. However, there have been no attempts in using these texts for compiling a parallel corpus. A domain-specific sentence-aligned parallel Croatian-Italian corpus of administrative texts would be of high value in creating different language tools and resources. The aim of this paper is, therefore, to explore the value of parallel documents which are publicly available mostly in pdf format and to investigate the use of automatically-built dictionaries in corpus compilation. The effects that a document format and, consequently sentence splitting, and the dictionary input have on the sentence alignment process are manually evaluated.

1 Introduction

Parallel corpora constitute a unique resource, not only for the development of machine translation (MT) systems, but also for providing assistance to human translators. They have been used to develop computer-assisted translation (CAT) tools and resources for human translators, such as translation memories (TM), terminology management tools and resources, bilingual concordances, and translator oriented word processors (cf. McEnery and Xiao, 2007; Kenning, 2010, Somers, 2001). The selection and preparation of the parallel corpora also conditions the quality of the resulting MT engine, since both dominant approaches to MT, statistical machine translation (SMT) and neural machine translation (NMT), rely on high quality parallel corpora.

In bilingual or multilingual areas in which the equal status of two or more languages is officially recognized, a large amount of parallel texts is produced on a daily basis. Due to the officiality of the minority languages and the official nature of the texts and of the context of language use, having a precise and uniform terminology as well as developed translation/language technologies that facilitate the whole translation process is of high importance (Trosterud, 2002). In order to improve the quality of translation, to reduce the time and the cost of the translation, and to preserve the official bilingualism and multilingualism, a number of actions have been initiated over the years in different bilingual and multilingual countries, regions or organizations. The full insight into the tools and resources necessary for facilitating and supporting the multilingual text production is given by the European Commission (Steinberger et al., 2014; European Commission, 2016). Supports have been given to the minority language engineering with a focus on MT development (e.g. for the Basque-Spanish language pair (Alegria et al., 2005) and for the Catalan-Spanish language pair (Arranz et al., 2006)), on terminology (e.g. for Welsh (Jones and Prys, 2006), for Italian, German and Ladin (Streiter et al., 2004)), and on parallel corpus building (e.g. the Trilingual Allegra-Corpus of German, Italian and Romansh (Scherrer and Cartoni, 2012), the Hansard French-English corpus and The United Nations Parallel Corpus v1.0 (Ziemski et al, 2016)).

Unfortunately, this is not the case of Istria County in Croatia, where existing parallel texts

Temnikova, I, Orăsan, C., Corpas Pastor, G., and Mitkov, R. (eds.) (2019) *Proceedings of the 2nd Workshop on Human-Informed Translation and Interpreting Technology (HiT-IT 2019)*, Varna, Bulgaria, September 5 - 6, pages 11–18.

https://doi.org/10.26615/issn.2683-0078.2019_002

have not been used so far for compiling a parallel corpus needed for MT and other human language technology (HLT) applications.

According to the Statute of the Istrian County (Art. 6, 21, 22, 23, and 24/2009), the Croatian and the Italian language are in equal official use in institutions of the County and of the official bilingual cities and municipalities. The Italian language is officially recognized as a minority language in seven cities and twelve municipalities in Istria County. Due to the equal status of Italian and Croatian, legal and administrative documents have to be published in both languages. The texts are usually written in Croatian and then translated into Italian.

The analysis of the current translation practice and terminology use shows that there is a need to develop translations tools and language resources which would enable a more efficient and faster translation process and ensure the usage of precise and unambiguous Italian terminology in Croatia.

Although parallel corpora for both Croatian and Italian exist, they are mostly in combination with English, as emphasized by Tadić et al. (2012) for Croatian and Calzolari et al. (2012) for Italian. There are also few parallel corpora including both languages of interest, Croatian and Italian – the OPUS2 parallel corpus (Tiedemann, 2012), the EUR-Lex Corpus (Baisa et al., 2016), the Eur-Lex judgments corpus (Baisa et al., 2016), the DGT-Translation Memory (Steinberger et al., 2012), the EAC-TM, the InterCorp (Čermák and Rosen, 2012), the Bulgarian-X language Parallel Corpus (Koeva et al., 2012), etc. These corpora, although few of them belong to the public administration domain, cannot fully satisfy the needs of the local translators and cannot be considered high quality corpora for facilitating the development of translation technology due to the specific bilingual terminology. Since Italian, which is a national language in Italy, has a minority language status in Croatia, differences and particularities of the two legal systems should be taken into account and a consistent and comprehensive Italian terminology adapted to the Croatian legal system should be prepared and used accordingly. The availability of parallel texts abundant in the respective terminology makes the goal of preparing a high quality domain-specific parallel corpus achievable.

Therefore, the aim of this work is to create a domain-specific sentence-aligned parallel Croatian-Italian corpus of administrative texts, which would be valuable in the Istrian case for the creation of different language tools and resources. Sentence alignment is the task of mapping the sentences of two given parallel corpora which are known to be translations of each other. Since the problem of correct sentence alignment is additionally burdened by erroneous sentence splitting (Biçici, 2007), in this paper we explore the value of parallel documents which are publicly available mostly in pdf format.

The research conducted in this paper can be divided into two parts. The first part is related to the preparation of the parallel documents and the second to sentence alignment. Since dictionary input affects sentence alignment, one line of this research explores the difference between sentence alignment without a dictionary input and sentence alignment with a dictionary input. Although both methods rely on the dictionary usage, the first makes use of the dictionary compiled from the same parallel corpus based on the sentence length information, while the latter makes use of the dictionary compiled from another corpus, similar in nature, which is already sentence-aligned.

Related work is presented in section 2. Section 3 deals with the corpus preparation and is divided into corpus and dictionary descriptions, and the description of automatic sentence alignment procedure. Evaluation of the sentence alignment approaches and of the dictionary compiled from the corpus which is not sentence-aligned is given in section 4. A short conclusion along with the directions for future work is given in the last section of the paper.

2 Related Work

The aim of this work is similar to the work in Soares and Krallinger (2019) and Doğru et al. (2018). Soares and Krallinger (2019) build two bilingual and one trilingual corpus for MT purposes and then build NMT models and evaluate translations according to the BLEU score. They conduct evaluation of randomly selected 100 sentences per corpus and mark them as "correct", "partial", or "no alignment". Although in this work we use the labels as in Aker et al. (2014), their meaning is the same. Doğru et al. (2018) gather and prepare medical parallel corpora for the purpose of MT training. The authors report the automatic and semi-automatic methods they use for creating domain-specific (medical) custom translation memories as well as bilingual terminology lists, which include web-crawling, document alignment in CAT tools and term extraction.

Etchegoyhen et al. (2018) acknowledge that domain-specific resources are usually scarce. However, it is widely accepted that MT works better with domain-specific parallel corpora (Doğru et al., 2018). Evaluation of the benefits of domain adaptation for MT, on three separate domains and language pairs, with varying degrees of domain specificity and amounts of available training data is presented by Etchegoyhen et al. (2018). Doğru et al. (2018) believe that concentrating on the parallel corpora selection, collection and preparation processes is equally important and may have a positive impact on the MT system quality and post-editing.

The first part of the research is similar to the one in Aker et al. (2014). There are three main approaches to the problem of sentence alignment: length-based, dictionary-based, and similarity-based (Varga et al., 2007). In this work we focus on the dictionary-based method and investigate two approaches. The authors in Aker et al. (2014) additionally propose and apply three cleaning methods to the noisy dictionary created by GIZA++. In a method-by-method comparison the transliteration method performs the best, however, the combination of the methods proves to have the highest precision. In this paper we do not apply any dictionary cleaning methods. Our focus is drawn to spurious line breaks introduced by pdf to plain text conversion since, due to the structure of the administrative documents, a simple deletion of these line breaks would badly affect the sentence splitting procedure.

3 Preparation of the Corpus

Since Italian is officially recognized as a minority language in seven cities and twelve municipalities in Istria County, legal and administrative documents of the County and of these official bilingual cities and municipalities have to be published in both Italian and Croatian.

Parallel documents are collected from the Web using a semi-supervised approach. A manual examination of the web sites reveals that suitable parallel documents exist on only four web sites (Istria county[1], Novigrad[2], Pula[3], Umag[4]). We de-cide to restrict ourselves to the official gazettes as these are published the most frequently of all the bilingual content available. We exclude those sites that publish two-column bilingual pdf files in which the text in Croatian is in one column, and the text in Italian in another column or those that just partly translate the content.

Due to the diversity of web page languages and formats, the python library *Beautiful Soup* and the command *wget* are used for extracting URLs and automatically fetching documents. The identified web sites containing potential parallel documents are first manually inspected and then different types of content within these websites are recognized. Finally, the URLs of official gazette editions are acquired and the respective documents fetched. The alignment on a document-level is performed based on the analyzed and manually detected naming conventions.

Since the downloaded files are mostly in pdf format, the conversion to plain text format is performed. Some basic pre-processing is also conducted, such as removing redundant spaces and empty lines. Please note that the documents contain a lot of numerical data which might give exaggerated perception of the size.

As evident from Table 1, less than half of the Croatian (hr) official gazette editions are available in Italian (it).

Subcorpus	# of hr docs	# of it docs	# of aligned parallel docs
Istria	660	429	251
Novigrad	126	106	65
Pula	65	57	37
Umag	286	71	70

Table 1: Number of documents per corpus.

[1] https://www.istra-istria.hr/index.php?id=8
https://www.istra-istria.hr/index.php?id=486

[2]
http://www.novigrad.hr/hr/administracija/dokumenti/category/sluzbene_novine
http://www.novigrad.hr/it/administracija/dokumenti/category/sluzbene_novine
[3] http://www.pula.hr/hr/opci-podaci/sluzbene-novine/
http://www.pula.hr/it/dati-generali/bollettino-ufficiale/
[4] http://www.umag.hr/hr/gradska-uprava/sluzbene-novine-grada-umaga?syear=
http://www.umag.hr/it/gradska-uprava/sluzbene-novine-grada-umaga?syear=

3.1 Sentence-Aligned Parallel Corpus

The software *hunalign* (Varga et al., 2007) is used for sentence alignment. The tool can be run by providing a dictionary but also without one. If no dictionary is provided, *hunalign* resorts to Gale and Church algorithm which is based on the notion that character lengths of source and target sentences are correlated. A dictionary is built based on such alignment, and then the second iteration of the algorithm does the realignment by combining sentence length information with the dictionary. If a dictionary is provided as input, the first step is skipped.

Input files contain Croatian and Italian corpora, both segmented into sentences (one sentence per line) and into tokens (delimited by space characters). We use a version of the tokenizer provided with the *moses* toolkit[5] to which we add the abbreviation list for Croatian[6]. The output contains the aligned sentences (one aligned sentence per line). The entire process of building the sentence-aligned Croatian-Italian corpus of Istria county and cities is shown in Figure 1.

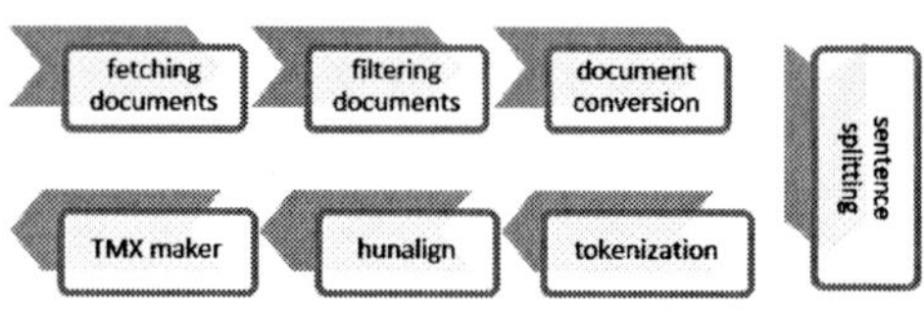

Figure 1: Building the Croatian-Italian corpus.

Since the structure of the public administration documents is such that they contain a wealth of long titles, subtitles, tabular data, lists, references, etc., which often span over multiple lines, the conversion from pdf to plain text format results in many spurious line breaks. We determine that removing these line breaks badly affects sentence splitting, i.e. titles and subtitles stay merged, data from multiple cells stay merged, list items often stay merged, etc. If there are no sentences with appropriate sentence markers in-between, a multi-line text might even end up as a single line. Therefore, we keep the splits introduced by the format conversion and can thus talk about segment splitting rather than sentence splitting.

The descriptions of the four subcorpora of which our corpus consists are given in Table 2. In parallel, we select only those documents that are

[5] http://www.statmt.org/moses/
[6] https://github.com/clarinsi/reldi-tokeniser

Subcorpus	# lines	# tokens	
		Croatian	Italian
Istria	1.2M	3.2M	3.4M
Novigrad	378K	1.2M	1.7M
Pula	318K	858K	1.0M
Umag	638K	1.8M	2.3M

Table 2: Number of lines and tokens per corpus.

originally in doc format and perform the steps shown in Figure 1.

3.2 Dictionary

We download the freely available DGT's translation memory (DGT-TM) (Steinberger et al., 2012). We use it for producing a sentence-aligned parallel Italian-Croatian corpus of the European Union's legislative documents (Acquis Communautaire). The corpus statistics is presented in Table 3.

# of	Italian	Croatian
sentences	284 864	284 864
words	5 501 552	4 669 480
characters	38 281 881	34 233 328

Table 3: Description of the sentence-aligned DGT corpus used for automatic dictionary building.

The translation memory mostly consists of the Acquis Communautaire documents. Due to some pre-processing, the contents of the original documents might have somewhat changed. We process 1267 tmx documents and extract 284 864 Italian-Croatian sentence pairs.

A bilingual dictionary is automatically generated using the GIZA++ tool (Och and Ney, 2003), similarly to Aker et al. (2014). One of the major drawbacks of the tool, as the authors in Aker et al. (2014) point out, is the difficulty in using it for technically non-sophisticated users. In addition, the parallel corpus needs to be pre-processed prior to running the tool. Since every source language word is treated as a possible translation of every target language word, the dictionaries created by GIZA++ contain a lot of noise. Words with high translation probabilities may still be wrong. However, we do not perform any filtering at this point of time and only pre-process the dictionary to put it in a format suitable for *hunalign*.

The entire process of creating the dictionary to be used as input for the alignment process is shown in Figure 2. The dictionary contains 793 803 entries.

Figure 2: Dictionary creation pipeline.

4 Evaluation

4.1 Evaluation of Sentence Alignments

We conduct manual evaluation of the aligned pairs. The assessment is done by two different evaluators. We randomly select 100 aligned pairs in such a way that all four sub-corpora are represented proportionally to their size and that translation units starting with digits or one-word units are discarded. Aligned pairs are labelled as equivalent (label *equiv.*) if the target segment is an acceptable translation of the source segment, as containment (label *cont.*) if the entire source segment is acceptably translated by a proper sub-part of the target language segment, and none of the above (label *none*) if neither of the first two options applies (Aker et al., 2014). The results of evaluations of sentence alignments on the whole corpus, of sentence alignments on Novigrad subcorpus which is originally in doc format, and of sentence alignments based on the DGT dictionary on Novigrad subcorpus are presented in Table 4, Table 5, and Table 6, respectively. The first row gives sums of evaluations per category, while the second row shows only cases for which there is agreement. The precision is calculated by dividing the number of equal evaluations with the total number of evaluations considered. The interrater agreement is from substantial to almost perfect with the Cohen's kappa scores 66%, 92%, and 73%, respectively (Cohen, 1960). The interpretation of the scores is taken over from Landis and Koch (1977).

As evident from Table 4 and Table 5, the precision is affected by the line breaks introduced with pdf-to-txt conversion, which cannot be solved straightforwardly without affecting the sentence splitting procedure. The precision increases greatly if we consider only documents in doc format. However, the difference in sentence alignment

	Equiv.	Cont.	None	Precision
Sum of evaluations	92	56	52	46%
Evaluations in agreement	40	18	20	78%

Table 4: Evaluation of global sentence alignment without dictionary input.

	Equiv.	Cont.	None	Precision
Sum of evaluations	172	11	17	86%
Evaluations in agreement	85	5	8	98%

Table 5: Evaluation of sentence alignment on word processing documents without dictionary input.

	Equiv.	Cont.	None	Precision
Sum of evaluations	170	6	24	85%
Evaluations in agreement	82	1	10	93%

Table 6: Evaluation of DGT-dictionary-based sentence alignment on word processing documents.

performed by *hunalign* without the DGT-based dictionary and with the DGT-based dictionary is not pronounced. Therefore, it can be concluded that DGT-based dictionary adds no value to the sentence alignment process. This might prove different if we were to use some kind of dictionary filtering.

In order to have more reliable precision results, the evaluation might be amended with an arbitration phase, where a third annotator would judge the cases where the first two annotators disagree. Such approach is taken by Mihalcea and Pedersen (2003) in the evaluation of word alignment.

4.2 Evaluation of Dictionary

We also perform a manual evaluation of the automatically built Istrian-based dictionary by randomly selecting 100 different highest probability dictionary entries. We follow the same evaluation methodology as in the previous subsection.

Table 7 presents manual evaluation results. The Cohen's kappa score is almost 69% meaning that there is substantial agreement between evaluators according to the interpretation given by Landis and Koch (1977).

	Equiv.	Cont.	None	Precision
Sum of evaluations	115	32	53	57.5%
Evaluations in agreement	52	8	19	79%

Table 7: Dictionary evaluation.

5 Conclusion and Future Work

The aim of this work is to create a domain-specific sentence-aligned parallel Croatian-Italian corpus. Such resource could be used for training an MT system, automatic terminology extraction, domain adaptation, etc. However, it seems there is a need to correct/validate alignment pairs when working with public administration documents converted from pdf. This would greatly enhance the quality of parallel corpus.

Based on the results of this research, in our future work we plan to extend our corpus and experiment with different methods for compiling or cleaning the dictionary, e.g. neural network-based word alignment, active learning, etc.

Creating such a valuable resource would enable us to train MT systems or to perform domain-adaptation on generic Croatian-Italian MT systems and thus facilitate the work of our public administration. For example, manually revised domain-specific terms extracted from such a resource would enable applying a domain adaptation technique available for SMT which adds phrasal term translations as favored translation options using the XMLmarkup functionality.

Acknowledgments

This work has been fully supported by the University of Rijeka under the grant number 17.14.2.2.01 and the bilateral Croatian-Slovenian project (2018-2019) of the Ministry of Science and Education.

References

Ahmet Aker, Monica Lestari Paramita, and Robert Gaizauskas. 2014. Bilingual Dictionaries for All EU Languages. In *Proceedings of the Ninth International Conference on Language Resources and Evaluation (LREC-2014)*. European Languages Resources Association (ELRA), Reykjavik, Iceland, pages 2839–2845. http://www.lrec-conf.org/proceedings/lrec2014/pdf/803_Paper.pdf.

Iñaki Alegria, Arantza Díaz de Ilarraza, Gorka Labaka, Mikel Lersundi, Aingeru Mayor, et al. 2005. An Open Architecture for Transfer-based Machine Translation between Spanish and Basque. In *Proceedings of the MT Summit X Workshop. Workshop on Open-Source Machine Translation*. Asia-Pacific Association for Machine Translation (AAMT), pages 7–14. https://pdfs.semanticscholar.org/d346/7010dd32f2f317f66cdc0bb532fcb045a97b.pdf.

Victoria Arranz, Elisabet Comelles, and David Farwell. 2006. Speech-to-Speech Translation for Catalan. In Isabella Ties, editor, *Proceedings of the Lesser Used Languages and Computer Linguistics Conference (LULCL 2005)*. Accademia Europea Bolzano, Bolzano.

Vít Baisa, Jan Michelfeit, Marek Medveď, and Miloš Jakubíček. 2016. European Union Language Resources in Sketch Engine. In *The Proceedings of tenth International Conference on Language Resources and Evaluation (LREC 16)*. European Language Resources Association (ELRA). Portorož, Slovenia, pages 2799–2803. https://www.aclweb.org/anthology/L16-1445.

Ergun Biçici. 2007. Local Context Selection for Aligning Sentences in Parallel Corpora. In Boicho Kokinov, Daniel C. Richardson, Thomas R. Roth-Berghofer, editors, *Modeling and Using Context. CONTEXT 2007. Lecture Notes in Computer Science*, volume 4635 (82–93). Springer, Berlin, Heidelberg. https://doi.org/10.1007/978-3-540-74255-5_7.

Nicoletta Calzolari, Bernardo Magnini, Claudia Soria, and Manuela Speranza. 2012. *The Italian language in the digital age / La lingua italiana nell'era digitale*. Berlin: Springer Verlag. http://www.meta-net.eu/whitepapers/e-book/italian.pdf.

Jacob Cohen. 1960. A Coefficient of Agreement for Nominal Scales. *Educ. Psychol. Meas.*, 20(1), pages 37–46.

European Commission. 2016. *Translation tools and workflow*. Luxemburg: Publication Office of the

European Union. https://doi.org/DOI: 10.2782/703257.

František Čermák and Alexandr Rosen. 2012. The case of InterCorp, a multilingual parallel corpus. *International Journal of Corpus Linguistics*, 13(3), 411–427. https://doi.org/10.1075/ijcl.17.3.05cer.

Gökhan Doğru, Adrià Martín, and Anna Aguilar-amat. 2018. Parallel Corpora Preparation for Machine Translation of Low-Resource Languages: Turkish to English Cardiology Corpora. In *Proceedings of the Eleventh International Conference on Language Resources and Evaluation (LREC 2018)*. European Language Resources Association (ELRA), Paris, France, pages 12–15. http://lrec-conf.org/workshops/lrec2018/W3/pdf/5_W3.pdf.

Thierry Etchegoyhen, Anna Fern, Andoni Azpeitia, and Eva Mart. 2018. Evaluating Domain Adaptation for Machine Translation Across Scenarios. In *Proceedings of the Eleventh International Conference on Language Resources and Evaluation (LREC 2018)*. European Language Resources Association (ELRA), Miyazaki, Japan, pages 6–15. https://www.aclweb.org/anthology/L18-1002.

Dewi B. Jones and Delyth Prys. 2006. The Welsh National Online Terminology Database. In *Proceedings of the Lesser Used Languages and Computer Linguistics Conference (LULCL 2005)*. Accademia Europea Bolzano, Bolzano, Italy, pages 149–169.

Marie-Madeleine Kenning. 2010. What are parallel and comparable corpora and how can we use them? In Anne O'Keeffe and Michael McCarthy, editors, *The Routledge handbook of corpus linguistics*. Routledge, London, pages 487–500. https://doi.org/10.4324/9780203856949.ch35.

Svetla Koeva, Ivelina Stoyanova, Rositsa Dekova, Borislav Rizov, and Angel Genov. 2012. Bulgarian X-language Parallel Corpus. In *Proceedings of the 8th International Conference on Language Resources and Evaluation (LREC 2012)*. European Language Resources Association (ELRA), Istanbul, Turkey, pages 2480–2486. http://www.lrec-conf.org/proceedings/lrec2012/pdf/587_Paper.pdf.

Richard Landis and Gary Koch. 1997. The Measurement of Observer Agreement for Categorical Data Data for Categorical of Observer Agreement. *Biometrics*. 33(1), pages 159–174. https://doi.org/10.2307/2529310.

Tony McEnery and Richard Xiao. 2007. Parallel and comparable corpora: What are they up to? In Gunilla M. Andermann and Margaret Rogers, editors, *Incorporating Corpora: Translation and the Linguist* (Translating Europe). Multilingual Matters, Clevedon, pages 1–13.

Rada Mihalcea and Ted Pedersen. 2003. An Evaluation Exercise for Word Alignment. In *Proceedings of the HLT-NAACL 2003 Workshop on Building and Using Parallel Texts: Data Driven Machine Translation and Beyond*. Association for Computational Linguistics Stroudsburg, PA, USA, pages 1–10. https://www.aclweb.org/anthology/W03-0301.

Franz J. Och and Hermann Ney. 2003. A Systematic Comparison of Various Statistical Alignment Models. *Computational Linguistics*. 29(1), pages 19–51. https://doi.org/10.1162/089120103321337421.

Yves Scherrer and Bruno Cartoni. 2012. The Trilingual ALLEGRA Corpus: Presentation and Possible Use for Lexicon Induction. In *Proceedings of the 8th international conference on Language Resources and Evaluation (LREC 2012)*, European Language Resources Association (ELRA), Istanbul, Turkey, pages 2890–2896. http://www.lrec-conf.org/proceedings/lrec2012/pdf/685_Paper.pdf.

Felipe Soares and Martin Krallinger. 2019. BVS Corpus : A Multilingual Parallel Corpus of Biomedical Scientific Texts. CoRR,arXiv:1905.01712 [cs.CL], pages 1–8. https://arxiv.org/abs/1905.01712.

Harold Somers. 2001. Bilingual Parallel Corpora and Language Engineering. In *Proceedings.of the Workshop on Language Engineering for South-Asian Languages*. pages 1–16. http://www.emille.lancs.ac.uk/lesal/somers.pdf.

Ralf Steinberger, Andreas Eisele, Szymon Klocek, Spyridon Pilos, and Patrick Schlüter. 2012. DGT-TM: A Freely Available Translation Memory in 22 Languages. In *Proceedings of the 8th international conference on Language Resources and Evaluation (LREC 2012)*, European Language Resources Association (ELRA), Istanbul, Turkey, pages 454–459. http://www.lrec-conf.org/proceedings/lrec2012/pdf/814_Paper.pdf.

Ralf Steinberger, Mohamed Ebrahim, Alexandros Poulis, Manuel Carrasco-Benitez, Patrick Schlüter, Marek Przybyszewski, and Signe Gilbro. 2014. An overview of the European Union's highly multilingual parallel corpora. *Lang. Resour. Eval.* 48(4), pages 679–707. https://doi.org/10.1007/s10579-014-9277-0.

Oliver Streiter, Mathias Stuflesser, and Isabella Ties. 2004. CLE, an Aligned, Tri-lingual Ladin-Italian-German Corpus. Corpus Design and Interface. In *Proceedings of the 4th International Conference on Language Resources and Evaluation (LREC 2004)*. European Language Resources Association (ELRA), Lisbona, Portugal, pages 84–87. http://citeseerx.ist.psu.edu/viewdoc/download?doi=10.1.1.616.3181&rep=rep1&type=pdf.

Marko Tadić, Dunja Brozović-Rončević, and Amir Kapetanović. 2012. *The Croatian language in the digital age / Hrvatski jezik u digitalnom dobu*. Heidelberg: Springer Verlag. http://www.meta-net.eu/whitepapers/e-book/croatian.pdf.

Jörg Tiedemann. 2012. Parallel Data, Tools and Interfaces in OPUS. In *Proceedings of the 8th International Conference on Language Resources and Evaluation (LREC 2012)*. European Language Resources Association (ELRA), Istanbul, Turkey, pages 2214–2218. http://www.lrec-conf.org/proceedings/lrec2012/pdf/463_Paper.pdf.

Trond Trosterud. 2002. Parallel corpora as tools for investigating and developing minority languages. In Lars Borin, editor, *Parallel corpora, Parallel worlds. Language and Computers*. Studies in practical linguistics no 43. Rodopi, Amsterdam, pages 111–122. https://doi.org/10.1163/9789004334298_007.

Dániel Varga, Péter Halácsy, András Kornai, Viktor Nagy, László Németh, and Viktor Trón. 2007. Parallel Corpora for Medium Density Languages. In *Recent Advances in Natural Language Processing IV: Selected papers from RANLP 2005*, Current Issues in Linguistic Theory 292, pages 247–258. https://doi.org/10.1075/cilt.292.32var.

Michał Ziemski, Marcin Junczys-Dowmun, and Bruno Pouliquen. 2016. The United Nations Parallel Corpus v1.0. In *The Proceedings of tenth International Conference on Language Resources and Evaluation (LREC 16)*. European Language Resources Association (ELRA). Portorož, Slovenia, pages 3530–3534. https://www.aclweb.org/anthology/L16-1561.

What Influences the Features of Post-Editese? A Preliminary Study

Sheila Castilho[1], Natália Resende[1] and Ruslan Mitkov[2]

[1]ADAPT Centre, Dublin City University
[2]University of Wolverhampton

[1]{sheila.castilho,natalia.resende}@adaptcentre.ie
[2]r.mitkov@wlv.ac.uk

Abstract

While a number of studies have shown evidence of translationese phenomena, that is, statistical differences between original texts and translated texts (Gellerstam, 1986), results of studies searching for translationese features in post-edited texts (what has been called *"post-editese"* (Daems et al., 2017)) have presented mixed results. This paper reports a preliminary study aimed at identifying the presence of post-editese features in machine-translated post-edited texts and at understanding how they differ from translationese features. We test the influence of factors such as post-editing (PE) levels (full vs. light), translation proficiency (professionals vs. students) and text domain (news vs. literary). Results show evidence of post-editese features, especially in light PE texts and in certain domains.

1 Introduction

Over the past three decades, differences between translations and original texts have been substantially debated and empirically studied. Overall, research on these differences has shown that translations are usually normalised to conform to the linguistic norms and cultural aspects of the target language (Kenny, 2001). It has also been shown that translations tend to present less varied vocabulary (lower type/token ratio) and lower information load than original texts (Johansson, 1995; Laviosa, 1998). Statistical differences observed between originals and translations have been named *translationese* (Gellerstam, 1986; Baker, 1993; Volan-

sky et al., 2013; Daems et al.; 2017; Toral, 2019). According to Volansky et al. (2013), translationese phenomena are the result of two coexisting forces with which translators have to cope during the translation process: on one hand, fidelity to the source text and, on the other hand, fluency in the target language.

The term "translationese" had been put forward by Gellerstam (1986), but it was Baker (1993, 1996) who proposed and described the linguistic and stylistic natures of translationese, naming them *Translation Universals*. Translation Universals are hypotheses of linguistic features common to all translated texts regardless of the source and target languages. The hypothetical features proposed by Baker are: *Simplification, Explicitation, Normalisation* (or *Conservatism*) and *Levelling out* (or *Convergence*, as named by Pastor et al. (2008).[1]

Simplification means that translated texts are easier to understand than original texts because translators tend to simplify the language of the original text for the readers. *Explicitation* is the tendency to spell things out in translation; consequently, translations tend to be longer than original texts. Moreover, linguistic features that are typical of the source language are more explicit on the surface of the translation even though they are optional. *Levelling out* or *Convergence* means that there is less variation among translated texts than among non-translated texts. In other words, translated texts seem to be more similar to each other

---

[1]In their paper, Corpas et al. 2008 dispute the validity of the concept of universals. Therefore, we believe it is more accurate to speak about "trends" or "features" rather than "universals" and hence we prefer the more neutral (and not "universal") term "translationese".

Temnikova, I, Orăsan, C., Corpas Pastor, G., and Mitkov, R. (eds.) (2019) *Proceedings of the 2nd Workshop on Human-Informed Translation and Interpreting Technology (HiT-IT 2019)*, Varna, Bulgaria, September 5 - 6, pages 19–27.

https://doi.org/10.26615/issn.2683-0078.2019_003

than original texts (Baker, 1996).

Within translation and machine translation (MT) literature, a number of studies (Baroni and Bernardini, 2006; Pastor et al., 2008; Volansky et al., 2013; Rabinovich and Wintner, 2015) have shown that computers can distinguish to a high degree of accuracy between translations and original texts. On the other hand, Daems et al. (2017) found that computers are not capable of accurately distinguishing between human translation (HT) and post-editing (PE), that is, the authors did not find any indication of *post-editese* in HT and PE texts. However, Toral (2019) has shown strong evidence that there is such a distinction. He found that PE texts contain post-editese features since they represent more interference from the original text than translationese features. A similar pattern was found by Čulo and Nitzke (2016) who compared MT, PE and HT in terms of terminology and found that the way terminology is used in PE texts is closer to MT than to HT and it has less variation than HT. The study carried out by Vanmassenhove et al. (2019) also found evidence of post-editese features. In this study, the researchers compared MT and HT and found that current MT system processes cause a general loss in terms of lexical diversity and richness when compared to human-generated translations.

Although evidence for post-editese has been reported in the literature, current results do not point to a clear conclusion. For example, in the studies previously mentioned, no distinction has been made between the levels of translation proficiency. In addition, the convergence feature has not been tested. In the present study, we fill in this gap. We base our experiments on studies by Toral (2019) and Daems et al. (2017) addressing post-editese. We aim to investigate the features that distinguish translationese from post-editese, that is, the unique characteristics of a post-edited text that set it apart from a translated text and an original text. We will simultaneously test whether linguistic patterns present in PE texts change as a function of three factors: the proficiency level of the translators (professional translators vs. student translators), text domain (news domain vs. literary domain) and PE type (full PE vs. light PE).

In the next section, we present our methodology in detail describing all the features investigated. The results are presented and discussed in Section 3. In Section 4, we present our conclusions with suggestions for future research.

2 Methodology

This section describes the corpora used for the experiment, the PE process, and the features we consider to verify the existence of translationese and post-editese in both human translation and the post-edited text versions.

2.1 Study Rationale

The rationale behind our experiments is the following: we will look for typical features in both HT and PE texts. If differences in feature patterns between those translation types are observed, then we assume that our corpus presents evidence of post-editese features. If, on the other hand, no differences between HT and PE texts are found, we assume that PE and HT are not distinguishable, as show by Daems et al. (2017). The research questions that guided our experiments are:

- **RQ1-** Is it possible to find translationese features in PE texts?

- **RQ2-** If RQ1 is true, are there differences between the features extracted from PE texts and HT texts?

- **RQ3-** If RQ1 is true, do the domains of the texts, the proficiency of the translators and the type of PE influence the features analysed? If so, how?

2.2 Corpus

Two corpora were used for this experiment: the *New York Times* (NYT) and the Opus corpus. The NYT corpus is a collection of English headlines from *The New York Times* online newspaper, human-translated into Brazilian Portuguese (PT-BR) (Antiqueira et al., 2002). The NYT corpus consists of nine different texts[2] about general news. Because the corpus was not aligned, we decided to align it manually as some English source sentences were split into more sentences in PT-BR during the translation (one to many). The alignment was carried out looking into the source sentence and aligning all the correspondents in PT-BR in the same line.[3] In total, eight texts from the

---

[2]For this experiment, one of the texts was dismissed as problems were encountered when setting up the PE process.

[3]For example, when one source sentence in EN was translated into 2 sentences in PT-BR, the line corresponding to the EN sentence would contain 2 sentences in the PT-BR version.

NYT corpus were used, with 251 sentences, and 6097 tokens in the source.

From the Opus corpus (Tiedemann, 2012), we used a part of the subsection Opus Book[4] EN-PT. In total, 250 in-context sentences from *Alice in Wonderland* were used, with 5920 tokens in the source. In total, nine texts were post-edited by the translators: eight from NYT corpus (news) and one from the OPUS corpus (literature).

2.3 Translators, Tools and Guidelines

The corpus was translated using Google translate.[5] Four translators - two students and two professional translators - post-edited the corpus on two PE levels: light post-editing and full post-editing. Light PE was performed by one professional translator (PL) and by one student (SL), while full PE was performed by the second professional translator (PF), and by the second student (SF). Translators were given specific guidelines and were asked to follow them thoroughly. The tool used for the PE task was the PET tool (Aziz et al., 2012), and no time constraints were set for the task. A warm-up task for the translators to get acquainted with the tool and guidelines was set up. Translators were encouraged to ask questions about the tool and/or guidelines if needed.

2.4 Features

A set of linguistic features were extracted from our corpus with the purpose of identifying the existence of *post-editese* as well as to test the effect of translation domains, translation proficiency and PE levels on the features analysed. The features examined are listed below.

Simplification - According to Baker (1993), *simplification* can be determined by comparing the vocabulary range and information load of the translated and original texts. As translators tend to split long sentences into smaller ones to facilitate text comprehension, *simplification* can also be reflected by number of sentences and sentence length. In the present study, *simplification* is computed by calculating lexical density (content words/words ratio), lexical richness (type/token ration), as well as sentence count and mean sentence length. (Daems et al., 2017; Toral, 2019).

Explicitation - Because translated texts tend to be more explicit than originals, they tend to be longer than original texts. Moreover, translated texts tend to follow the original in using pronouns even when they are optional in the target language (Volansky et al., 2013). This is the case of the language pair studied here: English does not allow subject omission, while for PT-BR an explicit subject is optional as tense, person and number information expressed by the subject can also be inferred from the structure of the verbs (Chomsky, 1993). In order to investigate explicitation phenomena, we test whether translations are longer than originals (length ratio), and whether the amount of personal pronouns (personal pronoun ratio) is different between translations and original texts.

Convergence - Translated texts tend to be more similar to each other than non-translated texts (Baker, 1993, 1996; Pastor et al., 2008). Convergence can be computed by calculating the variance of the features extracted within the original texts and within the translated texts (HT and PEs).

3 Results and Discussion

A series of *ad hoc* programs was written in the Python programming language to extract the linguistic patterns from the corpus and to identify the features. Descriptive statistical analysis was carried out in Language R. The automatic metric (h)TER was calculated using MulteEval.[6] Statistical significance was not calculated as we are aware that the size of the corpus and the number of participants is relatively small. It is noteworthy to mention that boxplots are presented to illustrate only the striking differences.

3.1 Automatic Metrics

We compute (h)TER (Snover et al., 2006) scores to measure the distance between the MT output against the HT, and the distance between the MT output and the PE versions. The higher the score, the more different MT is from HT, and the PEs from the MT.

Table 1 shows the overall results for the automatic metrics for each translation type, while Figure 1 shows the results per domain. In both Figure 1 and Table 1, the first column/bar shows the scores for MT against HT, and the following

---

[4] http://opus.nlpl.eu/Books.php. The selection consisted of chapters 1-3.

[5] https://translate.google.com/. The online tool was used in April 2019

[6] https://github.com/jhclark/multeval

Translation Type	MT	PF	PL	SF	SL
(h)TER	51.70	24.68	01.69	08.92	01.77

Table 1: Overall TER scores comparing MT and HT, and overall hTER scores comparing MT vs PEs

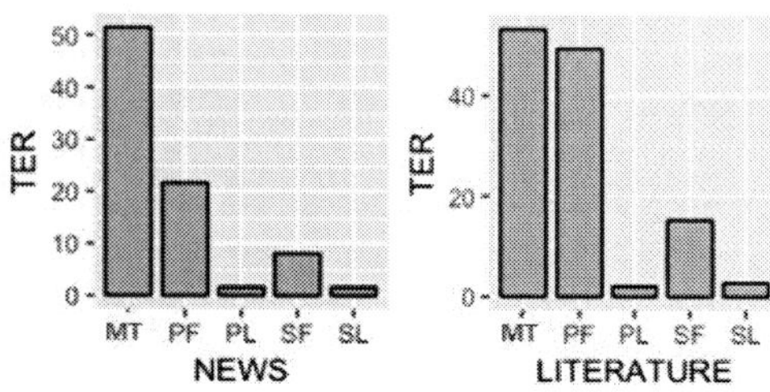

Figure 1: (h)TER scores per domain

columns/bars show the difference between the PE versions against the MT output.

We observe that the MT is indeed quite different from the HT version (51.70), and that all the light PE versions were indeed lightly post-edited with both professionals and students reaching <2 in terms of hTER in average. Interestingly, we can see that there is more PE being performed in the literature domain than in the news domain (Figure 1), where PF reaches 49 in terms of hTER against 21 in the news domains, and SF stands at 15 in literature against 8 in news domain, evidencing a domain effect on the amount of edits.

3.2 Simplification

Lexical Richness (LR) - In order to measure how varied the vocabulary range of original and translated texts is, we calculated type-token ratio (TTR), which is the number of token types, divided by the number of total tokens. We hypothesise that original texts will present higher lexical richness than the HT, MT and PEs versions. Because literature domain may involve more verbal artistry (e.g. paraphrase of figurative language and metaphors in the target language) (Baker, 1992), we hypothesise that the difference between originals and translation versions will be lower in the literature domain. Table 2 shows the overall results while Figure 2 illustrates the results per domain.

As previously mentioned, the literature on translationese shows that translated texts tend to be less lexically varied than original texts. When looking at the results per domain (Figure 2), we confirm our initial hypothesis. In the news domain, the original texts present higher lexical richness than the HT, while the MT version is very close to the PEs and the originals.

Translation Type	Ratio		
	News	Literature	Average of ratios
O	0.49	0.18	0.45
HT	0.47	0.23	0.44
MT	0.49	0.23	0.46
PF	0.49	0.23	0.46
PL	0.49	0.23	0.46
SF	0.49	0.22	0.46
SL	0.49	0.23	0.46

Table 2: Lexical Richness

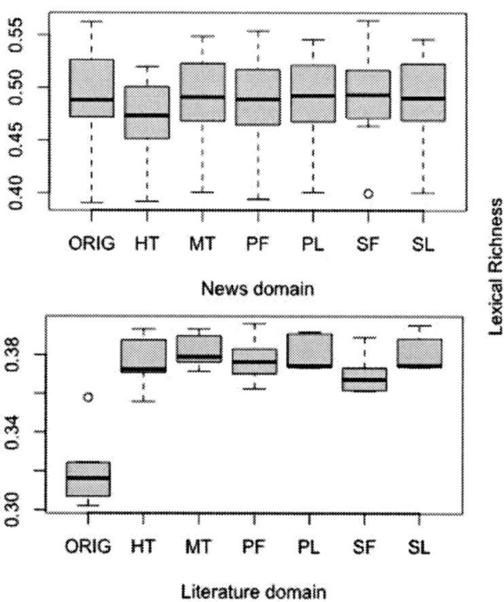

Figure 2: Lexical Richness per domain

In the literature domain, the difference between originals and translated texts is more notable, where all the translation types present more lexical variety than the original. More interestingly, HT and the full PE versions seem to have less lexical variety than the MT and the light PE versions. We assume that this reverse pattern in lexical richness for literature could be due to two main reasons, one of a linguistic and the other one of a stylistic nature. As PT-BR contains more verbal forms than English, these forms increased the number of types per verb root. We found, for instance, 128 occurrences of auxiliary verbs in the HT version, but only 38 in the original texts. Thus, we as-

Translation	Ratio		
Type	News	Literature	Average of ratios
O	0.65	0.56	0.63
HT	0.60	0.58	0.60
MT	0.61	0.57	0.60
PF	0.61	0.58	0.60
PL	0.61	0.57	0.60
SF	0.61	0.57	0.60
SL	0.61	0.57	0.60

Table 3: Lexical Density

sume that, when rendering the original message in the target language, translators could have used more lexical resources increasing, consequently, the number of types in the translated texts.

In spite of the unexpected results per domain, a pattern holds in both data sets: Because professional translators tend to pull the vocabulary range down in order to simplify text reading and comprehension and avoid redundancy, HT and PF versions tend to be similar. MT, on the other hand, tend to be closer to the original as observed by Toral (2019), and light PE, either professional or student, tends to keep the MT pattern.

It seems that this simplification feature is present in all translation types in the news domain, but its manifestation is more evident in translation types involving more human interference, namely: HT, PF, SF. Moreover, these results show a visible effect from domain, the proficiency levels of the translators.

Lexical Density (LD)   - To measure the amount of information present in the original text and in the translated texts, we extracted LD features by calculating the ratio of the number of content words (nouns, verbs, adjectives, adverbs) to total number of words. In this experiment, we excluded auxiliary verbs. As lower lexical density is a way of building redundancy and making a text simpler, we hypothesise that HT texts, PF and SF present lower lexical density than originals, but the pattern for MT, PL and SL will be similar. Table 3 displays the overall results and Figure 3 illustrates the results per domain.

In the news domain, our results confirm our hypothesis, as original texts show a higher lexical density than the HT texts. The MT texts show higher lexical density than the HT and is followed by the PE versions. We hypothesise that lexical density is higher for MT texts because this translation type tends to be close to the original texts than HT texts, corroborating teh results of Toral

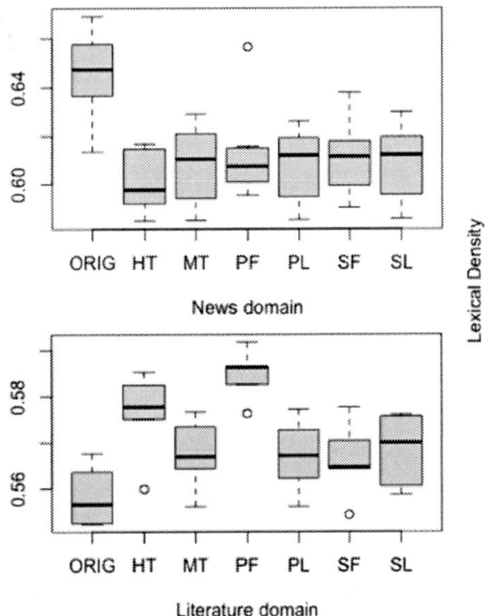

Figure 3: Lexical Density per domain

(2019).

Regarding the literature domain, our results contradict our hypothesis. The original texts present lower lexical density than the HT versions. As noted by the analysis of lexical richness, literary texts may feature more varied vocabulary of either lexical and function words as a way to conform to the linguistic norms and cultural aspects of the target language. In the literature domain, the PF version is equal to the HT, suggesting the number of edits performed has an effect on the translationese features. Interestingly, in both the literary and news domains, we confirm that MT and PEs present similar patterns.

Sentence Count (SC) and Sentence Length (SL) are calculated by simply counting the total number of sentences and the mean sentence length (in words). As mentioned previously, because translations tend to be simplified, we expect them to have a higher number of sentences and that those sentences will be shorter than the sentences in the original texts.

Table 4 shows that original texts present, on average, slightly fewer sentences than the other translation types. In the news domain, the MT version presents a lower sentence count than the HT. Also, PE versions are closer to the MT than to the HT version. In the literature domain, no strong pattern can be observed, but light PE versions (PL and SL) tend to reduce the number of sentences compared to the full PE versions (PF and SF).

Translation	Ratio		
Type	News	Literature	Total Average
O	251	315	62.9
HT	262	317	64.3
MT	253	322	63.9
PF	249	310	62.1
PL	254	317	63.4
SF	252	312	62.7
SL	252	321	63.7

Table 4: Sentence Count

Translation	Ratio		
Type	News	Literature	Total Average
O	27.7	23	27.2
HT	27.6	22	26.9
MT	27.9	21	27.2
PF	28.4	22	27.7
PL	27.6	21.4	26.9
SF	28	22.2	27.4
SL	27.9	21.3	27.2

Table 5: Mean Sentence Length

Regarding mean sentence length (Table 5, the original texts present slightly longer sentences on average. The MT version tends to follow the same sentence length of the original, and PE versions tend to keep the same pattern of the MT. Together, these results show that original texts tend to contain fewer sentences on average than HT texts as predicted, but PE versions tend to keep MT patterns, especially for light PE.

3.3 Explicitation

Length Ratio (LgtR) - According to Baker (1993), translated texts tend to be longer than originals. We test this hypothesis by calculating the difference between the length of the original text (measured in characters) and the length of the translated versions, divided by the length of the original. We expect translated texts to be longer than original texts. In Table 6, we observe that, overall, HT is 5% longer than the original, while the MT is even longer with 8%. The PE versions are closer to the HT than the MT version.

As predicted, overall results as well as results per domain confirm that translations are longer than the original. In Figure 4 and Table 6, we note that the literature domain does not, on average, differ in length from the original text. In the news domain, on average, the differences in length are more accentuated. MT texts present a

greater variation (0 to -0.25), having its median further from the original, that is, further from 0.

Translation	Ratio		
Type	News	Literature	Total Average
HT	-0.05	-0.08	-0.05
MT	-0.09	-0.08	-0.08
PF	-0.05	0.00	-0.05
PL	-0.05	-0.04	-0.05
SF	-0.07	-0.02	-0.06
SL	-0.05	0.20	-0.05

Table 6: Length Ratio per domain and overall. (*Ratios closer to 0 are closer to the original. A positive ratio means that the original is longer, while negative ratio means the original is shorter)

Theses results suggest a domain effect and a post-editese effect since PE versions tend to be closer to the original texts in terms of length than HT versions. It is noteworthy, however, that differences in text length between originals and translation could be explained by English being a more concise language than Portuguese, not necessarily by the presence of explicitation. Therefore, in order to obtain a better picture of the explicitation phenomena, we tested if elements that are optional in the target language, such as the personal pronouns, were kept in the translations.

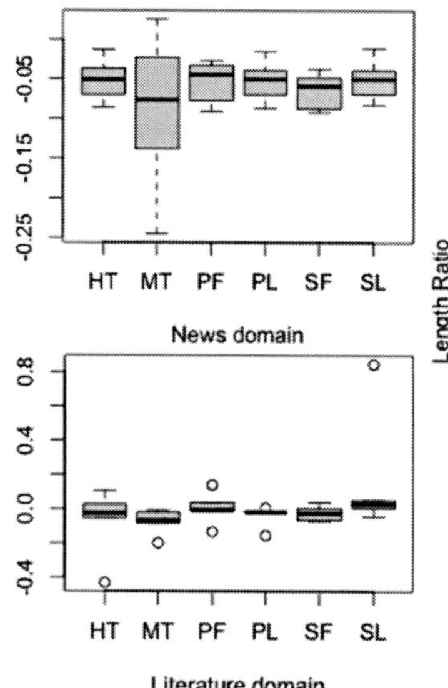

Figure 4: Length Ratio per domain

Personal Pronoun Ratio (PPR) - To test if translated texts tend to follow the original in using pronouns even when they are optional in the target language, we calculated the difference in the number of personal pronouns (PP) between original and translated text. While we expect the original texts to have a higher number of personal pronouns since they are optional in Portuguese, we expect that the MT version will be closer to the original than the HT, and that the full PE versions will be closer to the HT. Table 7 shows that, indeed, the original presents a higher ratio for PPR, given the positive ratio for all the translation types. Overall, the MT version is closer to the original (0.55) than the HT (0.59). While the PL keeps the

| Translation | Ratio | | |
Type	News	Literature	Total Average
HT	0.61	0.61	0.59
MT	0.49	0.50	0.55
PF	0.67	0.69	0.86
PL	0.48	0.49	0.55
SF	0.50	0.51	0.57
SL	0.49	0.50	0.58

Table 7: Personal Pronoun Ratio per domain and overall. (*Ratios closer to 0 are closer to the original. A positive ratio means that the original contains more PPs, while negative ratio means the original contains fewer PPs)

same ratio as MT, both student versions (SF and SL) slightly increase the ratio, revealing a PE effect and a professional proficiency effect.

3.4 Convergence

According to Baker (1993), translated texts tend to be more similar to each other than to the original texts. To investigate this hypothesis, we compare the variance scores obtained for the set of original texts, translated texts and post-edited texts for each of the simplification and explicitation features extracted from our corpus (literary domain and news domain): mean sentence length (MSL), sentence count ratio (SCR), lexical richness (LR), lexical density (LD), length ratio (LgtR) and personal pronoun ratio (PPR). For this comparison, we opted to calculate the variance within the translated texts involving only human translation (original and HT) separately from translations involving a MT (MT, PF, PL, SF, SL) to test the hypothesis that variance within MT and PEs is not as high as the previous experiments have shown, as well as to verify whether variance within the PE texts is higher or lower than the variance within the set of MT + PE texts.

Overall, Table 8 shows that original texts vary more than all translated texts for all features (MSL, SC, LR, LD), suggesting that the original texts are les similar to each other, while the trans-

lated texts are more similar to each other. When comparing variance between the set of HT and the set of other translation types (MT+PEs and PEs), it is possible to observe that the variance scores are very close to each other for all translationese features, suggesting that translation type has little effect. Variance scores obtained for the MT + PEs set do not differ from the PEs set. This indicates that MT texts are very close to PEs texts in all features, except for a tiny difference in variance score obtained for the LgthR feature between the MT + PEs set and PEs text set.

Features	Orig	HT	MT+PEs	PEs
MSL	11.26	9.84	8.43	8.28
SCR	0.14	0.13	0.13	0.13
LR	0.01	0.007	0.008	0.008
LD	0.001	0.0002	0.0003	0.0003
LgtR	-	0.0005	0.002	0.0005
PPR	-	0.01	0.005	0.005

Table 8: Variance scores within texts types for features SCR, LR, LD, LgtR and PPR (*The higher the variance score, the higher the dissimilarity within the text sets)

4 Conclusion

This study investigated the presence of post-editese features in a corpus composed by HT, MT and PE texts post-edited by either professional translators or student translators in two domains: news and literature.

Our results have revealed translationese features on the surface of HT and also PE texts, answering in the affirmative **RQ1**. Most of the features described by Baker (1993) were confirmed in the news domain for both HT versions and MT versions, namely LR, LD, LgthR, PPR, SC, except for mean sentence length. In the literature domain, not all translationese features were confirmed and, thus, we can assume that text domain plays a role in the prevalence of translationese features. This finding suggests that, looking for translationese features exactly as described by Baker (1993), may lead to erroneous conclusions, especially in the literary domain. This domain contain certain stylistic features that reflects the translator's verbal artistry, and issues inherently related to the language combination.

The most important finding of our study is the difference observed in the manifestation of translationese features between HT and PE texts, thus revealing evidences of post-editese features. Post-editese features were found to be reflected as more interference from the original than HT texts and also more interference from the raw MT output. Our results show that the greater the human interference in the raw MT texts, the greater their distance from the original text and, consequently, their distance from the MT output. This is the case when the raw MT is fully post-edited. In this case, the PF version tends to be closer to HT, and further from MT, PL and original versions, suggesting a great similarity in terms of features between HT and PF.

Together, these results show that simplification, explicitation and convergence features are present on the surface of translated text, although this picture is somewhat blurred for the literature domain. In spite of the differences between text domains, our results allow us to affirmatively answer **RQ2** and **RQ3**. We consider the differences between the manifestation of features between HT and PE texts as an evidence for post-editese. However, the post-editese features were found more prominently in the light PE performed by either professional or students. Likewise, we consider the differences encountered between domains, translator's proficiency levels and types of PE as evidence of the effect of these factors on the way post-editese features are manifested on the surface of the texts. Further, our findings corroborate Toral (2019) in confirming that MT translated texts and PE's are more influenced by the original texts. Like Toral (2019), we hypothesise that this behaviour is due to a priming effect between the MT output and the post-editor resulting in texts that are more aligned between these two. Additionally, our study adds a new finding to Toral (2019) and Daems et al. (2017): a high number of human edits in the raw MT by means of PE results, on the one hand, in a wider distance between the other PE versions, MT, and original; and, on the other hand, in an approximation of the HT version.

The limitations of this study lie in the number of translators and the size of the corpus. Statistical significance tests as well as the convergence experiment would benefit from a wider range of translators and a bigger corpus in order to allow for broader generalisations regarding the differences and similarities found. Nonetheless, the study allowed us to pose research questions that merit exploration in future research. Given that we found, in the news domain, that a greater loss in lexical richness and lexical density was present in HT and PF than in MT texts, does this mean that HT and PF convey less of the original meaning than a MT? Can we be sure that the greater the differences between the original and the translation (as the revealed by HT and PF versions), the higher the quality? To achieve MT quality, should systems be less influenced by the original text but rather convey a more simplified message in terms of lexical and syntactical features? Answering these questions has implications not only for the translation studies field but also for MT quality improvement as it will allow researchers to explore the features that constitute a high-quality MT output.

Acknowledgments

We would like to thank the professional translators and the students for providing us with the post-editing versions for both corpora. The ADAPT Centre for Digital Content Technology (`www.adaptcentre.ie`) at Dublin City University is funded by the Science Foundation Ireland Research Centres Programme (Grant 13/RC/2106) and is co-funded by the European Regional Development Fund. This project was partially funded by the European Union's Horizon 2020 research and innovation programme under the Marie Sklodowska-Curie grant agreement No 843455.

References

Lucas Antiqueira, Marcela Franco Fossey, Tatiana Pedrolongo, Juliana Galvani Greghi, Ronaldo Teixeira Martins, and Maria das Graças Volpe Nunes. 2002. A construção do corpus e dos dicionários inglês-unl e unl-português para o projeto ept-web.

Wilker Aziz, Sheila Castilho, and Lucia Specia. 2012. PET: a Tool for Post-editing and Assessing Machine Translation. In *Proceedings of the Eight International Conference on Language Resources and Evaluation (LREC'12)*. Istanbul, Turkey.

Mona Baker. 1992. London New York:Routledge.

Mona Baker. 1993. Corpus linguistics and translation studies: Implications and applications. In Gill Francis and Elena Tognini-Bonelli, editors, *Text and Technology: In Honour of John Sinclair*, John Benjamins Publishing Company, Netherlands, pages 233–252.

Mona Baker. 1996. chapter corpus-based translation studies: The challenges that lie ahead. In *Terminology, LSP and Translation: Studies in Language*

Engineering, in Honour of Juan C. Sager. Amsterdam: John Benjamins Publishing Company, page 175–186.

Marco Baroni and Silvia Bernardini. 2006. A new approach to the study of translationese: machine-learning the difference between original and translated text. *Literary and Linguistic Computing* 21(3):259–274.

Noam Chomsky. 1993. In *Lectures on Government and Binding: The Pisa Lectures*. Holland: Foris Publications.Reprint. 7th Edition, Berlin and New York: Mourton de Gruyter.

Oliver Čulo and Jean Nitzke. 2016. Patterns of terminological variation in post-editing and of cognate use in machine translation in contrast to human translation. In *Proceedings of the 19th Annual Conference of the European Association for Machine Translation*. pages 106–114. https://www.aclweb.org/anthology/W16-3401.

Joke Daems, Orphée De Clercq, and Lieve Macken. 2017. Translationese and post-editese: How comparable is comparable quality? *Linguistica Antverpiensia New Series - Themes in Translation Studies* 16:89–103.

Martin Gellerstam. 1986. Translationese in swedish novels translated from english. In *In Wollin, L. and Lindquist, H. Translation Studies in Scandinavia*. CWK Gleerup, Lund, volume 4, pages 88–95.

Stig Johansson. 1995. Mens sana in corpore sano: on the role of corpora in linguistic researc. *The European English Messenger* 4:19–25.

Dorothy Kenny. 2001. In *Lexis and creativity in translation: a corpus-based study*. Manchester: St. Jerome.

Sara Laviosa. 1998. Core patterns of lexical use in a comparable corpus of english lexical prose. *Meta* 43(4):557–570.

Gloria Corpas Pastor, Ruslan Mitkov, and Viktor Pekar. 2008. V.: Translation universals: Do they exist? a corpus-based nlp study of convergence and simplification. In *In: Proceedings of the AMTA*.

Ella Rabinovich and Shuly Wintner. 2015. Unsupervised identification of translationese. *Transactions of the Association for Computational Linguistics* 3:419–432.

Matthew Snover, Bonnie Dorr, Richard Schwartz, Linnea Micciulla, and John Makhoul. 2006. A study of translation edit rate with targeted human annotation. In *AMTA 2006: Proceedings of the 7th Conference of the Association for Machine Translation in the Americas*. Cambridge, MA, USA, pages 223–231.

Jörg Tiedemann. 2012. Parallel data, tools and interfaces in OPUS. In *Proceedings of the Eighth International Conference on Language Resources and Evaluation (LREC-2012)*. European Languages Resources Association (ELRA), Istanbul, Turkey, pages 2214–2218. http://www.lrec-conf.org/proceedings/lrec2012/pdf/463_Paper.pdf.

Antonio Toral. 2019. Post-editese: an exacerbated translationese. In *Proceedings of Machine TRanslation Summit*. Dublin, Ireland.

Eva Vanmassenhove, Dimitar Shterionov, and Andy Way. 2019. Lost in translation: Loss and decay of linguistic richness in machine translation. In *Proceedings of MT Summit XVII*. Dublin, Ireland.

Vered Volansky, Noam Ordan, and Shuly Wintner. 2013. On the features of translationese. *Digital Scholarship in the Humanities* 30(1):98–118. https://doi.org/10.1093/llc/fqt031.

Designing a Frame-Semantic Machine Translation
Evaluation Metric

Oliver Czulo[1], Tiago Timponi Torrent[2], Ely Edison da Silva Matos[2],
Alexandre Diniz da Costa[2], Debanjana Kar[3]

[1] Universität Leipzig, Germany
[2] Federal University of Juiz de Fora, Brazil
[3] Indian Institute of Technology Kharagpur, India

[1]czulo@uni-leipzig.de
[2]{tiago.torrent, ely.matos, alexandre.costa}@ufjf.edu.br
[3]debanjana.kar@iitkgp.ac.in

Abstract

We propose a metric for machine translation evaluation based on frame semantics which does not require the use of reference translations or human corrections, but is aimed at comparing original and translated output directly. The metric is developed on the basis of an existing manual frame-semantic annotation of a parallel corpus with an English original and a Brazilian Portuguese and a German translation. We discuss implications of our metric design, including the potential of scaling it for multiple languages.

1 Introduction

Meaning is the central dimension in translation. This entails that even if an original and a translation do not match very well on the formal side, they can still be related to each other in terms of semantic similarity. Current machine translation (MT) evaluation algorithms, however, are limited in evaluating the meaning of original and translation: they mostly rely on matching MT output to some reference translation, but the meaning may have been expressed by some sort of paraphrase or a creative solution, the adequacy of which cannot be thoroughly evaluated by means of simple matches. Using reference translations for evaluation furthermore requires the involvement of human translators which may prove a challenge if the aim is to evaluate large proportions of machine translated text.

This paper describes the outline for and a first application of a Frame Semantic Evaluation Measure (FSEM) designed to perform semantic evaluation of machine translated texts. While the first version operates on manually annotated texts, FSEM should eventually be able to incorporate automatic annotation of semantic frames.

2 Background

The evaluation method we propose here is based on the application of frame semantics to translation which was first formulated for human translation. We briefly introduce frame semantics (2.1) and the *Primacy of Frame* model of translation (2.2). We then explain how the primacy of frame model can be expressed algorithmically as a spread activation network (2.3).

2.1 Frame Semantics

Frame semantics (FS; Fillmore 1982, 1985) is a semantics of understanding. A frame is defined as

"[...] system of concepts related in such a way that to understand any one concept it is necessary to understand the entire system; introducing any one concept results in all of them becoming available." (Petruck 1996: 1)

The theory of FS is closely entrenched in a linguistic paradigm. While FS in many ways is a theory of the system of concepts prevalent in a culture (or more generally a collective of speakers), it also captures the relation between linguistic material and mental concepts. A frame is evoked by means of linguistic expressions, and by this evocation our background knowledge is activated and helps us interpret an expression. One of the most popular examples to describe this, is by means of the Commercial_transaction frame. In this frame, a Buyer

Temnikova, I, Orăsan, C., Corpas Pastor, G., and Mitkov, R. (eds.) (2019) *Proceedings of the 2nd Workshop on Human-Informed Translation and Interpreting Technology (HiT-IT 2019)*, Varna, Bulgaria, September 5 - 6, pages 28–35.

https://doi.org/10.26615/issn.2683-0078.2019_004

and a Seller are involved in a transfer of Goods in exchange for Money. This frame can be perspectivized in various ways: in the Commerce_buy scenario, the focus is on the Buyer, in the Commerce_sell scenario on the Seller. But the fact that the frame is linked to the evoking lexical units such as *buy*, *purchase*, *sell*, *price*, etc. and that the frame as a whole is activated in the process of interpretation allows us to fully understand partial instantiations of a frame. So even when we read/hear a sentence like

(1) Jane sold her house.

we understand that it was sold to someone and for a certain amount of money, even though this is not explicitly mentioned. At the same time this example highlights the notion of *perspective*: The scene that is instantiated in this example is reported on from the viewpoint of the seller, not the buyer.

Berkeley FrameNet is a computational modeling of Frame Semantics for English (Fillmore, Johnson, and Petruck 2003) and comprises a network of frames together with the linguistic expressions they are connected to based on corpus data. Each frame entry lists a definition, a list of core and peripheral frame elements and of lexical units which evoke this frame. For lexicalized frames, a list of lexical units which evoke the frame is given, and for each list the corpus examples and the annotation scheme can be viewed. Frames do not stand just for themselves, but are also connected to each other via frame-to-frame relations. The frames Filling and Fullness, for instance, are connected via the causative_of-relation, where Filling is the causative alternation of Fullness. Other relations currently defined include such relations as inheritance, precedence or perspective. FrameNets exist in various other languages, with differences in coverage, database structure and annotation policies, e.g. for German (named SALSA, Burchardt et al. 2006), Japanese (Ohara et al. 2004), Spanish (Subirats Rüggeberg and Petruck 2003), Swedish (Borin et al. 2010), or Brazilian Portuguese (Torrent et al. 2018a).

2.2 The *Primacy of Frame* Model of Translation

The Primacy of Frame model of translation (POF; Czulo 2017) seeks to provide a descriptive basis for the measurement of semantic similarity between an original and its translation. This is in line with Tymoczko's (2005) proposal, which advocates viewing equivalence not as an identity relation, but as a similarity relation. A measure based on the POF model should thus not make a binary decision about something being adequate (or even "correct") or not, but should pose the relation between an original and its translation(s) on a scale of degree of similarity. The notion of semantic similarity is of priority here, but POF takes other dimensions into account.

On the semantic scale, POF is based on a number of pre-existing works in which frame semantics has been applied to translation. The main goal of defining the model was to consolidate the various existing works and to identify a common underlying hypothesis. Indeed, this is a trivial step: though, to the knowledge of the authors, it has not been made explicit, the common underlying assumption in frame analyses of translation is that, ideally, there is a one-to-one correspondence on the frame level between an original and a translation. In such a model, the frame level provides a means to abstract away from purely formal considerations on the lexical level, such as cases of n:m-correspondences, e. g. between the German verb *einschlafen* and the English correspondence *fall asleep*.

The principle of a one-to-one relation on the frame level can be overridden depending on various factors. The classification of these can be very detailed, such as those performed by Vinay & Darbelnet (1958). POF remains on a more general level. We can distinguish between the purely formal level, such as the above example of an n:m-correspondence on the lexical level, but not on a semantic level. These formal factors can be more complex, though, such as in multimodal settings, where number of syllables or lip movement (in dubbing) or number of characters per line (in subtitling) may play a role and may lead to motivated departures from an exact rendering of the original message.

What POF stresses in contrast to other approaches is the importance of the functional level. Function here is seen as a conventionalized understanding of what a linguistic expression conveys on a pragmatic level, e. g. considering the level of formality or of politeness, or such aspects as focus and information structure. Sometimes, functional considerations can be prioritized over exact semantic representation such as in (2):

(2) DE: Handlungsbedarf wird
    Need-for-action will.3.PERS.PRES

es auch weiterhin   geben.
it also furthermore give.INF
Lit. 'Need-for-action will there also furthermore be.'
EN: More changes will take place in the future.

As reported in (Čulo 2016), there are various
strategies to deal with this when translating from
German to English. The simplest would be to just
switch the order of subject and object, losing the
focus on *Handlungsbedarf*. In (3), the translator
apparently decided to keep the word order of the
original sentence, but by shifting the element
which was the sentence-initial direct object in
German into the subject in English, the main verb
of the sentence needs to be accommodated. This
results in a frame shift between the sentences:
While the German original speaks of the Existence of a need for change, the English version describes the very likely Event of a change happen-
ing in the future. Despite this shift in semantics we
can still relate the two sentences to each other in
terms of "semantic similarity" and model this relation by means of exploiting frame-to-frame relations as proposed by Ellsworth and colleagues
(2006).

The Existence frame is preceded by the Com-
ing_to_be frame which, in turn, inherits from the
Event frame (Figure 1). The frames Existence and
Event are thus closely related and we can state that
the two sentences in (2) are semantically similar.

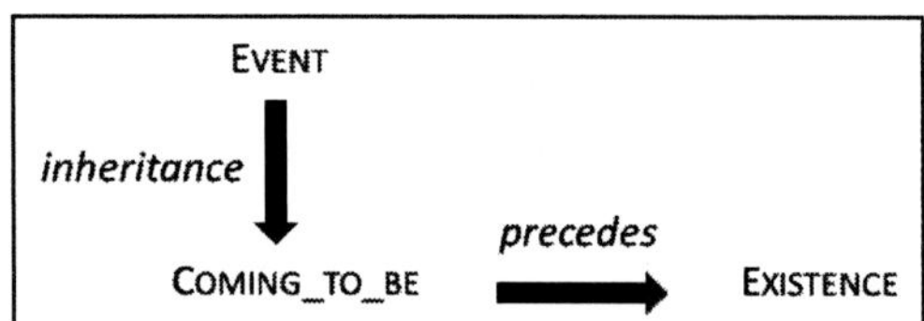

Figure 1: Frame to frame relations for Event and
Existence

There are various other factors, such as typological or systematic contrastive differences, e. g.
concerning the agentivity of the subject between
German or English (Hawkins 1986), in information encoding in the verb for motion events in
different languages (Talmy 2000, Slobin 2004),
and other factors which could lead to frame shifts.
Questions arising from this are:

A. Can a frame shift be described ade-
    quately by means of the frame hierar-
    chy?
B. If not, is this due to a lack of
    -   frame coverage in FrameNet?
    -   recorded relations in the frame
        hierarchy?
    -   cultural specificity of frames or
        frame relations?

The project presented here sets out to test in
how far current versions of FrameNet can be applied cross-linguistically (currently ignoring more
complex cases of cultural differences) and cover
the basic semantic space well enough in order to
make it usable for cross-linguistic comparison of
originals and translations.

2.3 Spread Activation and the Frame Hier-archy

The FrameNet network can be handled as a seman-
tic/conceptual network. A common technique used
to query this kind of network is Spread Activation
(SA). Although SA is mainly a cognitive theory
modeling semantic memory (Collins and Loftus,
1975), the algorithm has been used in various NLP
and Information Retrieval processes. Hirst (1988)
presents an initial proposal to apply SA for Word
Sense Disambiguation. Diederich (1990) discusses
SA in the context of NLP systems. The algorithm
was also used for similarity measures in Okazaki
(2003), Gouws (2010) and Thiel (2010).

The SA algorithm can be described as an iterative process of propagating real-valued energy
from one or more source nodes over a network using weighted links. Each propagation is called a
pulse. Basically, pulses are triggered from one (or
more) initial node(s) and propagates through the
network, activating linked nodes. This process of
activating more and more nodes and checking for
termination conditions is repeated pulse after
pulse, until all termination conditions are met,
which results in a final activation state for the network.

This general process can be implemented in
specific ways depending on the problem and the
network characteristics. Given FrameNet structure, the network can be handled as a directed acy-
clic graph (DAG) Figure 2 shows the schematic
network topology.

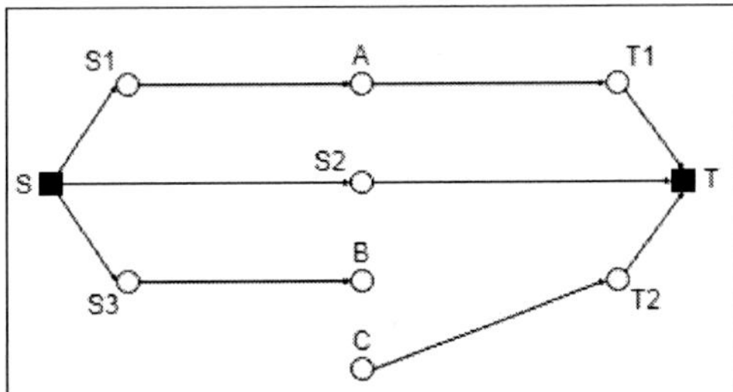

Figure 2: Network topology

The network comprises:
- a source node (S) representing the sentence in the source language,

- a target node (T) representing the sentence in the target language,

- nodes directly evoked by the source sentence (S1, S2, S3),

- nodes directly evoked by the target sentence (T1, T2, S2),

- and nodes from the frame hierarchy (A, B, C).

Three situations can occur in the network: (i) common frames evoked directly by both sentences (S2), (ii) common frames in the hierarchy (A), (iii) unshared frames (B, C), leading nodes C and T2 to not being activated.

The process starts with the source node activation. This node propagates activation for the neighbour nodes as a function of its activation level (a real-value) and the weights from its input links. For each interaction p, node j has an activation level $Aj(p)$ and an output level $Oj(p)$ defined as a function of the activation level, as in (3).

$$(3) \qquad O_j(p) = f(A_j(p))$$

An output from a node j affects the activation level of the next node k linked to node j. All weights were set to 1.0 (meaning that every FrameNet relation is supposed to have the same importance to the process), as in (4).

$$(4) \quad A_k(p) = \Sigma_j^{\boxed{}} O_j(p-1)W_{jk}$$

The output function (O) in (5) was chosen as a logistic function variation to avoid excessive activation in the nodes. The variation in the numerator — the multiplication by 5 — is meant to smooth the resulting curve.

$$(5) \quad O_j(p) = \frac{1-\exp(5*(-Aj(p)))}{1+\exp(-Aj(p))}$$

As the propagation ends (when the target sentence node is reached), the calculated output level for this node (a real-value in $(0,1)$) is considered the similarity measure in relation to the source sentence node.

3   A Frame-Semantic Spread Activation Evaluation Measure (FSEM)

FSEM is designed to take up on some of the shortcomings of the above described metrics. In short, it should

- not require human involvement (such as HTER; Snover et al. 2006),

- not be based on pure lexical matching, such as BLEU (Papineni et al., 2002), even if synonyms are considered, such as METEOR (Banerjee and Lavie, 2005),

- maximally describe the semantic content of a sentence, not just shallow and generic argument structure configurations as those provided by Propbank based SRL, such as MEANT (Lo and Wu, 2011; Lo and Wu 2017).

FSEM shall thus
- be fully automatic (in its final version),

- capture meaning rather than surface form (using FrameNet frames and the hierarchy network behind them),

- evaluate frames not just for the main verb of the sentence, but for as many semantically relevant segments as possible.

FSEM has so far been applied only to a corpus which was manually annotated for the frames using the Berkeley FrameNet 1.7 data release. This corpus is made up of the English transcript and the Brazilian Portuguese and German translations of this transcript of the TED talk "Do schools kill creativity", the most viewed TED talk at the time of writing. In (Torrent et al. 2018b), the corpus and the project setting are described and early annotations for English and Brazilian Portuguese are compared. English is annotated by the Berkeley FrameNet team, Brazilian Portuguese by the FrameNet Brazil Computational Linguistics Lab team and German by a working group consisting of members of the Universities Düsseldorf and

Leipzig. Currently, annotation standards are harmonized and a set of sentence pairs has been prepared for developing and tuning the FSEM algorithm.

Unlike the MEANT family of metrics, FSEM does not rely on argument structure, and, therefore does not currently require the existence of SRL applications for all languages involved in the translation task. FSEM only takes into consideration the frames evoked in the sentence. Also, it considers the FrameNet network of relations to address cases of frame shifts.

As an example of the application of FSEM, consider the sentence extracted from the TED Talk transcript in (6), followed by the translations provided by TED for the same sentence in Brazilian Portuguese (7) and German (8).

(6) We have a huge vested interest in it, partly because it's education that's meant to take us into this future that we can't grasp.

(7) Nos   interessamos
    us.REFL   be-interested.PRES.1PL
    tanto   por   ela   em parte
    so-much   for   she.ACC   in part
    porque   é   da
    because   be.PRES.3SG   of-the
    educação   o papel de nos
    education   the role of us
    conduzir   a esse futuro
    conduct.INF to this future
    misterioso.
    misterious

(8) Wir haben   ein großes,
    We have.PERS.1PL   a   big
    persönliches Interesse, teilweise Bildung

personal   interest   partly   education
dazu   gedacht   ist,
for-this   think.PART.PERF be.PERS.3SG
uns in diese Zukunft zu bringen,
us in this future   to bring.INF
die   wir nicht fassen   können.
which we not   grasp.INF can.PERS.1PL

Note that there are important structural differences between the original in (6) and the Brazilian Portuguese translation in (7), mainly due to a difference in the POS of the main predicator: interest.n in English versus interessar-se.v in Brazilian Portuguese. Torrent et al. (2018b) demonstrate that this difference triggers a cascade of other structural differences, such as the use of an adjective - *huge.a* - to intensify the interest in English, as opposed to a degree adverb in - *tanto.adv* - to do the same with the verb in Brazilian Portuguese. Nonetheless, the final activation score obtained when comparing the frames evoked by the words in both sentences is 0.9808, since the formal differences observed between the two sentences are not capable of precluding them from evoking the same core frames used in understanding them (see Figure 3):

- Mental_stimulus_experiencer_focus, indicating interest,

- Causation, indicating the causative relation between the role of education to take us into the future,

- Education_teaching, the topic of the talk,

- Bringing, the metaphorical action performed by education, and

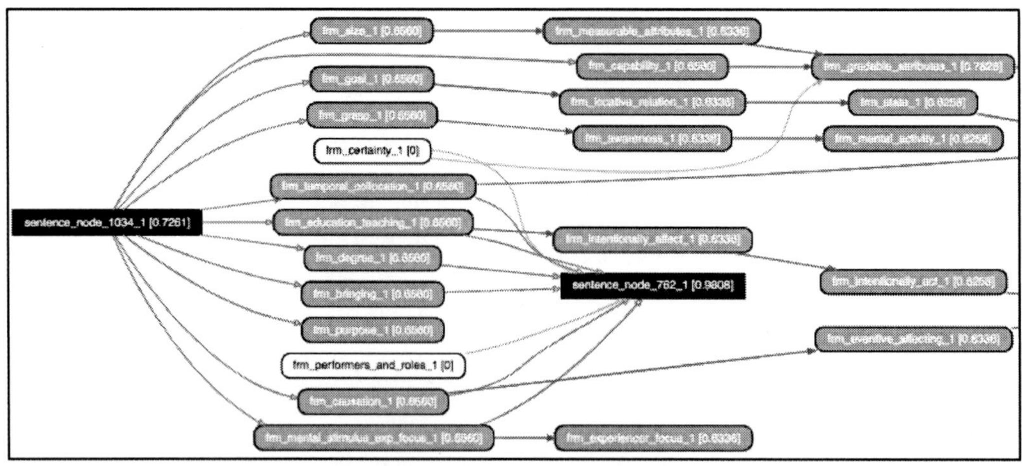

Figure 3: Spread activation network for the sentence pair (7-8)

- Temporal_collocation, indicating the future.

As for the German translation in (8), the activation score is even slightly higher with 0.9899, despite the fact that one frame is not being realized in the German version: a connector indicating Causation is missing in the subordinate clause (e. g. *da* or *weil*). Apart from this, the German translation is structurally closer to the English original than the Brazilian translation with one notable difference: In English, the construction *it is X that* which has the function to strengthen the focus on *education* is not reproduced as such in German even though a formally and functionally analogous construction exists in German. We suspect that this construction was not rendered as such in German due to space and reading time restrictions of the subtitling. On a purely frame semantic level, however, this does not have an effect.

4 Implications of FSEM

FSEM is a semantically informed evaluation algorithm which can not only abstract away from surface form but can also point to differences in the semantic make-up of original and translation which could point to phenomena such as differences in conceptualization of a scenario between source and target language.

For this paper, we used the English Berkeley FrameNet as means of comparing an English original, a Brazilian Portuguese and a German translation. This was possible as the language of the text analyzed was general enough to be well covered by the Berkeley FrameNet, and to assume that a FrameNet describing similar portions of German and Brazilian Portuguese could be analogously structured. This raises a number of questions, though, concerning the cross-linguistic applicability of large portions of the Berkeley FrameNet. The more culture specific the topic, the less can we expect a structural overlap between FrameNets of different languages.

A practical issue is that of granularity: depending on the process of development, different FrameNets may have a more general or a very specific coverage of certain domains. The spread activation model of FSEM partially adjusts for this, as related frames (also more general and more specific frames) are taken into account in the analysis, but this comes with a penalty. For future implementations of FSEM, we plan to incorporate information obtained from the shared annotation task discussed in Torrent et al. (2018b) as a means of calibrating the weights of different types of frame-to-frame relations for each language pair.

In order to complete the implementation of FSEM and to include automatic semantic parsing for the identification of the frames evoked by each LU in the sentence through tools such as SEMAFOR (Chen et al. 2010), Open Sesame (Swayamdipta el al. 2017) and Sling (Ringgaard et al., 2017), a Google Summer of Code project was started.[1] This project also aims explore alternative possibilities for comparing frame annotations and to test the inclusion of frame elements in the evaluation. In the first round of evaluation, around 30 sentence pairs from the human translated TED talk were scored from 4 (acceptable without changes) to 1 (unusable) by 7 annotators for each language pair. A normalized score between 0 to 1 was computed for each sentence by considering a weighted average of the scores provided by the annotators. To remove class bias, 30 more negative samples (i.e. sentence pairs with score 0) were generated. The scores obtained were tested against a model which incorporated frames evoked and BERT lexical unit embeddings. Usage of multilingual embeddings allowed us to combine the samples from both language pairs to have an increased sample size of 120 sentences in total. The model was trained against 100 sentence pairs and tested on the remaining pairs. It made good predictions with a root mean squared error (RMSE) of 0.41 and mean square error (MSE) of 0.17, probably due to data bias and a small sample size.

Future development will include increasing the data size using bootstrapping techniques and moving towards a language independent model. Moreover, testing a model incorporating the annotation of frame elements is on the plans. Also, sample sizes of human-evaluated translations shall be increased. Finally, more research shall be done on the pragmatics of constructions, which is a necessary prerequisite to include this information in later iterations of FSEM.

5 Acknowledgements

Research presented in this paper is funded by the CAPES PROBRAL and DAAD PPP programs,

---

[1]https://summerofcode.withgoogle.com/projects/#5495810450522112

under the grant numbers 88887.144043/2017-00 and 57390800, respectively. Costa's research is funded by CAPES PROBRAL, grant number 88887.185051/2018-00.

References

Banerjee, Satanjeev, and Alon Lavie. 2005. "METEOR: An Automatic Metric for MT Evaluation with Improved Correlation with Human Judgments." In Proceedings of the ACL Workshop on Intrinsic and Extrinsic Evaluation Measures for Machine Translation and/or Summarization, 65–72. Ann Arbor, Michigan: Association for Computational Linguistics.

Borin, Lars, Dana Dannélls, Markus Forsberg, Maria Toporowska Gronostaj, and Dimitrios Kokkinakis. 2010. "The Past Meets the Present in Swedish FrameNet++." In 14th EURALEX International Congress, 269–281.

Burchardt, Aljoscha, Katrin Erk, Anette Frank, Andrea Kowalski, Sebastian Pado, and Manfred Pinkal. 2006. "The SALSA Corpus: A German Corpus Resource for Lexical Semantics." In Proceedings of LREC 2006, 969–74. Genoa, Italy.

Chen, Desai, Nathan Schneider, Dipanjan Das, and Noah A. Smith. 2010. "SEMAFOR: Frame Argument Resolution with Log-Linear Models." In Proceedings of the 5th International Workshop on Semantic Evaluation, 264–267. Uppsala, Sweden: Association for Computational Linguistics.

Collins, Allan M., and Elizabeth F. Loftus. 1975. "A Spreading-Activation Theory of Semantic Processing." Readings in Cognitive Science: A Perspective from Psychology and Artificial Intelligence, 126–136.

Čulo, Oliver. 2016. "Translationswissenschaftliche Analyse der Übersetzung des Direkten Objekts Im Vorfeld ins Englische und Anregungen Daraus für die Kontrastive Linguistik." Deutsche Sprache. Zeitschrift Für Theorie, Praxis Und Dokumentation, no. 3: 214–34.

Czulo, Oliver. 2017. "Aspects of a Primacy of Frame Model of Translation." In Empirical Modelling of Translation and Interpreting, edited by S. Hansen-Schirra, Oliver Czulo, and Sascha Hofmann, 465–90. Translation and Multilingual Natural Language Processing 6. Berlin: Language Science Press.

Diederich, Joachim. 1990. "Spreading Activation and Connectionist Models for Natural Language Processing." In Theoretical Linguistics, edited by Hans-Martin Gärtner, 16:25. Mouton de Gruyter.

Ellsworth, Michael, Kyoko Ohara, Carlos Subirats, and Thomas Schmidt. 2006. "Frame-Semantic Analysis of Motion Scenarios in English, German, Spanish, and Japanese." presented at the Fourth International Conference on Construction Grammar, Tokyo, Japan.

Fillmore, Charles J. 1982. "Frame Semantics." In Linguistics in the Morning Calm, edited by The Linguistic Society of Korea, 111–137. Hanshin.

———. 1985. "Frames and the Semantics of Understanding." Quaderni Di Semantica 6: 222–254.

Fillmore, Charles J., Christopher R Johnson, and Miriam R. L. Petruck. 2003. "Background to Framenet." International Journal of Lexicography 16 (3): 235–250.

Gouws, Stephan, G-J van Rooyen, and Herman A Engelbrecht. 2010. "Measuring Conceptual Similarity by Spreading Activation over Wikipedia's Hyperlink Structure." In Proceedings of the 2nd Workshop on Collaboratively Constructed Semantic Resources, Coling 2010, 46–54.

Hawkins, John A. 1986. A Comparative Typology of English and German. Unifying the Contrasts. London: Croom Helm.

Hirst, Graeme. 1988. "Semantic Interpretation and Ambiguity." Artificial Intelligence 34 (2): 131–177.

Kußmaul, Paul. 2010. Verstehen Und Übersetzen. 2., aktualisierte Aufl. Narr Studienbücher. Tübingen: Narr.

Levý, Jiří. 1969. Die Literarische Übersetzung: Theorie Einer Kunstgattung. Athenäum Bücher Zur Dichtkunst. Bonn: Athenäum-Verlag.

Lo, Chi-kiu. 2017. "MEANT 2.0: Accurate Semantic MT Evaluation for Any Output Language." In Proceedings of the Second Conference on Machine Translation, 589–597.

Lo, Chi-kiu, Meriem Beloucif, Markus Saers, and Dekai Wu. 2014. "XMEANT: Better Semantic MT Evaluation without Reference Translations." In ACL (2), 765–771. The Association for Computer Linguistics.

Lo, Chi-kiu, and Dekai Wu. 2011. "MEANT: An Inexpensive, High-Accuracy, Semi-Automatic Metric for Evaluating Translation Utility Based on Semantic Roles." In Proceedings of the 49th Annual Meeting of the Association for Computational Linguistics: Human Language Technologies, 220–229. Portland, Oregon, USA: Association for Computational Linguistics.

Lyngfelt, Benjamin, Lars Borin, Kyoko Ohara, and Tiago Timponi Torrent. 2018. Constructicography: Constructicon Development across Languages. John Benjamins.

Miller, George A., Richard Beckwith, Christiane Fellbaum, Derek Gross, and Katherine Miller. 1990.

"WordNet: An on-Line Lexical Database." International Journal of Lexicography 3: 235–244.

Ohara, Kyoko, Seiko Fuji, Toshio Ohori, Ryoko Suzuki, Hiroaki Saito, and Shun Ishizaki. 2004. "The Japanese FrameNet Project: An Introduction." In Proceedings of the Satellite Workshop "Building Lexical Resources from Semantically Annotated Corpora," 9–11. European Language Resources Association.

Okazaki, Naoaki, Yutaka Matsuo, Naohiro Matsumura, and Mitsuru Ishizuka. 2003. "Sentence Extraction by Spreading Activation with Refined Similarity Measure." IEICE Transactions on Information and Systems (Special Issue on Text Processing for Information Access) E86-D: 1687–1694.

Papinieni, Kishore, Salim Roukos, Todd Ward, and Wei-Jing Zhu. 2002. "BLEU: A Method for Automatic Evaluation of Machine Translation." In Proceedings of the 40th Annual Meeting of the Association for Computational Linguistics, 311–18. Philadelphia, USA.

Petruck, Miriam R. L. 1996. "Frame Semantics." In Handbook of Pragmatics, edited by Jef Verschueren, Jan-Ole Östman, Jan Blommaert, and Chris Bulcaen. Philadelphia: John Benjamins.

Ringgaard, Michael, Rahul Gupta, and Fernando C. N. Pereira. 2017. "SLING: A Framework for Frame Semantic Parsing." CoRR abs/1710.07032.

Slobin, Dan I. 2004. "The Many Ways to Search for a Frog: Linguistic Typology and the Expression of Motion Events." In Relating Events in Narrative: Typological Perspectives, edited by S. Strömqvist and L. Verhoeven, 219–57. Mahwah, N.J.: Lawrence Erlbaum Associates.

Snover, Matthew, Bonnie Dorr, Richard Schwartz, Linnea Micciulla, and John Makhoul. 2006. "A Study of Translation Edit Rate with Targeted Human Annotation." In Proceedings of Association for Machine Translation in the Americas, 223–231.

Subirats Rüggeberg, Carlos, and Miriam Petruck. 2003. "Surprise: Spanish FrameNet!" In Proceedings of the Workshop on Frame Semantics, edited by Eva Hajičová, Anna Kotěšovcová, and Jiří Mirovský. Prague: Matfyzpress.

Swayamdipta, Swabha, Sam Thomson, Chris Dyer, and Noah A. Smith. 2017. "Frame-Semantic Parsing with Softmax-Margin Segmental RNNs and a Syntactic Scaffold." CoRR abs/1706.09528.

Talmy, Leonard. 2000. Toward a Cognitive Semantics: Vol. II: Typology and Process in Concept Structuring. Cambridge, MA: MIT Press.

Thiel, Kilian, and Michael R Berthold. 2010. "Node Similarities from Spreading Activation." In 2010 IEEE International Conference on Data Mining, 1085–1090. IEEE.

Tiago Torrent, Ely Matos, Ludmila Lage, Adrieli Laviola, Tatiane Tavares, and Vânia Almeida. 2018a. "Towards continuity between the lexicon and the constructicon in FrameNet Brasil." In Constructicography: Constructicon development across languages, edited by Benjamin Lyngfelt, Lars Borin, Kyoko H. Ohara, and Tiago T Torrent. Amsterdam: John Benjamins.

Tiago Torrent, Collin Baker, Michael Ellsworth, and Ely Matos. 2018b. "The Multilingual FrameNet Shared Annotation Task: A Preliminary Report." In Proceedings of the Eleventh International Conference on Language Resources and Evaluation (LREC 2018) edited by Tiago Timponi Torrent, Lars Borin, and Collin F. Baker 7-12. Paris, France: European Language Resources Association (ELRA).

Tymoczko, Maria. 2005. "Trajectories of Research in Translation Studies." Meta 4 (50): 1082–1097.

Vinay, Jean-Paul, Jean Darbelnet, and Gerhard Helbig. 1958. Stylistique Comparée Du Français et de l'anglais. Méthode de Translation. Paris: Didier.

Human Evaluation of Neural Machine Translation:
The Case of *Deep Learning*

Marie Escribe
Guildhall School of Business and Law
London Metropolitan University
escribe.marie@gmail.com

Abstract

Recent advances in artificial neural networks now have a great impact on translation technology. A considerable achievement was reached in this field with the publication of *L'Apprentissage Profond*. This book, originally written in English (*Deep Learning*), was entirely machine-translated into French and post-edited by several experts. In this context, it appears essential to have a clear vision of the performance of MT tools. Providing an evaluation of NMT is precisely the aim of the present research paper. To accomplish this objective, a framework for error categorisation was built and a comparative analysis of the raw translation output and the post-edited version was performed with the purpose of identifying recurring patterns of errors. The findings showed that even though some grammatical errors were spotted, the output was generally correct from a linguistic point of view. The most recurring errors are linked to the specialised terminology employed in this book. Further errors include parts of text that were not translated as well as edits based on stylistic preferences. The major part of the output was not acceptable as such and required several edits per segment, but some sentences were of publishable quality and were therefore left untouched in the final version.

1 Introduction

The concept of a computer system designed for translation assistance is several decades old. While the first computers were created just before World War II to perform calculations (in ballistics), it quickly became apparent that they could be used as decoding tools (to decipher enemy encrypted transmissions such as the Enigma code). This achievement is often considered as one of the first steps towards Machine Translation (MT) (Planas, 2017). Obviously, translation is not exactly a matter of deciphering codes, but rather raises issues of equivalence between languages. However, this paved the way for MT, and experts began to build more and more tools (Rule-Based MT, Statistical MT). While the first studies on the use of neural networks for MT dates back to the 1990s (Ñeco and Forcada, 1997), Neural Machine Translation (NMT) has largely benefited from the advances in Artificial Intelligence (AI) and has thus grown considerably in recent years.

In November 2018, the first book translated by a NMT system (English>French), *L'Apprentissage Profond*, was published in France. The title says it all: *Deep Learning* is the very promising technology based on artificial neural networks used by Quantmetry and DeepL GmbH to translate this book. This has been widely publicised in both national and international media and it is often referred to as the first book entirely translated by an AI system (Zaffagni, 2018), since the amount of post-editing prior to the publication of this book is considered to be minimal. These advances in MT technology sometimes lead professionals to think that their jobs will entirely be performed by machines in the coming years: Bawa-Mason et al. (2018) pointed out that 38% of practising translators are worried that MT tools will end up replacing them. In this context, it appears crucial to conduct research in the area of recent MT systems in order to have a clear vision of the performance of NMT nowadays. This is precisely the objective of the present study. Implementing quality assessment methods is essential to monitor the evolution of MT systems. This is why several quality assessment frameworks have been

Temnikova, I, Orăsan, C., Corpas Pastor, G., and Mitkov, R. (eds.) (2019) *Proceedings of the 2nd Workshop on Human-Informed Translation and Interpreting Technology (HiT-IT 2019)*, Varna, Bulgaria, September 5 - 6, pages 36–46.

https://doi.org/10.26615/issn.2683-0078.2019_005

proposed, including both human judgment and automatic metrics.

This research project proposes a method for the analysis of NMT output based on human evaluation. The aim is to establish a comparative study between the raw translation output and the post-edited version of *Deep Learning* in order to identify and analyse differences between the two versions. The edits performed were thus quantified and classified in order to identify recurring patterns of errors. The analysis of the outcomes obtained allowed to determine typical situations in which the performance of NMT is still insufficient.

2 MT Evaluation

2.1 Automatic Metrics vs Human Judgment

With the increasing development of MT systems, it became necessary to implement assessment techniques to evaluate the translations obtained and thus design more efficient systems. As a matter of fact, MT evaluation became a field in its own right.
Many scholars claim that automatic metrics are the most efficient solution because they are objective, fast and inexpensive compared to human evaluation. Among the many automatic metrics created, BLEU (BiLingual Evaluation Understudy) appears to be the most popular (Do, 2011) because it is considered to provide very accurate results that are strongly correlated with human judgments (Papineni et al., 2002). Similar metrics include the NIST metric (National Institute of Standards and Technology, Doddington, 2002) and METEOR (Metric for Evaluation of Translation with Explicit Ordering, Banerjee and Lavie, 2005). Other metrics are based on the error rate and the Levenshtein distance, such as the WER (Word Error Rate) score and the improved versions of this metric – i.e. PER (Position-independent Word Error Rate, Tillmann et al., 1997), TER (Translation Edit Rate or Translation Error Rate, Snover et al., 2006) and HTER (Human-targeted Translation Edit Rate, Snover et al., 2006).

The popularity of such metrics can be explained by the weaknesses of human evaluation. Having human evaluators judge a MT output, either by rating it or by post-editing it according to a reference, is a difficult task because such techniques are time-consuming, rather expensive and generally not re-usable. Moreover, such studies are highly subjective, as human evaluators do not necessarily agree on the quality of the MT output. In addition to this, error categorisation is a particularly difficult task when it comes to human evaluation.

Despite this, human judgment is paramount for designing effective evaluation systems and interpreting the scores they provide. The human input is crucial when it comes to informing experts in order to improve MT evaluation systems, since human analyses often serve as a framework for the creation of such tools. Vilar et al. (2006) argued that the interpretation of scores provided by automatic metrics can sometimes be unclear and that error classification and analysis by humans is therefore needed. Turian et al. (2003) also insisted on the importance of human judgment. In fact, several experts disagreed with the statement that automatic metrics show a good correlation with human judgments (Doddington, 2002; Callison-Burch et al., 2006). In this regard, Sennrich (cited in Pan, 2016) also pointed out that BLEU only focuses on precision and does not consider syntactic structures and grammar. Furthermore, Tinsley (cited in Pan, 2016), noted that BLEU scores are not efficient when it comes to evaluation of NMT.

The limitations of automatic metrics therefore make human judgment extremely valuable. Only human evaluators can tell whether the type of language used is adequate according to the context (register) or if a change in grammar or lexis at the post-editing stage is considerably affecting the meaning of a sentence. Indeed, Ulitkin (2013), who tested several automatic metrics such as BLEU and TER, stated that these tools could not provide quality assessment at the semantic or pragmatic levels. Consequently, it is necessary to conduct human evaluation of NMT output. Such methods usually focus on adequacy (i.e. whether the meaning has been rendered correctly) and fluency (i.e. grammaticality and fluency of the output) (Lavie, 2011) and generally require to elaborate an error classification.

2.2 Previous Work

Llitjós et al. (2005), who aimed to find an automation process for post-editing, were among the first experts to present an error typology. The classification they proposed served as a model for that presented by Vilar et al. (2006) for human evaluation of SMT. These two classifications are indeed very similar, with three categories in common ("missing word", "word order" and "incorrect words"). Vilar et al. (2006) used a more comprehensive typology, with more sub-categories, thus allowing a more precise error identification. For instance, the sub-category "sense" (belonging to "word order") has, in turn, been divided into two categories (namely "wrong lexical choice" and "incorrect disambiguation"). Daems et al. (2017) also came up with a typology including similar categories – even though the aim of their study was to quantify the post-editing effort. Although the general classification appears to be different, these frameworks share common features (for instance the "lexicon" category in Daems et al., 2017 is similar to that of "wrong lexical choice" in Vilar et al., 2006).

It is important to note that these typologies were established before the creation of NMT, and it could therefore be argued that they concentrate mostly on features for which more recent MT systems are not likely to produce errors (even though their study was conducted in 2017, Daems et al. worked with a SMT system). Isabelle et al. (2017) argued that the performance of NMT was outstanding compared to other MT systems and, for this reason, one can think that the classifications mentioned above are now antiquated and cannot be used for NMT evaluation. However, this is not the case. Ahrenberg (2017), who established a comparison of a NMT output and a human translation, mostly built on Vilar et al. (2006) to create an error typology and even acknowledged that five categories out of six are directly inspired by their taxonomy. The framework for human analysis of NMT used by Hassan et al. (2018) also shares several features with those introduced before, with categories such as "missing word" and "word order" that were already present in the study of Vilar et al. (2006). These error types can also be found in Popovic (2018). Moreover, these typologies share a number of categories with several guidelines for post-editing. For instance, DePalma (2013) presented a categorisation (adapted from LISA QA Model) explaining the differences between "light" and "full" post-editing. Some of the errors that should be addressed by post-editors are similar to the categories mentioned above (with "omissions"/"additions" corresponding to "missing word"/"extra word" in Llitjós et al., 2005, for example). Further studies, such as the 'QT21 Harmonised Metric' (Lommel et al., 2015) and 'From Quality Evaluation to Business Intelligence' (TAUS Quality Dashboard, 2016) introduced DQF (Dynamic Quality Framework) tools allowing users to categorise and count errors segment-by-segment using issue type hierarchies (i.e. error typologies). Here again, several error categories are identical to other frameworks mentioned before (for instance, "addition", "omission", "punctuation", "spelling" and "grammar").

2.3   Performance of NMT

Isabelle et al. (2017) tested NMT systems with particularly challenging linguistic material and pointed out the cases in which NMT failed to provide a satisfying output thanks to a specific error typology. This study proved the efficiency of NMT over other MT systems and provided a list of strengths (such as the capacity to overcome many limitations of *n*-gram language modelling) and weaknesses (such as the translation of idioms) of NMT. However, some experts, such as Hassan et al. (2018), argue that the performance of NMT now equals human quality. This study proved to be highly controversial as other experts criticised their approach, especially regarding the definition of human parity (as pointed out by Diño, 2018). The authors claimed that human parity is achieved if the output is considered to be equivalent to a human translation according to bilingual human judges. This definition can appear as not rigorous enough, in particular when compared to other metrics (such as BLEU) in which human parity is achieved only if a candidate translation is completely identical to a translation produced by a human.

Of course, this discrepancy is due to an intrinsic problem in Translation Studies. The concept of equivalence itself is a controversial topic in the field (Hatim and Munday, 2004), and, very often, there is not only one possible translation for a given sentence, but rather several valid options. Therefore, establishing a comparison based only on a limited number of possible translations seems restrictive. On the other hand, evaluations established by human judges allow for more possibilities to be included, but they are subjective.

Several studies brought nuances to the findings of Hassan et al. (2018). Amongst them, Läubli et al. (2018) suggest that given the good quality of NMT output at the sentence level, analyses of NMT should focus on the document level. This suggestion was also made by Toral et al. (2018), who argue that important variables were not considered in the experiment of Hassan et al. (such as the languages involved, the translation expertise of the evaluators, etc.).

In fact, the need for MT evaluation is more important than ever with the development of NMT systems. They have become more and more popular in recent years, in particular because they are able to produce translations of high quality, compared to Statistical MT, as pointed out by Sennrich (2016). Furthermore, NMT is a relatively recent technology, whereas most automatic evaluation metrics were created more than 15 years ago. Consequently, it appears relevant to conduct human evaluation of NMT output in order to identify recurrent error patterns and thus to investigate how to integrate the recognition of such patterns in automatic metrics. Ahrenberg (2017) stressed the fact that Translation Studies and MT evaluation have mostly evolved separately and therefore lack common terminology. This is unfortunate because cooperation between translators and computer engineers is paramount to create efficient evaluation systems, since knowledge from linguists is important feedback for the creation of adequate assessment methods. This is particularly true when it comes to NMT. For instance, Monti et al. (2018, pp. 19-20) pointed out that only a few studies were implemented regarding multiword units NMT output, and further research is therefore needed.

3 Experimental Setup

3.1 Material Investigated

The material investigated for this project consists of an excerpt from *Deep Learning* (Goodfellow, Bengio and Courville, 2016). This manual is extremely comprehensive, which is why it is known to be a 'must-have' for Data Science students or practitioners aiming to use deep learning models and is recommended by several universities, even in non-English-speaking countries (Bousquet, 2018). However, the English language can be perceived as a barrier to a full understanding of the book. On the other hand, translating this monumental work (800 pages) would be both long and expensive – estimations showed that it would require approximately an entire year of work and up to 150,000 euros (Stora, cited in Zaffagni, 2018). Quantmetry and DeepL GmbH came up with a bold solution to this problem – translating *Deep Learning* by using deep learning methods. This incredible *mise en abîme* was successful, as *L'Apprentissage Profond*, the French translation of *Deep Learning*, was published in 2018 and this achievement received strong media attention. To do this, the developers had to create a glossary of 200 specialised terms (Zaffagni, 2018) and to implement a tool capable of handling LaTeX format. The system thus developed showed impressive results, as the book was translated in no more than 12 hours, for a total budget of 30,000 euros, including printing (Bousquet, 2018). The translation was then entirely post-edited by several experts from the ENSAI, INRIA and CNRS [1] (Bousquet, 2018 and Zaffagni, 2018), but linguists were not involved in the revision process. Even though changes had to be implemented, the translation is considered to be of good quality, which is why this book is known to be the first book translated by an AI-powered system (Zaffagni, 2018). Consequently, it appears relevant to identify and analyse the instances in which the machine-translated text had to be edited.

For the purpose of this research project, the scientific director of Quantmetry accepted to provide the raw translation output of the third chapter, entitled "Probability and Information Theory" (pp. 51-76 in the English version and pp. 75-98 in the French version) which is approximately 9,000 words long, and was divided into 431 segments for this study. Therefore, the

[1] ENSAI: *École Nationale de la Statistique et de l'Analyse de l'Information* (National School of Statistics and Information Analysis)
INRIA: *Institut National de Recherche en Informatique et en Automatique* (National Institute of Research in Computer Science and Automation)
CNRS: *Centre National de la Recherche Scientifique* (National Centre of Scientific Research)

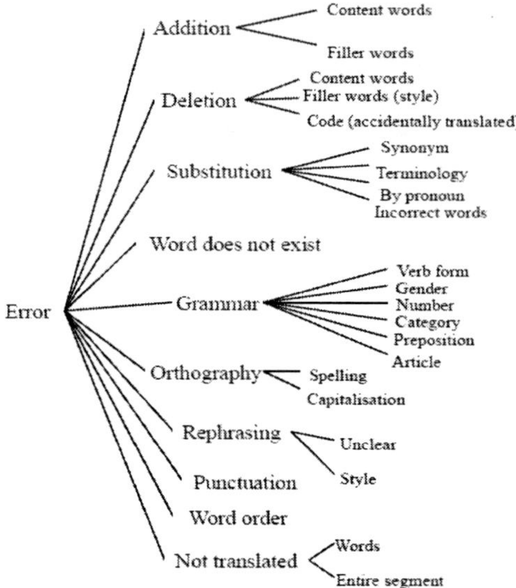

Figure 1: Error categorisation used for recording post-editing actions.

corpus consists of three texts – the original version of this chapter (English), the machine-translated text (French) and the published version (French).

3.2 Research Methods

Despite the popularity of automatic metrics such as BLEU, this research project is based on human evaluation, as it seems to be the most adequate method. Indeed, even though human evaluation is time-consuming and subjective, it allows for a more comprehensive classification of errors, and thus a more precise analysis of differences. Fundamentally, BLEU requires to have at least one reference human translation, which is not possible for this project. It could be argued that the post-edited version can be used as a reference. However, BLEU would still not be sufficient for the purpose of this research, in particular because it only focuses on the n-gram precision and it seems important to analyse larger units (as opposed to sequences of words).

Obviously, all of the taxonomies for human evaluation (mentioned in 2.2) were created with different purposes and are thus built differently. Error classification seems to be implemented on a case-by-case basis because the framework chosen to identify errors must be designed according to a number of characteristics. Two of the most important features are the type of text to be analysed and the languages involved (Vilar et al., 2006). However, previous studies do share some common features, as several categories appear to be recurrent (the major ones being the following: missing or additional words, incorrect words, word order, grammar, spelling and punctuation) and were therefore incorporated in the present research.

The material was analysed by a single bilingual annotator – the author of the present paper –, whose native language is French and who is entering the translation profession (one-year experience). The corpus was first gathered in a table with three main columns – the original text (English), the raw translation output and the post-edited, published version (French). Then, each segment of the corpus (i.e. sentences, titles, captions) was analysed manually and the changes spotted in the final version were recorded in a separate table. The classification adopted for recording errors was largely adapted from the error typologies proposed by Llitjós et al. (2005), Vilar et al. (2006), DePalma (2013), Lommel et al., (2015), TAUS Quality Dashboard (2016), Ahrenberg (2017), Daems et al. (2017), Hassan et al. (2018), and Popovic (2018). These are only a few examples of the studies presenting error typologies, and it is generally considered that the Multidimensional Quality Metrics (MQM) core (German Research Center for Artificial Intelligence, 2014) is a standard classification in the field (used in the study of Knowles et al., 2019, for instance). Consequently, the classification proposed here is also inspired by the MQM. The classification thus obtained is presented in Figure 1.

Errors were recorded by units of meaning. One error generally corresponds to one word edit (for example, a substitution edit corresponds in most cases to a single word edit). However, in the case that a post-editing action is affecting a unit of meaning composed of several words (e.g. "in terms of"), it was counted as one error.

Furthermore, a series of features above the sentence level was added to this classification. In particular, the instances in which sentences were split, merged, added or deleted were recorded. A particular emphasis was placed on the textual level, including in particular the consistency of terminology employed throughout the document as well as coherence. Moreover, the translation procedures identified by Ahrenberg (2017) as being beyond the capacity of NMT (sentence splitting, shifts, explicitation, modulation and paraphrasing) were also studied.

4 Presentation of Results

Edit category	Edit sub-category	Total per sub-category	Total per category
Addition	Content words	63 (5.25%)	120 (10%)
	Filler words	57 (4.75%)	
Deletion	Content words	85 (7.08%)	148 (12.33%)
	Filler words (Style)	40 (3.33%)	
	Code	23 (1.92%)	
Substitution	Synonym	141 (11.75%)	389 (32.42%)
	Terminology	209 (17.42%)	
	By pronoun	12 (1%)	
	Incorrect words	27 (2.25%)	
Word does not exist		1 (0.08%)	
Grammar	Verb form	22 (1.83%)	238 (19.82%)
	Gender	76 (6.33%)	
	Number	58 (4.83%)	
	Category	24 (2%)	
	Preposition	33 (2.75%)	
	Article	25 (2.08%)	
Orthography	Spelling	0 (0%)	11 (0.92%)
	Capitalisation	11 (0.92%)	
Rephrasing	Unclear	36 (3%)	70 (5.83%)
	Style	34 (2.83%)	
Punctuation		57 (4.75%)	
Word order		19 (1.58%)	
Translation	Words in a segment	136 (11.33%)	147 (12.22%)
	Entire segment	11 (0.92%)	
Total number of edits		1200	

Table 1: Number of post-editing actions recorded per edit category presented as percentages.

Segments that did not require any edit	94 (21.81%)
Average number of edits per segment	2.78
Merged segments	4
Split segments	3
Added segments	1
Deleted segments	1
Untranslated segments	11 (2.55%)
Total number of segments in the corpus	431

Table 2: Segment analysis.

5 Evaluation

First, it should be pointed out that 21.81% of the output analysed did not require any edit, which proves that the NMT system was able to provide an output of publishable quality in certain cases. Moreover, the average number of edits per segment is 2.78, which corroborates the results obtained by Ahrenberg (2017).

While an error typology was used to easily record post-editing actions, it is deemed essential to point out that the types of edits identified belong to different severity levels. This concept was already used in previous studies, and it is the case in particular for the MQM, which relies on a scoring algorithm to assign a weight to the different errors encountered. Indeed, while untranslated words are obviously a critical issue, substituting a word by a synonym is a preferential edit (corresponding to the "preferential changes" master category in de Almeida, 2013) and thus belongs to a lower severity level.

5.1 Serious Errors

The most serious errors are attributed to cases of mistranslations. This happens when the raw output does not convey the meaning expressed in the Source Language (SL). A few words were translated incorrectly (2.25% of the edits performed), but they mostly correspond to bad translation choices and they generally do not interfere with the general meaning of an entire segment. Most of the time, errors belonging to the "incorrect words" category constituted a barrier to a good understandability and readability of the text because the formulation remained too close to that of the SL. At the sentence level, it was sometimes necessary to rephrase an entire clause or segment because the raw translation was not clearly formulated. Nevertheless, only 3% of the edits correspond to rephrasing an unclear segment in the output.

Other serious errors correspond to instances in which the output is not intelligible for the end reader. This obviously includes words that were left untranslated in the output. The post-editing action "translate" accounts for 12.22% of the changes made in the final version. In fact, 11/431 segments were not translated. It can be assumed that some words that were not translated are not commonly used, and since the material fed to the system did not contain instances of these words, it could not translate them ("cassowary" for instance, appeared in English in the raw output). However, given that the segments that were not translated are not particularly challenging, it can be argued that this is due to a bug in the NMT system because this mostly happened in cases where the code surrounding these segments was particularly dense, in the case of captions for instance (6/11 occurrences).

Further serious errors include cases in which the output is not clear to the end reader. This happens in particular when the output presents a grammatical issue. For instance, the NMT system sometimes made errors of conjugation (especially regarding the sequence of tenses). On a few occasions, the grammatical category used in the output was not correct. However, it can also be the case that the sentence produced is grammatically correct, but the output is too close to the SL (literal translation) and therefore, the formulation does not seem natural to a French reader.

Moreover, even though a few serious grammatical errors were spotted in the NMT output, it is important to mention that most edits related to grammar were not implemented because the output was ungrammatical, but rather for the sake of consistency when other types of edits had to be performed. Indeed, changing even a single word in a sentence can have several repercussions and can thus considerably increase the number of edits necessary to produce a correct sentence, as already pointed out by Vilar et al. (2006). If a masculine noun was substituted by a feminine noun, it is likely that other elements in the sentence have to be modified (adjective and verb agreement, for instance). Nevertheless, the presence of acronyms resulted in recurring grammatical inconsistences, since acronyms seem to be identified as masculine by default in the NMT output.

One could think that segments in which it was necessary to add or delete words are severe cases of errors (especially for "content words"), but most often, this did not affect the general meaning of a segment. These changes are sometimes preferential, and in other cases, words were added in order to make the target text more precise or when it was deemed necessary to include additional information. When it comes to deleting words, this could be done when a concept was implied or simply for stylistic reasons (to avoid repetitions in particular). In fact, the most serious

case in which words needed to be deleted was when the code was accidentally translated (for example: "**\newterm**{multinomial distribution}" translated as "*nouvelle distribution multinomiale*" [new multinomial distribution], instead of "*distribution multinomiale*" [multinomial distribution]).

Furthermore, only one word that does not exist was spotted in the output ("*prioror*", which resembles both the English "prior" and the French "*à priori*").

As far as orthography is concerned, spelling mistakes were included in the classification, but none was found in the raw output. Only a few capitalisation errors were spotted, accounting for 0.92% of the edits performed.

5.2   Contextual Errors

The following severity level corresponds to errors related to the context. In fact, this is the case for most of the errors in the output analysed. Most of the output was grammatically correct and understandable, but the lexical items employed needed to be adjusted to comply with terminological standards. The specialised terminology apparently constituted a genuine challenge: 32.42% of the edits were substitutions, and 54% of the substitutions were performed to comply with terminological requirements. In most cases, specialised terms were not identified and were translated as general words, which is a rather unexpected finding, given that a glossary of specialised terms was used for the translation of *Deep Learning*. Furthermore, on a few occasions, some inconsistencies in terminology were spotted in the NMT output.

It is also essential to point out that, even though substitutions performed because of the specialised terminology correspond to the most common type of edit, several errors were in fact replicated but recorded as often as they appeared in the raw MT output. As a result, an important number of changes were performed to correct the same error appearing multiple times. This is particularly true for this error category and thus contributed to make it the most prominent in the results.

5.3   Stylistic Preferences

The last level of severity corresponds to preferential changes. These edits were not performed to correct grammatical or terminological errors, but are rather based on stylistic preferences. In particular, the authors are clearly present in the SL, which is particularly reflected by the use of personal pronouns ("we provide this chapter to ensure…", p.51 of *Deep Learning*). This is not common in French: Pontille (2006) underlined that markers of the authors' presence should be carefully erased in scientific texts in order for the readers to focus on the facts presented. This element was thus modified at the post-editing stage in order to make the French version more impersonal. Other preferential changes include instances in which a noun was substituted by a synonym (11.75%) as well as reformulation of a sentence based on stylistic preferences (2.83%).

Moreover, even though most standards of scientific writing encourage repetition in French (for instance, Boudouresque, 2006) for the sake of precision, Baker (2018) pointed out that the acceptability of this procedure varies greatly across languages. In fact, even in scientific discourse, French generally tends to avoid repetition in order to enhance readability. For this reason, pronouns were used in the final version of the text ("substitution by pronoun"). Alternatively, some words could be deleted when they were not deemed necessary or when they were mentioned shortly before.

5.4   Procedures Beyond Reach of NMT

The outcomes of this study confirmed the observations made by Ahrenberg (2017) regarding the translation procedures beyond reach of NMT systems. No sentence was split in the raw output. On one occasion, two sentences were merged in the raw output, which demonstrates the ability of NMT technology to handle sentences, but this would need to be analysed in more detail. Modulation and explicitation also appear to be beyond the capacity of NMT. Similarly, category shifts and paraphrasing seem to be procedures that the NMT system did not implement, which sometimes caused the output to be too literal. In addition to these procedures, it appears important to mention that the NMT system was not capable of making adjustments regarding the readability (e.g. substitution by pronoun to avoid repetition) and the register (some sentences were translated literally and would certainly have been acceptable in oral discourse, but needed to be changed to a more formal tone).

6   Limitations of the Research

The first limitation of this research corresponds to the size of the corpus analysed (only one chapter of *Deep Learning*). Even though the chapter analysed can be considered as representative of the entire book, verifying whether the results obtained in this study apply to the whole text would certainly constitute a valuable analysis. Beyond a larger sample of the same book, it would also be relevant to extend this study to different text genres in order to verify whether it would show similar results.

The same goes for the linguistic combination. This research project only focused on the English-French language pair, whereas several NMT systems offer a number of different combinations. It would therefore be relevant to evaluate NMT output for more distant languages. This could help in identifying strengths and weaknesses of such technology that are independent of the language pair studied.

Another limitation lies in the MT system itself. Indeed, Quantmetry has developed a NMT tool in partnership with DeepL GmbH for the purpose of translating *Deep Learning* into French. It was announced at the DataJob conference (2018) that the company aimed at making this tool available for free to the public in the months following the publication of the book in France, but it was not the case by the time this research project was conducted. Nevertheless, after comparing some fragments of the raw translation obtained and a translation of the same text performed by DeepL's online NMT tool (excerpt of 40 segments), it seemed that both outputs were particularly similar (about 80% of the segments tested were identical), which is understandable given the contribution of DeepL GmbH to this project. Therefore, the data analysed in this research project can be considered as representative of NMT output. However, conducting human evaluation on more NMT systems would allow to verify whether the results obtained in the present study are applicable to more NMT systems.

The methodology adopted for this research also constitutes a limitation. The classification implemented for the analysis of the corpus was inspired by previous studies, and only the features that seemed relevant to this project were selected. One can argue that a more exhaustive typology should be built, thus allowing to analyse more aspects in future projects. Beyond this point, establishing a new error typology makes the experiment hardly reproducible and comparable to other research in the same area.

Moreover, this research project is based on human evaluation only, and relying on a single annotator compromises the analysis. Hence, a suggestion for further research would be working with more evaluators, as inter-rater agreement testing is particularly valuable when assessing post-editing. It would also appear relevant to analyse the same corpus with automatic metrics and to compare the results thus obtained with the findings of the present study, as already suggested in the research of Vilar et al. (2006).

Finally, it must be acknowledged that the present research would have benefitted from more information regarding the NMT system used for the translation of *Deep Learning* (i.e. training methods used, post-editing guidelines followed, etc.). Unfortunately, this information was not available by the time the present research was conducted.

7   Conclusion

This research project provided a detailed analysis of the changes performed at the post-editing stage in the case of *Deep Learning*. The interpretation of the results obtained allowed to meet the objective of this project by identifying recurring patterns of errors, thus providing an evaluation of the raw NMT output.

What emerges from this study is that the NMT tool produced critical errors in some instances, but several changes made in the final text were preferential and the majority of edits were performed to comply with terminological standards. Of course, this evaluation is largely subjective, and the raw NMT output would not have been acceptable without any post-editing. But it seems reasonable to say that the NMT tool developed for the translation of *Deep Learning* was efficient and that the raw translation is satisfactory for the intended use of this kind of material nowadays, knowing that machine-translated texts are still reviewed.

The evaluation of NMT conducted for this research provides translation professionals and scholars with an insight of the performance of NMT in the case of *Deep Learning* as well as a list of predominant errors in NMT, which correspond to aspects that should be carefully controlled at the post-editing stage in the English-French combination.

As things stand currently, NMT tools are still not efficient enough for producing translations of human quality, as the raw output analysed in this project is not comparable to a human translation. Nevertheless, artificial neural networks are a very promising technology and with the increasing amount of data produced, NMT seems to be an ideal solution to meet the translation demand. But even in this scenario, human translators will play a key role, as the development of more efficient MT tools will mostly depend on collaboration between computer engineers and professional translators. Therefore, it seems essential to implement an 'orchestrated symbiosis' (in the words of Bawa-Mason et al., 2018); it is crucial that translators do not consider technology as a competitor but as a means to enhance their performance. Working hand in hand with computer engineers is essential to improve MT systems. Such collaboration would allow engineers to understand better the equivalence issues between languages as well as typical translation problems and thus to design new systems able to provide even better results.

The analysis conducted for this project provides a list of features that NMT specialists should endeavour to improve when developing new tools (language in context, the importance of specialised terminology, etc.). Furthermore, receiving feedback from linguists working with NMT systems is also essential for the implementation of more sophisticated automatic metrics suitable for the evaluation of more recent MT tools.

Acknowledgments

I would like to express my sincere gratitude to Nicolas Bousquet. I would not have been able to conduct this research project without his help and the raw translation output he kindly accepted to provide me.

References

Lars Ahrenberg. 2017. Comparing Machine Translation and Human Translation: a Case Study. In *RANLP 2017 The First Workshop on Human-*

Informed Translation and Interpreting Technology (HiT-IT): Proceedings of the Workshop, ACL, Shoumen, Bulgaria, pages.21-28. https://doi.org/10.26615/978-954-452-042-7_003.

Mona Baker. 2018. *In Other Words: A Coursebook on Translation*. Routledge, London, UK, 3rd edn.

Satanjeev Banerjee and Alon Lavie. 2005. METEOR: An Automatic Metric for MT Evaluation with Improved Correlation with Human Judgments. In *Proceedings of Workshop on Intrinsic and Extrinsic Evaluation Measures for MT and/or Summarization at the 43rd Annual Meeting of the Association of Computational Linguistics*, ACL, Ann Arbor, USA, pages 65-72. https://www.aclweb.org/anthology/W05-0909.

Sarah Bawa-Mason, Lindsay Bywood, Charles Gittins, Paul Kaye, Raisa McNab, Maeve Olohan and Michael Wells. 2018. Translators in the Digital Era: What Kind of Jobs Will We Have Ten Years from Now? Presented at *The Language Show*, Olympia, London, UK, 11 November 2018.

Charles-François Boudouresque. 2006. Manuel de Rédaction Scientifique et Technique. Centre d'Océanologie de Marseille. 4th edn.

Nicolas Bousquet. 2018. Deep Learning: Histoire d'une Traduction. Presented at *Data Job*, Carrousel du Louvre, Paris, France, 22 November 2018.

Chris Callison-Burch, Miles Osborne and Philipp Koehn. 2006. Re-Evaluating the Role of BLEU in Machine Translation Research. In *Proceedings of the 11st Conference of the European Chapter of the Association for Computational Linguistics*, ACL, Trento, Italy, pages 249-256. https://www.aclweb.org/anthology/E06-1032.

Joke Daems, Sonia Vandepitte, Robert J. Hartsuiker and Lieve Macken. 2017. Identifying the Machine Translation Error Types with the Greatest Impact on Post-Editing Effort. Frontiers in Psychology, vol. 8, 1282. https://doi.org/10.3389/fpsyg.2017.01282.

Giselle de Almeida. 2013. *Translating the Post-Editor: an Investigation of Post-Editing Changes and Correlations with Professional Experience across Two Romance Languages*. PhD thesis, Dublin City University.

Don DePalma. 2013. *Post-Editing in Practice*. TCworld.

Deutsches Forschungszentrum für Künstliche Intelligenz GmbH (German Research Center for Artificial Intelligence). 2014. *Multidimensional Quality Metrics (MQM) Definition*. http://www.qt21.eu/mqm-definition/definition-2015-06-16.html

Gino Diño. 2018. 'Human Parity Achieved' in Machine Translation — Unpacking Microsoft's Claim. *Slator*.

Thi Ngoc Diep Do. 2011. *Extraction de Corpus Parallèle pour la Traduction Automatique Depuis et Vers une Langue Peu Dotée*. MSc Thesis, Université Grenoble Alpes, France; Hanoi University, Vietnam.

George Doddington. 2002. Automatic Evaluation of Machine Translation Quality Using n-gram Co-occurrence Statistics. In *Proceedings of the Second Conference on Human Language Technology*, ACL, San Diego, USA, pages 138-145. https://doi.org/10.3115/1289189.1289273.

Ian Goodfellow, Yoshua Bengio and Aaron Courville. 2016. *Deep Learning*. MIT Press, Cambridge.

Ian Goodfellow, Yoshua Bengio and Aaron Courville. 2018. *L'Apprentissage Profond*. Florent Massot, Paris, France.

Hany Hassan, Anthony Aue, Chang Chen, Vishal Chowdhary, Jonathan Clark, Christian Federmann, Xuedong Huang, Marcin Junczys-Dowmunt, William Lewis, Mu Li, Shujie Liu, Tie-Yan Liu, Renqian Luo, Arul Menezes, Tao Qin, Frank Seide, Xu Tan, Fei Tian, Lijun Wu, Shuangzhi Wu, Yingce Xia, Dongdong Zhang, Zhirui Zhang, and Ming Zhou. 2018. Achieving Human Parity on Automatic Chinese to English News Translation. Microsoft AI & Research. https://www.microsoft.com/en-us/research/uploads/prod/2018/03/final-achieving-human.pdf.

Basil Hatim and Jeremy Munday. 2004. *Translation: An Advanced Resource Book*. Routledge, London, UK.

Pierre Isabelle, Colin Cherry and George Foster. 2017. A Challenge Set Approach to Evaluating Machine Translation. In *Proceedings of the 2017 Conference on Empirical Methods in Natural Language Processing*, ACL, Copenhagen, Denmark, pages 2486-2496. https://aclweb.org/anthology/D17-1263.

Rebecca Knowles, Marina Sanchez-Torron, and Philipp Koehn. 2019. A User Study of Neural Interactive Translation Prediction. *Machine Translation Journal Special Issue on Human Factors in Neural Machine Translation*. vol. 33, pages 135-154.

Alon Lavie. 2011. Evaluating the Output of Machine Translation Systems. Presented at the *13th MT Summit Tutorial*, 19 September 2011, Xiamen, China.

Samuel Läubli, Rico Sennrich and Martin Volk. 2018. Has Machine Translation Achieved Human Parity? A Case for Document-level Evaluation. In

Proceedings of EMNLP, ACL, Brussels, Belgium pages 4791-4796. https://aclweb.org/anthology/D18-1512

Ariadna Font Llitjós, Jaime G Carbonell and Alon Lavie. 2005. A Framework for Interactive and Automatic Refinement of Transfer-Based Machine Translation. In *Proceedings of the 10th Annual Conference of the European Association for Machine Translation*, EAMT, Budapest, Hungary, pages 87-96. https://pdfs.semanticscholar.org/ba58/aa555d6be8f d5b5c148ff3daf992c3a1803d.pdf.

Arle Lommel, Attila Görög, Alan Melby, Hans Uszkoreit, Aljoscha Burchardt and Maja Popović. 2015. QT21 Harmonised Metric. QT21 Consortium.

Johanna Monti, Violeta Seretan, Gloria Corpas Pastor and Ruslan Mitkov (eds). 2018. *Multiword Units in Machine Translation and Translation Technology*. John Benjamins, Amsterdam and Philadelphia.

Hazel Mae Pan. 2016. How BLEU Measures Translation and Why It Matters. Slator.

Ramón P. Ñeco and Mikel L. Forcada. 1997. Asynchronous Translations with Recurrent Neural Nets. In *Proceedings of the International Conference on Neural Networks*, IEEE, Houston, TX, USA, vol. 4, pages 2535-2540.

Kishore Papineni, Salim Roukos, Todd Ward and Wei-Jing Zhu. 2002. BLEU: a Method for Automatic Evaluation of Machine Translation. In *Proceedings of the 40th Annual Meeting on Association for Computational Linguistics*, ACL, Philadelphia, USA, pages 311-318. https://www.aclweb.org/anthology/P02-1040.

Emmanuel Planas. 2017. État de l'Art et Futur de la TAO en 2017. Presented at *Penser la Traduction 2017-2018*, Faculté des Lettres, Langues et Sciences Humaines de l'Université de Haute Alsace, France, 27 November 2018.

David Pontille. 2006. Qu'est-ce qu'un Auteur Scientifique? *Sciences de la Société, Presses universitaires du Midi*, pages 77-93. https://halshs.archives-ouvertes.fr/halshs-00261793/document

Maja Popovic. 2018. Error Classification and Analysis for Machine Translation Quality Assessment. In *Translation Quality Assessment*. pages 129-158. https://www.researchgate.net/publication/3258962 50_Error_Classification_and_Analysis_for_Machi ne_Translation_Quality_Assessment.

Rico Sennrich. 2016. *Neural Machine Translation: Breaking the Performance Plateau*. Presented at the META-FORUM 2016, Lisbon, Portugal. http://www.meta-net.eu/events/meta-forum-2016/slides/09_sennrich.pdf

Matthew Snover, Bonnie Dorr, Richard Schwartz, Linnea Micciulla, and John Makhoul. 2006. A Study of Translation Edit Rate with Targeted Human Annotation. In *Proceedings of the 7th Conference of the Association for Machine Translation in the Americas: Visions for The Future of Machine Translation*, AMTA, Cambridge, Massachusetts, USA, pages 223-231. https://www.cs.umd.edu/~snover/pub/amta06/ter_a mta.pdf.

TAUS Quality Dashboard. 2016. From Quality Evaluation to Business Intelligence. TAUS BV, De Rijp, The Netherlands.

Christoph Tillmann, Stephan Vogel, Hermann Ney, A. Zubiaga and Hassan Sawaf. 1997. Accelerated DP-Based Search for Statistical Translation, In *Proceedings of the 5th European Conference on Speech Communication and Technology*, EUROSPEECH 1997, Rhodes, Greece, pages 22-25. https://pdfs.semanticscholar.org/2472/ad58de68c6 5d54e05470cceee70b4f4f8bb3.pdf.

Antonio Toral, Sheila Castilho, Ke Hu and Andy Way. 2018. Attaining the Unattainable? Reassessing Claims of Human Parity in Neural Machine Translation. In *Proceedings of the Third Conference on Machine Translation*, ACL, Brussels, Belgium, pages 113-123. https://www.aclweb.org/anthology/W18-6312

Joseph P. Turian, Luke Shen and I. Dan Melamed. 2003. Evaluation of Machine Translation and its Evaluation. In *Proceedings of Machine Translation Summit IX*, AMTA, New Orleans, LA, USA, pages 386-393. https://nlp.cs.nyu.edu/publication/papers/turian-summit03eval.pdf.

Ilya Ulitkin. 2013. Human Translation vs. Machine Translation: Rise of the Machines. Translation Journal. vol. 17. https://translationjournal.net/journal/63mtquality.ht m.

David Vilar, Jia Xu, Luis Fernando D'Haro, and Hermann Ney. 2006. Error Analysis of Statistical Machine Translation Output. In *Proceedings of the International Conference on Language Resources and Evaluation 2006*, Genoa, Italy, pages 697-702. http://www.lrec-conf.org/proceedings/lrec2006/pdf/413_pdf.pdf.

Marc Zaffagni. 2018. Une IA Traduit un Livre de 800 Pages en 12 heures. Futura Tech.

Translationese Features as Indicators of Quality
in English-Russian Human Translation

Maria Kunilovskaya
University of Tyumen
University of Wolverhampton
maria.kunilovskaya@wlv.ac.uk

Ekaterina Lapshinova-Koltunski
Saarland University
e.lapshinova@mx.uni-saarland.de

Abstract

We use a range of morpho-syntactic features inspired by research in register studies (e.g. Biber, 1995; Neumann, 2013) and translation studies (e.g. Ilisei et al., 2010; Zanettin, 2013; Kunilovskaya and Kutuzov, 2018) to reveal the association between translationese and human translation quality. Translationese is understood as any statistical deviations of translations from non-translations (Baker, 1993) and is assumed to affect the fluency of translations, rendering them foreign-sounding and clumsy of wording and structure. This connection is often posited or implied in the studies of translationese or translational varieties (De Sutter et al., 2017), but is rarely directly tested. Our 45 features include frequencies of selected morphological forms and categories, some types of syntactic structures and relations, as well as several overall text measures extracted from Universal Dependencies annotation. The research corpora include English-to-Russian professional and student translations of informational or argumentative newspaper texts and a comparable corpus of non-translated Russian. Our results indicate lack of direct association between translationese and quality in our data: while our features distinguish translations and non-translations with the near perfect accuracy, the performance of the same algorithm on the quality classes barely exceeds the chance level.

1 Introduction: Aim and Motivation

In the present paper, we test if the linguistic specificity of translations that makes them distinct from non-translations may also reflect their quality. The possible link between translationese and translation quality has been assumed in corpus-based translation studies ever since translationese has become one of the most attractive research topics. At the onset of machine learning approach to translationese detection, Baroni and Bernardini (2006) suggested using machine learning techniques to develop an automatic translationese spotter to be used in translator education. Attempts has been made to correlate translation quality and statistical differences between translations and non-translations in the target language (TL, Scarpa, 2006) and to describe translational tendencies with the view of using them as translation quality assessment tools (Rabadán et al., 2009). Generally, it seems reasonable to posit that the more rigorous the translationese effects, the stronger they signal the low quality of translation. Mostly, the presence of translationese is assumed to affect the fluency of translations, hampering their readability and giving them the distinct flavour of foreignness. While it is true that fluency is one of the traditional aspects of translation quality evaluation, along with pragmatic acceptability and semantic accuracy (as set out in Koponen, 2010; Secara, 2005, for example), it is not clear whether the features that capture translationese can be related to the quality in human translation evaluation. Therefore, we test whether linguistic features responsible for translationese effects are also good indicators of human translation quality as perceived by human experts in real-life educational environment. To the best of our knowledge, the direct application of automatically retrieved translationese features for learning human translation quality has not been attempted before. If successful, this application could be useful for a number of translation technologies, especially those involving automatic quality assessment of both human and machine translation

Temnikova, I, Orăsan, C., Corpas Pastor, G., and Mitkov, R. (eds.) (2019) *Proceedings of the 2nd Workshop on Human-Informed Translation and Interpreting Technology (HiT-IT 2019)*, Varna, Bulgaria, September 5 - 6, pages 47–56.

https://doi.org/10.26615/issn.2683-0078.2019_006

(MT).

We select a range of lexico-grammatical features that have originated in register studies (Biber, 1995; Neumann, 2013) and are known to capture translationese, i.e. to reflect the systemic differences between translated and non-translated texts (see, for example Evert and Neumann, 2017, where they use a similar set to register features to reveal asymmetry in translationese effects for different translation directions in English-German language pair). Importantly, our features are designed as immediately linguistically interpretable as opposed to surface features, such as n-grams and part-of-speech frequencies commonly used in machine translation evaluation, and include manually-checked frequencies of less easily extractable linguistic phenomena such as correlative constructions, nominalisations, by-passives, nouns/ proper names in the function of core verbal arguments, modal predicates, mean dependency distance, etc., along with the more traditional and easily-extractable features like lexical density, frequency of selected parts-of-speech (e.g. subordinating conjunctions and possessive pronouns).

These features are believed to reflect language conventions of the source and target languages (English and Russian in our data) as well as potential 'translationese-prone' areas.

We represent English and Russian texts as feature vectors and use these representations to automatically learn differences between translations/non-translations and high-scoring/low-scoring translations. Assuming that a shift in the translations linguistic properties (away from the target language norm manifested in non-translations) may be related to the translation quality, we use classification techniques to automatically distinguish between good and bad translations. However, we are not only interested in the performance of classifiers, but also in identifying discriminative linguistic features specific either for good or bad translations.

We believe that the findings of this study will contribute to both translation studies and translator training. On the one hand, the knowledge about differences between good and bad translations is important from a didactic point of view, as it delivers information on the potential problems of the novice translators. On the other hand, they provide new insights and new methodological approaches (as our features are automatically retrieved from a corpus) to the area of translation studies and translation technologies.

The remainder of the paper is structured as follows: In Section 2, we report on the related studies and the theoretical background of the paper. Section 3 provides details on our methodology and the resources used. In Section 4 we explore the ability of our features to distinguish between (1) translated and non-translated texts (2) good and bad translations. We report results in terms of accuracy and f-score, and provide a feature analysis. And finally, in Section 5, we conclude and describe the future work.

2 Related Work and Theoretical Background

2.1 Specificity of Translations

Our analyses are based on the studies showing that translations tend to share a set of lexical, syntactic and/ or textual features (e.g. Gellerstam, 1986; Baker, 1995; Teich, 2003). The choice and number of features investigated in translationese studies varies. Corpas Pastor et al. (2008) and Ilisei (2012) use about 20 features to demonstrate translationese effects in professional and student translations from English to Spanish. They used supervised machine learning techniques to distinguish between translated and non-translated texts in this language pair. The authors use two different groups of features – those that grasp general characteristics of texts, e.g. distributions of grammatical words, different part-of-speech classes and the proportion of grammatical words to lexical words, and those that reflect simplification effect (the tendency of translations to be less complex than non-translated texts), such as average sentence length, sentence depth as the parse tree depth, proportion of simple sentences and lexical richness. Our feature set is inspired by the research reported in Evert and Neumann (2017). They adopted 27 features from the feature set developed for the contrastive study in English-German register variation in Neumann (2013) and effectively applied it to the study of translationese effects. This research shows a remarkable similarity between the register features and translationese features: the two sets have a big area of intersection, including, for example, such indicators as sentence length, type-to-token ratio, number of simple sentences, the distributions of some parts-of-speech and function words such as conjunctions, etc. Our own feature set (described in Section 3.2) has considerable extensions and modifications on the one suggested in the works referred above. The feature selection is based on the assumption that the translationese effect is immediately related to quality, and we included the features that are known, or expected, indicators of translationese, which are, incidentally, mostly lexico-grammatical features.

2.2 Translation Features and Quality Estimation

Automatic human translation evaluation is an emerging direction in Natural Language Processing (NLP). For instance, Vela et al. (2014a) and Vela et al. (2014b) used automatic metrics derived from machine translation evaluation and applied them for the evaluation of human translations. They correlated the automatic scores with the human evaluations showing that these automatic metrics should be used with caution. One of the latest work in this strand of research is (Yuan et al., 2016). The authors use easily extractable monolingual features to capture fluency and their bilingual ratios as well as bilingual embeddings features to account for adequacy of content transfer. Their models return the best predictions on the embedding features for both fluency and accuracy. The advantage of using other features such as part-of-speech and dependency frequencies is in their interpretability: the best-performing features selected in their experiments helped the authors to determine grammatical features that are likely to be responsible for lower translation quality scores. They show that human translations typically contain errors beyond the lexical level, to which proximity-based MT evaluation metrics are less sensitive.

The only study that make use of genre features for quality analysis is (Lapshinova-Koltunski and Vela, 2015). However, the authors compare English-German translation (both human and machine) with non-translated German texts that, as the authors claim, represent target language quality conventions. Their main aim is to show that the usage of translation corpora in machine translation should be treated with caution, as human translations do not necessarily correspond to the quality standards that non-translated texts have. Rubino et al. (2016) use features derived from machine translation quality estimation to classify translations and non-translations motivating their work by the fact that automatic distinction between originals and machine translations was shown to correlate with the quality of the machine translated texts (Aharoni et al., 2014). However, their data does not contain human quality evaluation. Translationese as quality indicator was also used by Rabadán et al. (2009) who claims that the smaller the disparity between native and translated usage in the use of particular grammatical structures associated with specific meanings, the higher the translation rates for quality. De Sutter et al. (2017) use a corpus-based statistical approach to measure translation quality (interpreted as target language acceptability) by comparing the features of translated and original texts. They believe that acceptability can be measured as distance to the target language conventions represented in the linguistic behaviour of the professional translators and professional writers. Their analysis is based on the visual estimation of the linguistic homogeneity of professional and original fiction books that are expected to form separate clusters on the Principal Components biplots. The acceptability of student translations is interpreted as the location of a given translation on the plot with regard to these clusters. The PCA-based multivariate analysis was supported by univariate AVOVA tests. The features that were used in this research include a 25 language-independent (overwhelmingly, simple frequencies of parts-of-speech, types, tokens, n-grams, as well as sentence length, TTR, hapax) and 5 language dependent features. The differences observed between professional and student translations are not clear-cut and "only seven features (out of 30) exhibit a significant difference between students and professionals" in their first case study, for example. Their data does not contain manual quality evaluation and it remains unclear how selected linguistic features relate exactly to translation quality. This work is particularly relevant to us, because it is explicitly bringing together translational quality and professionalism.

2.3 Translation Competence

A few other works, like the last one commented above, attempted to capture the specificity of the two translational varieties – the professional and the student translations. If professionalism in translation could be reliably linked to the linguistic properties of translations, (probably, the ones associated with translationese), then professional translations could be used to work around the scarcity and unreliability of the data annotated for translation quality. However, there is hardly any work that has successfully completed this challenging task: professional and learners' translations prove to be difficult to classify. Further product-oriented analyses of professional and student translations that do not exclusively focus on the analysis of errors include works by Nakamura (2007); Bayer-Hohenwarter (2010); Kunilovskaya et al. (2018). The idea to link the level of professional expertise and the performance of a translationese classifier was put to the test in Rubino et al. (2016). They used a range of features to analyse German translations of the two types and non-translated comparable texts in German. Their feature set included features inspired by MT quality estimation (13 surface features such as number of upper-cased letters, and over 700 surprisal and distortion features that were "obtained by computing the negative log probability of a word given its preceding context" based on regular and backward language models). Their result for the binary professional/student translation classification was "barely above the 50% baseline" demonstrating that the MT evaluation features were not helpful for that task. In a similar attempt, Kunilovskaya et al. (2018) used a set of 45 syntactic features (mostly Universal Dependencies relations) to achieve F1 = 0.761, which was lower that their baseline, based on part-of-speech trigrams.

3 Experimental Setup

3.1 Corpus Resources

For our translationese-related analysis, we use a corpus of Russian professional translations to English mass-media texts and a comparable subcorpus of newspaper texts from the Russian National Corpus (RNC, Plungian et al., 2005). Professional translations ('pro') are collected from a range of established electronic media, such as *Nezavisimaya Gazeta* and *InoSMI.RU* or Russian editions of global mass media such as *BBC*, *Forbes* and *National Geographic* (all publications either carry the name of the translator or the endorsement of the translation by the editorial board). Non-translated Russian texts (reference corpus, ref) come from a user-defined subcorpus of the RNC to represent the expected target language norm for the selected register, i.e. the current target language 'textual fit' (Chesterman, 2004). They were sampled on the frame limiting the extracted texts to the type 'article', intended for the large adult non-specialist readership, created after 2003 and marked as neutral of style. For our quality-related analysis, we use the total of 438 student translations from English into Russian labeled for quality in real-life translation competitions, exam or routine classwork settings. All translations were evaluated by the translation experts (either university teachers of translation and/or professional translators), who were asked to rank several translations of the same source text. Though each translation competition and each institution, where translations were graded, had their own descriptions of quality requirements, they were not limiting translation quality to a specific aspect. For the purposes of this research, we relied on the overall agreed judgment of the jury or exam board. For the purposes of this research, we use only 1–3 top ranking translations and/ or translations that received the highest grade and bottom translations and/ or translations that received the lowest grade, which gives us the binary labels 'best' and 'worst'. These translations and their quality labels were extracted from RusLTC (Kutuzov and Kunilovskaya, 2014), a collection of quality-annotated learner translator texts, available online (https://www.rus-ltc.org). The English source texts for both professional and student translations were published in 2001-2016 by well-known English media like *The Guardian, The USA Today, The New York Times, the Economist, Popular Mechanics*. All corpus resources used in this research are made comparable in terms of register and are newspaper informational or argumentative texts. The quantitative parameters of the corpus resources used in this research (based on the pre-processed and parsed data) are given in Table 1. We have different number of student translations of the two classes (best, worst), which is also distinct from the number of source texts, because we used several top-ranking translations and in some settings the worst translations were not determined (i.e. the ranking was done only for the top submissions).

Taking into account the small size of our data, we paid attention to its pre-processing to reduce the number of tagging and sentence-splitting errors that may have influence on the feature extraction. First, we normalised spelling and typographic conventions used. Second, we split sen-

		ref	pro	best	worst
EN	**words**	-	458k	49k	
	texts	-	385	98	
RU	**words**	737k	439k	141k	61k
	texts	375	385	305	134

Table 1: Basic statistics on the research corpora

tences with the adjusted NLTK sentence tokeniser, deleted by-lines, dates and short headlines (sentences shorter that 4 tokens, including punctuation) and corrected any sentence boundary errors. Finally, the corpora were tagged with UDpipe 1.2.0 (Straka and Straková, 2017). For each language in this experiments we used the pre-trained model that returned most accurate results for our features and had the highest accuracy for Lemma, Feats and UAS reported at the respective Universal Dependencies (UD) page among the available releases. At the time of writing it is 2.2 for English EWT, and 2.3 for Russian-SynTagRus treebank.

3.2 Features

For our experiments, we use a set of 45 features that include the following types:

- eight morphological forms: two degrees of comparison (`comp`, `sup`), past tense and passive voice (`pasttense`, `longpassive`, `bypassive`), two non-finite forms of verb (`infs`, `pverbals`), nominalisations (`deverbals`) and finite verbs (`finites`);

- seven morphological categories: pronominal function words (`ppron`, `demdets`, `possdet`, `indef`), adverbial quantifiers (`mquantif`), coordinative and subordinative conjunctions (`cconj`, `sconj`);

- seven UD relations that are known translationese indicators for the English-Russian translation pair (Kunilovskaya and Kutuzov, 2018). These include adjectival clause, auxiliary, passive voice auxiliary, clausal complement, subject of a passive transformation, asyndeton, a predicative or clausal complement without its own subject (`acl`, `aux`, `aux:pass`, `ccomp`, `nsubj:pass`, `parataxis`, `xcomp`).

- three syntactic functions in addition to UD relations: various PoS in attributive function

(`attrib`), copula verbs (`copula`), nouns or proper names used in the functions of core verbal argument (subject, direct or indirect object) to the total number of these relations (`nnargs`);

- nine syntactic features that have to do with the sentence type and structure: simple sentences (`simple`), number of clauses per sentence (`numcls`), sentence length (`sentlength`), negative sentences (`neg`), types of clauses – relative (`relativ`) and pied-piped subtype (`pied`), correlative constructions (`correl`), modal predicates (`mpred`), adverbial clause introduced by a pronominal ADV(`whconj`);

- two graph-based features: mean hierarchical distance and mean dependency distance (`mhd`, `mdd`) (Jing and Liu, 2015);

- five list-based features for semantic types of discourse markers (`addit`, `advers`, `caus`, `tempseq`, `epist`) and the discourse marker *but*[1] (`but`). The approach to classification roughly follows (Halliday and Hasan, 1976; Biber et al., 1999; Fraser, 2006). The search lists were initially produced independently from grammar reference books, dictionaries of function words and relevant research papers and then verified for comparability and consistency;

- two overall text measures of lexical density and variety (`lexdens`, `lexTTR`).

Special effort was made to keep our feature set cross-linguistically comparable. The rationale behind this decision is an attempt to reveal the most notorious effect in translation, namely, 'shining-through', the translational tendency to reproduce source language patterns and frequencies rather than follow the target language conventions. This form of translationese can be established by comparing the distributions of a feature values across three corpora: non-translations in the source language (SL), non-translations (or reference) in the TL and in the translated texts in the TL. We use several norms to make features comparable across different-size corpora, depending on the nature of the feature. Most of the features, including all

---

[1]If not followed by 'also' and not in the absolute sentence end.

types of discourse markers, negative particles, passives, relative clauses, are normalised to the number of sentences (30 features). Such features as personal, possessive pronouns and other noun substitutes, nouns, adverbial quantifiers, determiners are normalised to the running words (6 features). Counts for syntactic relations are represented as probabilities, normalised to the number of sentences (7 features). Some features use their own normalisation basis: comparative and superlative degrees are normalised to the total number of adjectives and adverbs, nouns in the functions of subject, object or indirect object are normalised to the total number of these roles in the text.

3.3 Methodology

We extract the instances of the features from our corpus relying on the automatically annotated structures (parts-of-speech, dependency relations, etc.). The accuracy of feature extraction is therefore largely related to the accuracy of the automatic annotation. However, care has been taken to filter out noise by using empirically-motivated lists of the closed sets of function words and typical annotation errors where possible. Each text in the data is represented as a feature vector of measures for a range of linguistic properties as described in 3.2.

For both tasks – (1) the analysis of the differences between translated and non-translated texts and (2) the comparison of the highest-ranking and lowest-ranking translations, we model the difference between our binary text classes using machine learning techniques. The experiments are arranged as text classification tasks, where we determine the utility of our features based on the performance of the classifier. For the consideration of space, we report the results of a Support Vector Machine (SVM) algorithm with the default sklearn hyper parameters only. To account for the generalization error of the classifier, we cross-validate over 10 folds. The results of the same learner on the full feature set are compared to the results on the most informative features only to reveal the comparative usefulness of our handcrafted features for each task. Below we report the results for the 15 best features selected with Recursive Feature Elimination (RFE) method, which seems preferable to the standard ANOVA-based SelectKBest, because some of our features do not comply with the normal distribution assumption

made by ANOVA. Besides, we use Principal Component Analysis (PCA) to visualise the distinctions between our classes, given our features.

In the first task, we automatically distinguish comparable Russian non-translations from professional and student translations. In the second task, we use the same algorithm and the same features to learn the difference between good and bad translations. The comparative outcome of this two-step methodology indicates whether the features described in 3.2 capture translationese, whether they correlate with the human evaluation of human translation quality, and whether there is an association between the two. Moreover, we analyse which features are most informative in the two classification tasks and intersect the resulting feature lists.

4 Results and their Interpretation

4.1 Translationese

As seen in Figure 1 illustrating the results of PCA, our features are good indicators of translationese: we get very similar, consistent results on the differentiation between the non-translations in our data and the two translational corpora that come from different sources and, in fact, represent two socio-linguistic translational varieties (student and professional translations).

These visual impressions are corroborated by the results of the automatic classification. Table 2 show that this feature set allows us to predict translations of any type with the accuracy of 92-94%.

	precision	recall	f1-score
pro	0.91	0.94	0.93
ref	0.94	0.91	0.92
macro avg	0.92	0.92	0.92
stu	0.93	0.95	0.94
ref	0.94	0.92	0.93
macro avg	0.94	0.94	0.94

Table 2: Cross-validated classification between translations and non-translations on the full feature set

As a sanity check measure, we ran a dummy classifier that randomly allocates labels with respect to the training set's class distribution to get the expected overall accuracy of 48%. Most informative features contributing to this distinction (as selected by RFE wrapped around a Random Forest algorithm) include `possdet, whconj,`

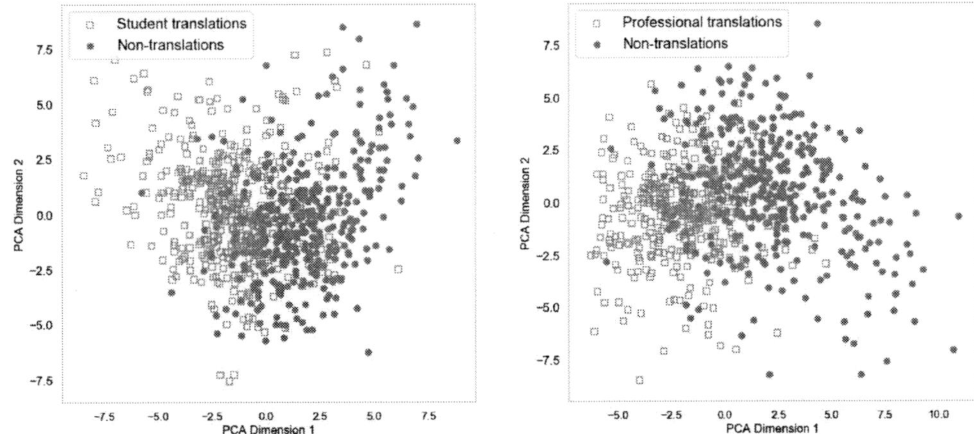

Figure 1: Student and professional vs. non-translations in Russian

relativ, correl, lexdens, lexTTR, finites, deverbals, sconj, but, comp, numcls, simple, nnargs, ccomp. It is the stable best indicators of translationese: 2/3 of this list is reproducible on the both translational collections, and the classification results on just these features are only 3% inferior to the whole 45-feature set.

4.2 Quality

Using the same feature set, we analyse differences between the top-scoring and lowest-scoring translations labelled as 'good' and 'bad' in our data. As seen from Figure 2 that plots the values for our data points on the first two dimensions from PCA (the x- and y-axis, respectively), the best and the worst translations are evenly scattered in the two-dimensional space and, unlike the previous experiment, no groupings are visible.

The cross-validated SVM classifier on the full feature set for good/bad translations returns the macro-averaged F1-measure of 0.64 (Table 3). The overall accuracy of this classification is 68%. Interestingly, good translations can be more easily modelled than the bad ones (76% vs. 51% respectively). This contradicts expectations from the teaching practice where examiners commonly better agree on what is a bad translation. But given that bad translations are a minority class in our classification and that the employed feature set performs worse than a dummy classifier which achieves 73% accuracy, these observations are unreliable anyway. The result on the 20 RFE features is the same as on the full feature set of 45, but

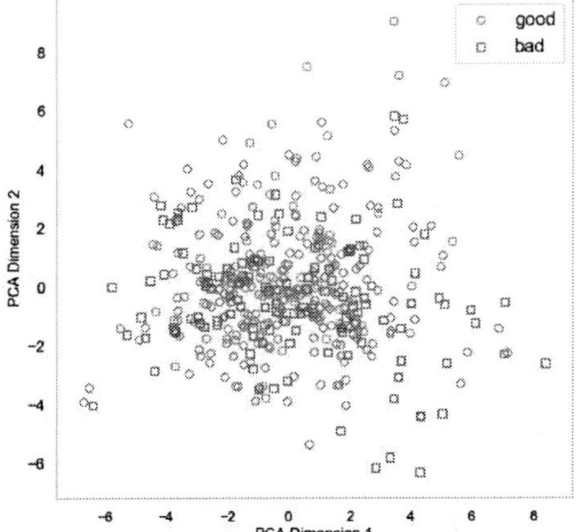

Figure 2: Best vs. worst translations

worse than that returned by the dummy classifier.

	precision	recall	f1-score
bad	0.48	0.55	0.51
good	0.79	0.74	0.76
macro avg	0.63	0.64	0.64

Table 3: Results for good/bad classification

If we attempt the classification on the 15 best translationese indicators established in the previous step of this research, we would see the overall classification results deteriorate to F1=0.56, while the results for the minority class ('bad') plummet to F1=0.36.

Even though the classification result can hardly

be found reliable, we calculated the features that
statistically return the best differentiation between
the labeled classes according to ANOVA. They
include `copula, finites, pasttense,
infs, relativ, lexdens, addit,
ccomp, but, sconj, nnargs, acl,
advers, ppron, sentlength`. The inter-
section with the 15 top translationese indicators
is limited to the six list items: `finites,
lexdens, but, relativ, nnargs,
sconj, ccomp`.

One of the major motivation behind this research was to reveal the existence and extent
of features responsible for one distinct form of
translationese, namely, shining-through. We visualise the difference (distance) between good and
bad translations with a kernel density estimation
(KDE) plot provided in Figure 3. This plot demonstrates how well the values learnt on one of the
PCA dimensions separate the text classes in our
experiment. In this way, we are able to observe
the extent of the shining through effects in our
data: while it is clear that all translations are lo-
cated in the gap between the source and the target language, this form of translationese does not
differentiate translations of different quality. If
shining through features were useful in discern-
ing bad translations (as we expected), the red line
should have been more shifted towards the yel-
low dashed line of the source language. Needless
to say, the professional translations demonstrate a
similar shining through effect, which we do not illustrate here for brevity.

5 Conclusion

In the present paper, we analyzed if morphosyntactic features used in register studies and
translationese studies are also useful for the analysis of quality in translation. It is often assumed that any differences of translations from
non-translations may affect the fluency of translations. If so, automatically extracted translationese
features can also be used for human translation
evaluation, which saves time and effort of manual
annotation for quality.

We tested this on a dataset containing English-
Russian translations that were manually evaluated
for quality. The results of our analysis show that
features that are good for predicting translationese,
i.e. separating translations from the comparable
non-translations, are not necessarily good in pre-

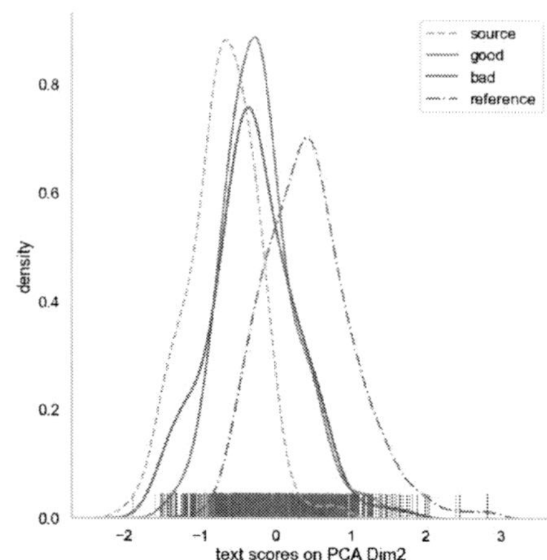

Figure 3: Good and bad translations vs. non-
translations in the source and the target languages

dicting translation quality, at least for the data at
hand. We have to admit that these results do not
align well with our expectations. One explanation
is that we relied on the morphology and syntax
for capturing translationese, while the most immediately perceptible lexical level remained unac-
counted for. Another reason for the lack of correlation between the quality labels and the fluency
(understood here as deviations from TL morphosyntactic patterns) is that quality is not entirely
about fluency, of course. The quality labels in
our data must reflect semantic faithfulness and
pragmatic acceptability of translations as well. If
anything, our results support the original interpretation of translationese as inherent properties
of translations exempt from the value judgment:
translationese is not the result of poor translation, but rather a statistical phenomenon: various
features distribute differently in originals than in
translations (Gellerstam, 1986).

To our knowledge, there are no further studies pursuing direct application of translationese
features for learning human translation quality.
In (De Sutter et al., 2017), the authors tried to
automatically assess translation quality of student
translations measuring their deviation from the
"normal" texts represented by professional translations and non-translated texts in a target language. Although they were able to show that student translations differ from both comparable originals and professional translations, it is not clear
if these differences were encountered due to other

influencing factors, as their data does not contain any manual evaluation. Besides that, they were not able to find out why certain linguistic features were indicators of deviant student translation behaviour in a given setting.

Similarly, we show that translationese, at least the features used in our analysis, are not necessarily good indicators of translation quality. We believe that these results provide valuable insights for both translation studies and translation technologies, especially those involving quality estimation issues.

Acknowledgments

This work is mostly produced in the University of Tyumen and is supported in part by a grant (Reference No. 17-06-00107) from the Russian Foundation for Basic Research.

References

Roee Aharoni, Moshe Koppel, and Yoav Goldberg. 2014. Automatic detection of machine translated text and translation quality estimation. In *Proceedings of ACL*, pages 289–295.

Mona Baker. 1993. Corpus linguistics and translation studies: Implications and applications. In G. Francis Baker M. and E. Tognini-Bonelli, editors, *Text and Technology: in Honour of John Sinclair*, pages 233–250. Benjamins, Amsterdam.

Mona Baker. 1995. Corpora in translation studies: An overview and some suggestions for future research. *Target*, 7(2):223–243.

Marco Baroni and Silvia Bernardini. 2006. A new approach to the study of translationese: Machine-learning the difference between original and translated text. *Literary and Linguistic Computing*, 21(3):259–274.

Gerrit Bayer-Hohenwarter. 2010. Comparing translational creativity scores of students and professionals: flexible problem-solving and/or fluent routine behaviour? In S. Göpferich, F. Alves, and I. Mees, editors, *New Approaches in Translation Process Research*, Copenhagen studies in language, pages 83–111. Samfundslitteratur.

Douglas Biber. 1995. *Dimensions of Register Variation: A Cross-Linguistic Comparison*. Cambridge University Press.

Douglas Biber, Susan Conrad, Edward Finegan, Stig Johansson, Geoffrey Leech, Susan Conrad, Edward Finegan, and Randolph Quirk. 1999. *Longman grammar of spoken and written English*, volume 2. MIT Press.

Andrew Chesterman. 2004. Hypotheses about translation universals. *Claims, Changes and Challenges in Translation Studies*, pages 1–14.

Gloria Corpas Pastor, Ruslan Mitkov, Naveed Afzal, and Lisette Garcia-Moya. 2008. Translation universals: do they exist? a corpus-based and nlp approach to convergence. In *Proceedings of the LREC-2008 Workshop on Building and Using Comparable Corpora*, pages 1–7.

Gert De Sutter, Bert Cappelle, Orphée De Clercq, Rudy Loock, and Koen Plevoets. 2017. Towards a corpus-based, statistical approach to translation quality: Measuring and visualizing linguistic deviance in student translations. *Linguistica Antverpiensia, New Series–Themes in Translation Studies*, 16.

Stefan Evert and Stella Neumann. 2017. The impact of translation direction on characteristics of translated texts : A multivariate analysis for English and German. *Empirical Translation Studies: New Methodological and Theoretical Traditions*, 300:47.

Bruce Fraser. 2006. Towards a Theory of Discourse Markers. *Approaches to discourse particles*, 1:189–204.

Martin Gellerstam. 1986. Translationese in Swedish novels translated from English. In L. Wollin and H. Lindquist, editors, *Translation Studies in Scandinavia*, pages 88–95. CWK Gleerup, Lund.

M A K Halliday and Ruqaiya Hasan. 1976. *Cohesion in English*. Equinox.

Iustina Ilisei. 2012. *A machine learning approach to the identification of translational language: an inquiry into translationese*. Doctoral thesis, University of Wolverhampton.

Iustina Ilisei, Diana Inkpen, Gloria Corpas Pastor, and Ruslan Mitkov. 2010. Identification of translationese: a supervised learning approach. In *Proceedings of CICLing-2010*, volume 6008 of *LNCS*, pages 503–511, Springer, Heidelberg.

Yingqi Jing and Haitao Liu. 2015. Mean Hierarchical Distance Augmenting Mean Dependency Distance. In *Proceedings of the Third International Conference on Dependency Linguistics (Depling 2015)*, pages 161–170.

Maarit Koponen. 2010. Assessing Machine Translation Quality with Error Analysis. In *Electronic proceedings of the VIII KäTu symposium on translation and interpreting studies*, volume 4, pages 1–12.

Maria Kunilovskaya and Andrey Kutuzov. 2018. Universal Dependencies-based syntactic features in detecting human translation varieties. *Proceedings of the 16th International Workshop on Treebanks and Linguistic Theories (TLT16)*, pages 27–36.

Maria Kunilovskaya, Natalia Morgoun, and Alexey Pariy. 2018. Learner vs. professional translations into Russian: Lexical profiles. *Translation & Interpreting*, 10.

Andrey Kutuzov and Maria Kunilovskaya. 2014. Russian learner translator corpus. In Petr Sojka, Aleš Horák, Ivan Kopeček, and Karel Pala, editors, *Text, Speech and Dialogue*, volume 8655 of *Lecture Notes in Computer Science*, pages 315–323. Springer International Publishing.

Ekaterina Lapshinova-Koltunski and Mihaela Vela. 2015. Measuring 'registerness' in human and machine translation: A text classification approach. In *Proceedings of the Second Workshop on Discourse in Machine Translation*, pages 122–131, Lisbon, Portugal. Association for Computational Linguistics.

Sachiko Nakamura. 2007. Comparison of features of texts translated by professional and learner translators. In *Proceedings of the 4th Corpus Linguistics conference*, University of Birmingham.

Stella Neumann. 2013. *Contrastive register variation. A quantitative approach to the comparison of English and German*. Mouton de Gruyter, Berlin, Boston.

Vladimir Plungian, Tatyana Reznikova, and Dmitri Sitchinava. 2005. Russian National Corpus: General description [Nacional'nyj korpus russkogo jazyka: obshhaja harakteristika]. *Scientific and technical information. Series 2: Information processes and systems*, 3:9–13.

Rosa Rabadán, Belén Labrador, and Noelia Ramón. 2009. Corpus-based contrastive analysis and translation universals A tool for translation quality assessment. *Babel*, 55(4):303–328.

Raphael Rubino, Ekaterina Lapshinova-Koltunski, and Josef van Genabith. 2016. Information density and quality estimation features as translationese indicators for human translation classification. In *Proceedings of NAACL HT 2006*, pages 960–970, San Diego, California.

Federica Scarpa. 2006. Corpus-based quality-assessment of specialist translation: A study using parallel and comparable corpora in English and Italian. In Maurizio Gotti and Susan Šarčevic, editors, *Insights into specialized translation*, volume 46 of *Linguistic Insights / Studies in Language and Communication*, pages 155–172. Peter Lang, Bern.

Alina Secara. 2005. Translation Evaluation - a State of the Art Survey. *Proceedings of the eCoLoRe/MeLLANGE Workshop, Leeds*, pages 39–44.

Milan Straka and Jana Straková. 2017. Tokenizing, POS Tagging, Lemmatizing and Parsing UD 2.0 with UDPipe. In *Proceedings of the CoNLL 2017 Shared Task: Multilingual Parsing from Raw Text to Universal Dependencies*, pages 88–99.

Elke Teich. 2003. *Cross-Linguistic Variation in System and Text. A Methodology for the Investigation of Translations and Comparable Texts*. Mouton de Gruyter, Berlin.

Mihaela Vela, Anne-Kathrin Schumann, and Andrea Wurm. 2014a. Beyond Linguistic Equivalence. An Empirical Study of Translation Evaluation in a Translation Learner Corpus. In *Proceedings of the EACL 2014 Workshop on Humans and Computer-assisted Translation*, pages 47–56, Gothenburg, Sweden. Association for Computational Linguistics.

Mihaela Vela, Anne-Kathrin Schumann, and Andrea Wurm. 2014b. Human Translation Evaluation and its Coverage by Automatic Scores. In *Proceedings of MTE Workshop at LREC 2014*, Reykjavik, Iceland. European Language Resources Association (ELRA).

Yu Yuan, Serge Sharoff, and Bogdan Babych. 2016. MoBiL: A Hybrid Feature Set for Automatic Human Translation Quality Assessment. In *Proceedings of the Tenth International Conference on Language Resources and Evaluation (LREC 2016)*.

Frederico Zanettin. 2013. Corpus Methods for Descriptive Translation Studies. *Procedia - Social and Behavioral Sciences*, 95:20–32.

The Punster's Amanuensis:
The Proper Place of Humans and Machines in the Translation of Wordplay

Tristan Miller
Austrian Research Institute for Artificial Intelligence (OFAI)
Freyung 6, 1010 Vienna, Austria
`tristan.miller@ofai.at`

Abstract

The translation of wordplay is one of the most extensively researched problems in translation studies, but it has attracted little attention in the fields of natural language processing and machine translation. This is because today's language technologies treat anomalies and ambiguities in the input as things that must be resolved in favour of a single "correct" interpretation, rather than preserved and interpreted in their own right. But if computers cannot yet process such creative language on their own, can they at least provide specialized support to translation professionals? In this paper, I survey the state of the art relevant to computational processing of humorous wordplay and put forth a vision of how existing theories, resources, and technologies could be adapted and extended to support interactive, computer-assisted translation.

1 Introduction

The creative language of humour and wordplay is all around us: every day we are amused by clever advertising slogans for which companies have paid vast sums to copy writers; our televisions and cinemas play an endless string of comedies, most of which get dubbed or subtitled into many different languages; and literary critics and scholars write volumes cataloguing and analyzing the wit of contemporary and classic authors. The ubiquity of humour and wordplay, and the constant need for creative professionals to evaluate, analyze, and translate it, would seem to make it a prime candidate for natural language processing (NLP) techniques such as machine translation (MT).

But despite being a recurrent and expected feature of many discourse types, humour and wordplay are necessarily out of scope for most real-world NLP applications. This is because these applications can only rigidly apply a fixed set of hand-crafted or automatically learned rules about the vocabulary, grammar, and semantics of a language. While these approaches work well enough on conventional language, they cannot robustly deal with texts that deliberately disregard or subvert linguistic conventions for a rhetorical effect. To computers, anomalies and ambiguities in the input, if they are detected at all, are seen as something that must always be resolved in favour of a single "correct" interpretation, rather than preserved and interpreted in their own right. For example, to native English speakers it is clear that the bank slogan "We feel loanley" contains a play on the words *loan* and *lonely*, but MT systems are stymied by the nonce term, leaving it untranslated, or else wrongly assuming it is a misspelling of *lonely* and losing the double meaning.

Recent years have seen a small flurry of NLP research aimed at changing the way computers process language by allowing them to recognize and interpret intentionally humorous ambiguity. While this work has laid some important groundwork, it is clear that there can never be a fully automatic, "one-size-fits-all" approach. Each expert user, whether a copy writer, a translator, or a literary scholar, has their own tasks, workflows, strategies, and goals. Customizing existing NLP tools to expert tasks has traditionally taken the form of automatically adapting existing data models to new languages and domains, or learning new data models with the help of "user-in-the-loop" techniques such as reinforcement learning. But neither of these approaches works around the "rigid rule" problem mentioned above: wordplay is by definition unpredictable and irreverent of rules and norms, and so cannot be easily captured in a predictive model.

In this paper, I survey the state of the art in

Temnikova, I, Orăsan, C., Corpas Pastor, G., and Mitkov, R. (eds.) (2019) *Proceedings of the 2nd Workshop on Human-Informed Translation and Interpreting Technology (HiT-IT 2019)*, Varna, Bulgaria, September 5 - 6, pages 57–65.
https://doi.org/10.26615/issn.2683-0078.2019_007

linguistics, computational linguistics, translation, and machine translation as it relates to humour and wordplay. On the basis of these findings, I argue that the proper place of machines in the translation of humorous wordplay is to support rather than replace human translators. In the vein of the *Translator's Amanuensis* proposed by Kay (1980), I make some specific proposals concerning how the hitherto disparate work in these fields can be connected with a view to producing "machine-in-the-loop" tools to assist human translators in selecting and implementing appropriate translation strategies for instances of puns and other forms of wordplay.

2 State of the Art

2.1 Linguistic Conceptions of Humour and Punning

The linguistic mechanisms of verbal humour have been studied since antiquity, by which time the roles of ambiguity and incongruity had already been recognized (Attardo, 1994, Ch. 1). Modern linguistics has significantly broadened and deepened this understanding, giving rise to formal theories of humour—that is, testable explanations of the necessary and sufficient linguistic conditions for a text to be humorous. Perhaps the most widely accepted of these today are Raskin's (1985) Script-based Semantic Theory of Humour (SSTH) and its extension, the Generalized Theory of Verbal Humour (GTVH; Attardo and Raskin, 1991).

Both the SSTH and the GTVH are based on the notion of *scripts*, or *semantic frames* as they are more commonly called in computational linguistics. A script is a collection of semantic information, internalized by a native speaker, that specifies "characteristic features, attributes, and functions of a denotatum, and its characteristic interactions with things necessarily or typically associated with it" (Alan, 2001, p. 251). Under the SSTH, humour is evoked when a given text is compatible, at least in part, with two different scripts that are "opposite" in some culturally significant sense (e.g., life vs. death). The GTVH incorporates this notion of *script opposition* (SO) as the first of six parameters, or *knowledge resources* (KRs), that, when instantiated, uniquely characterize a given joke. The other five KRs are, in descending order of salience, the *logical mechanism* (LM), the (often faulty) reasoning whereby the incongruity of the scripts is resolved; the *situation* (SI), the non-humorous set-

Figure 1: A multimodal pun from the 1984 film *Top Secret!*: Hearing it cough, the woman asks the driver if the horse is alright. The driver replies, "Oh, he caught a cold the other day and he's just a little hoarse."

ting and paraphernalia of the joke; the *target* (TA) or butt of the joke; the *narrative strategy* (NS) or "genre" of the joke; and *language* (LA), the lexical, syntactic, phonological, and other linguistic choices that express the other KRs. Empirical validation has shown the postulated dependency hierarchy of the six KRs to be fundamentally correct (Ruch et al., 1993), which has important implications (discussed in §2.3) for the translation of humour.

Punning is a form of language play in which a word or phrase is used to evoke the meaning of another word or phrase with a similar or identical pronunciation. The term *pun* can refer to such an instance of wordplay as a whole, or more specifically to the word/phrase in it with the more salient meaning; the *target*[1] is the secondary word/phrase that is evoked. Figure 1 presents an example for the pun *hoarse* and the target *horse*.

Puns are one of the most studied phenomena in the linguistics of humour. Most analyses of puns to date have been taxonomic or phonological, a survey of which can be found in Hempelmann and Miller (2017). These studies describe the permissible and preferential sound transformations between a pun and its target (in terms of the types of articulatory features, the number of segments affected, their positions in the lexical and syllabic structure, etc.). Though native speakers have implicit knowledge of these transformational rules (Aarons, 2017), they must be learned or explicitly modelled in computational applications. Such models are briefly discussed in the following subsection.

Whether and how phonological features contribute to the humorousness of a pun is an open

---

[1] Not to be confused with the *target* (TA) of the GTVH.

question. Lagerquist (1980) and Fleischhacker (2005) have posited a correlation between, on the one hand, the degree of phonetic similarity between the pun and its target, and on the other hand, the "successfulness" or funniness of the pun. Hempelmann (2003a) rejects this hypothesis, basing his arguments on semantic theories of humour and on informal evidence from non-humorous pseudo-punning wordplay. More recent empirical evidence from certain forms of humorous but non-punning wordplay, however, establishes that perceived humour is a quantifiable function of entropy distance to the source word (Westbury et al., 2016). Further empirical study would be necessary to determine whether this finding also applies to puns.

Other scholarship has targeted the semantics of puns. Guiraud (1976, pp. 111–113) discusses loss of meaning as a feature of humour and observes the "defunctionalization of language" in puns. Using the GTVH as a framework, more recent studies (Attardo et al., 2002; Hempelmann, 2004; Hempelmann and Attardo, 2011) have identified the LM of puns as *cratylistic syllogism* (Attardo, 1994, Ch. 4), the notion that if meaning motivates sound, then the meaning of similar-sounding words must be similar. This line of reasoning is an example of the faulty "local" logic underpinning much humour (Ziv, 1984). Cratylism is at odds with the canonical assumption of conventional linguistics that the relation between the signifier (sound sequence) and the signified (mental concept) is arbitrary and language-specific (de Saussure, 1995, pp. 97–103). The findings of these semantic studies support my contention that humour is not suitable for processing with methods from conventional computational semantics, but rather must be treated as a special case.

2.2 Computational Linguistics and Humour

An advantage of the GTVH is that its most central notions, scripts and logical mechanisms, are amenable to mathematical and computational modelling. Attardo et al. (2002) and Hempelmann (2010) present set- and graph-theoretic models of script overlap and opposition, as well as graph-theoretic models of certain logical mechanisms. In brief, if scripts are conceptualized as sets of slot–filler pairs, then two scripts are overlapping but opposed when they have a non-null intersection, and when the complementary sets of the intersection contain subsets that are (locally) antonymic.

Though the aforementioned authors do not provide an implementation of their model, such an implementation could be realized with a knowledge base of scripts, a knowledge base of word meanings, algorithms for tagging text with reference to these knowledge bases, and an inference engine for identifying the overlapping and opposing parts.

Many of these resources, and their attendant software tools, are by now available, and of sufficient maturity, to lay the groundwork for an automated, GTVH-based interpreter of humorous text. On the knowledge base side, these resources include WordNet (Fellbaum, 1998), a lexical-semantic network storing lexicalizations and linguistic relations for over 200 000 English word senses, and FrameNet (Ruppenhofer et al., 2016), a database of some 1200 scripts covering over 13 000 English word senses.[2] On the algorithm side, state-of-the-art techniques for word sense disambiguation (Navigli, 2009) and semantic role labelling (Palmer et al., 2010) can apply WordNet senses and FrameNet scripts to raw text with 70–80% accuracy (Täckström et al., 2015; Miller, 2016). The crucial missing component here is the inference engine, which would need to identify the overlap between the tagged FrameNet scripts, and then use WordNet to find contrasting relations between the non-overlapping parts.

However, a general-purpose GTVH-based interpreter would require explicit modelling of all possible LMs, an ambitious undertaking that is far beyond the current state of the art. Restricting the interpreter to the LM of cratylism—the purview of the present paper—would be much more feasible, in particular because it could draw from the growing body of work on the computational processing of puns. This work includes attempts to computationally model the phonological properties of puns, as well as semantics-focused work on the detection and interpretation of puns. The former camp aims at producing tables of edit probabilities for sound pairs in the pun and its target, using Optimality Theory (Hempelmann, 2003a,b) or patterns learned by weighted finite-state transducers (Jaech et al., 2016). The latter camp includes studies such as Kao et al. (2016) and Simpson et al. (2019), which em-

---

[2]WordNet, FrameNet, and their counterparts for other languages have also been aligned at the word sense level (Matuschek, 2014; Hartmann and Gurevych, 2013) and combined in linked lexical-semantic resources such as EuroWordNet (Vossen, 1998), UBY (Gurevych et al., 2012), and BabelNet (Navigli and Ponzetto, 2013).

ploy Gaussian processes or information-theoretic measures to predict human judgments of the humorousness of puns, and various approaches (surveyed in Miller et al. (2017)) for sense-tagging their double meanings. While few of these systems are informed by linguistic theories of humour, analysis points to the superiority of knowledge- and rule-based approaches over rote supervised techniques.

2.3 Translation of Wordplay

The translation of humour, and more specifically of puns and other forms of wordplay, is among the most intensively studied problems in the field of translation studies (Delabastita and Henry, 1996; Delabastita, 1994; Henry, 2003; Vandaele, 2011; Regattin, 2015). Modern treatments recognize several high-level strategies for translating puns, many of which are informed by Nida's (1964) notion of dynamic translational equivalence.[3] For example, Delabastita (1996) covers the following strategies: (S_1) replace the source-language pun with a target-language pun (which may deviate from the original semantics); (S_2) substitute non-punning language that preserves one or both of the original meanings; (S_3) replace the pun with some non-punning wordplay or rhetorical device (irony, alliteration, vagueness, etc.); (S_4) omit the language containing the pun; (S_5) leave the pun in the source language; (S_6) as a compensatory measure, introduce a new pun at a discourse position where the original had none; (S_7) as a compensatory measure, introduce entirely new material containing a pun; and (S_8) editorialize: insert a footnote, endnote, etc. to explain the pun.

The choice of strategy for a given case depends on the medium of translation, the aims of the translator, the possibilities for appropriate wordplay in the target language given the source context, and the translator's ability to find and exploit these possibilities. For example, in the foreign dubbing of motion pictures for mass-market audiences, S_7 and S_8 are generally not available. Similarly, the use of S_1 can be constrained by the presence of one or both meanings in the audio or visual channel (Bucaria, 2017). The *hoarse/horse* pun of Fig. 1 exemplifies these challenges: the animal and its cough are very conspicuously shown and heard, and so must

be acknowledged in the dialogue. In the German-language dub, the translator was able to implement S_1 by having the driver say that the horse's cold had made its voice *rostig* ("rusty", but also evoking *Ross*, meaning "horse"). The translation thus preserves the original's wordplay and semantics. By contrast, the Russian dub abandons any attempt at punning, presumably because Russian lacks (or the translator could not identify) any similar-sounding synonyms for "horse" (лошадь) and "hoarse" (охрипший), nor any other pair of words for things that would make sense for the characters to be discussing in the scene. Instead, S_2 is applied, with the driver giving the non-humorous explanation, "Вчера простудился. Лошадиный кашель." ("He caught a cold yesterday. A horse cough.")

S_1 is a particular focus of the present paper. Though the literature abounds with case studies, there does not yet exist a generalized, formalized methodology for producing or explaining such translations (Delabastita, 1997). Attardo (2002) provides an important step in this direction by viewing the translation of humour through the lens of the GTVH. He argues that since the degree of perceived difference between jokes increases linearly with the salience of the KRs in which they differ (Ruch et al., 1993), translation of humour should strive to respect all six KRs. Moreover, where deviation is necessary, it should occur at the lowest level necessary for the translator's pragmatic purposes. Attardo is quick to point out that puns constitute an exception to this rule: whereas referential jokes rank LA lowest and therefore afford its translations a great deal of latitude, in wordplay, the essential features of LA are preselected by the cratylistic LM. "Translatable" puns, therefore, are those that exhibit a set of LA features in the source language that is consistent with a set of LA features in the target language, such that the pragmatic goals of the translation are met. The notion of what constitutes "consistency" of features remains an open question.

2.4 Machine Translation and Computer-assisted Translation

Though MT has made impressive strides in the last few decades, it is not yet capable of producing publication-quality output for most conventional text domains, let alone for the stylistically and semantically aberrant constructs of creative language. To date, only a scattered handful of studies have treated the topic of MT and humour. Stede

---

[3]In contrast to formal ("word-for-word") equivalence, dynamic equivalence privileges target language solutions that aim at preserving the intention, rather than the literal meaning, of the source text. In the case of puns and other jokes, this intention is to amuse the reader in the context of the discourse.

and Tidhar (1999), recognizing the unsuitability of the prevailing statistical MT paradigm for the translation of humour, propose a transfer-based architecture (Nirenburg et al., 1992) where ambiguity and its mechanisms are explicitly modelled. The architecture produces a syntactic chart of the source text and employs a measure of script opposition to identify partial analyses suitable for humorous translation. These parts are then transferred to syntactic charts in the target language, from which generation commences. However, no system implementing this architecture was ever realized, and it seems that any attempt to do so would be blocked by the infeasibility of modelling the common-sense world knowledge necessary to identify script oppositions. Farwell and Helmreich (2006) propose a separate knowledge-based translation framework that differentiates between the author's locutionary, illocutionary, and perlocutionary intents,[4] and present a case study of its application to puns. However, as with Stede and Tidhar (1999), the framework is not actually implemented as it presupposes an extensive store of real-world knowledge and beliefs that is too expensive to model computationally.

Other past work has applied MT to other forms of creative language, such as poetry. However, these studies (Greene et al., 2010; Genzel et al., 2010) focus on the preservation of surface-level constraints such as rhyme and metre, rather than semantic ambiguity as in humour. A spiritually similar constraint satisfaction approach, which targets both creative language and semantic ambiguity (but not humour), is the hidden acrostic generator of Stein et al. (2014). It relies on automatic paraphrasing, a technique intimately connected to MT (Callison-Burch, 2007). While the work is not directly applicable to the translation support task of this paper, inspiration can be taken from their optimization approach.

While much of the research in the MT community has focused on end-to-end automation of the translation process, it has been convincingly argued (Kay, 1980) that the proper role of computers is automating that which is "mechanical and routine", leaving the "essentially human" aspects to the human translator. Accordingly, there has been increasing interest in integrating information technology into traditional, manual translation workflows. Translation is by now a highly

<hr>

[4]That is, how something is said, what is being said, and why something is being said (Austin, 1975).

technologized profession: electronic dictionaries, translation memories, terminology extraction systems, and concordancers are just some of the many computer-assisted translation (CAT) tools that professional translators have come to rely on (Kenny, 2011). Despite the extensive treatment creative language has received in translation studies, a survey of the available literature reveals no CAT tools that specifically support its translation. However, there exist a number of interactive, component-based CAT workbenches (Federico et al., 2014; Alabau et al., 2014; Albanesi et al., 2015) into which such support could conceivably be integrated. Some of these workbenches were designed for historical texts that pose special structural, stylistic, linguistic, and hermeneutical challenges. Their support for nonstandard text could provide useful, or at least inspirational, for handling contemporary wordplay.

3 Research Challenges

We have seen from the previous section that there exists a considerable body of foundational work on humour and wordplay in the fields of linguistics, computational linguistics, and translation studies. Linguistics provides us with semantic theories of humour that define the conditions for a text to be humorous, and with phonological models that characterize the patterns of sound changes in punning. Computational linguistics provides us with tools to automatically annotate texts with word meanings and semantic roles, to analyze lexical-semantic relationships, and to measure the semantic similarity between words and texts; the past couple of years has seen rudimentary attempts to apply these tools to the computational processing of puns. Translation studies has established a number of high-level strategies for dealing with puns, plus a wealth of case studies on the fine-grained application of these strategies. By and large, however, the past work in each of these three fields has been not been informed by work in the other two.

I contend that the time is now right to connect these separate channels of research—to start developing linguistically informed, computerized translation methodologies for dealing with the vagaries of creative language. Indeed, the need for such interdisciplinarity in the translation of wordplay has long been recognized: Delabastita (1997) acknowledged both the necessity and insufficiency of linguistic theory, arguing that pun translation mechanisms could be understood only with additional help from

61

"finer instruments... borrowed from neighbouring disciplines". And Attardo (2002) presciently remarked that "what a theory of translation really needs is a metric of similarity between meanings/pragmatic forces". Digital versions of these instruments and metrics have become realizable only recently, with the advent of large-scale multilingual lexical-semantic resources and distributional computational semantics.

But as we have seen, past work on MT of humour and wordplay is sketchy, the only two papers on the topic (Stede and Tidhar, 1999; Farwell and Helmreich, 2006) putting forth high-level plans but no implementation or evaluation. Both papers agree that automated translation must be knowledge-based, but they do not specify how to acquire and model all the non-linguistic knowledge required to understand arbitrary instances of humour. Nor do I think that this is even possible at the present time—despite ongoing work on addressing this bottleneck (e.g., Li et al., 2016; Gordon, 2014), translation of humour requires a familiarity with discourse, cultural, and commonsense knowledge that is far out of reach of today's artificial intelligence.

Nonetheless, I believe that contemporary AI could still be made to play an important role in the translation of humorous wordplay. Rather than trying to model the entire end-to-end translation task computationally, as in MT, I argue that it is instead necessary to study how human translators approach the problem, and then provide them with tools that support rather than replace these approaches. With this "machine-in-the-loop" paradigm, language technology would be applied to only those subtasks it can perform best, such as using lexical information retrieval (i.e., searching a large vocabulary space for words matching a given set of semantic and phonological features) to generate and rank lists of pun translation candidates. Subtasks that depend heavily on real-world background knowledge and pragmatic inference—such as making the final selection from such a candidate list—would be left to the human translator.

To fulfill this vision it will be necessary to develop innovative, interactive techniques for detecting and interpreting puns in their source-language contexts, assessing the applicability of different translation strategies to a given pun, determining the amount of semantic leeway afforded to the translator, generating a set of translation candidates adhering to this semantic leeway and to phonological constraints on

punning, and dynamically exploring this candidate space. Along these lines, I envisage three major research directions:

1. Systematic and wide-ranging studies of how human translators process puns. Such studies would need to go deeper than the coarse-grained taxonomies of Delabastita (1996) and others, aiming at fine-grained models of the implementation of various translation strategies. Low (2011) provides a step in this direction by describing one method by which puns could be systematically S_1-translated, though it is not clear whether this method, or one akin to it, had been or is in common use, nor what other methods may be in use.

2. Empirical validation of the competing hypotheses (Lagerquist, 1980; Fleischhacker, 2005; Hempelmann, 2003a) concerning the relationship between a pun's humorousness and the phonetic distance between the pun and its target. Resolving this issue is a prerequisite for computationally ranking pun translation candidates by fitness.

3. Building on the above, the development of interactive, NLP-based methodologies for helping a human translator to assess whether a given pun is S_1-translatable and, if so, to implement that translation. This will necessarily involve the development and synthesis of methods based on sense annotation and semantic role labelling of puns, cross-lingual similarity of word senses and sentiments, and exploration of lexical-semantic spaces.

Though the precise form and functionality of a "Punster's Amanuensis" tool implementing these methodologies will depend on the findings of the first two research directions, the following can serve as a rough sketch. The tool would first scan the source text and flag possible instances of humorous lexical ambiguity for special attention by the translator, who can interactively confirm or reject these flags, or flag additional instances missed by the system. For each confirmed pun in the source text, the system would construct an interpretation via word sense and semantic role annotation of the pun and its context, and (in the case of multimodal source data) automatic keyword captioning (Gong et al., 2014; Vinyals et al., 2017) of any associated sound or images; these annotations would be subject to interactive post-correction. This interpretation could then be used to identify a set of translation candidates that attempt to preserve the semantics of the original and adhere to phonological constraints on punning. These candidates could be found, for example, by looking up translations of the pun's two meanings and then searching for closely related senses in the target language whose lexicalizations have similar pronunciations. The candidates would be ranked according to various fitness measures (including phonological ones) and presented to the user in a manner that facilitates interpretation and exploration.

To expand upon this, consider the pun introduced in Fig. 1 and how the Punster's Amanuensis might help translate it into German. The tool, having detected the presence of the pun in the line, automatically interprets its two meanings and tags them with reference to their entries ("deep and harsh-sounding", with English lexicalizations *hoarse, gruff, husky*; and "solid-hoofed quadruped", with the English lexicalization *horse*) in a bilingual semantic network such as EuroWordNet. The system then looks up in the network the corresponding lexicalizations in German: *heiser* and *Pferd, Gaul, Ross*, respectively. Each possible pun–target pairing (*heiser–Pferd, heiser–Gaul, heiser–Ross*) is scored according to the phonetic similarity between the pun and the target (as determined by some phonological model of punning). For these naïve "direct" translations, the similarities are very low, indicating that they do not form valid puns in German. However, the tool can start searching the semantic neighbourhoods of the two senses for closely related senses whose German-language lexicalizations *are* similar-sounding. It might thereby arrive at *rostig* ("having a voice impaired in skill or tone by neglect") a hyponym of *heiser* that happens to have a relatively high phonetic similarity to the previously discovered *Ross*. The pun–target pair *rostig–Ross* would therefore be among the translation candidates highly scored by the system. Further candidates of this sort (*Bronchitis–Bronco*, etc.) would also be discovered and scored, either by having the system automatically expand the search space in the semantic network, or by allowing the user to manually explore it and possibly modify the search criteria.

4   Conclusion

In this paper I have surveyed the research on word-play translation. I have observed a need for support-ing translation technologies, but found that existing MT approaches are inappropriate and manual ones are as yet too vaguely defined to implement computationally. However, I have identified divers theories, methodologies, and resources that could be extended and integrated to produce such translation technologies. I have sketched a CAT tool encapsulating these ideas, whose exact form and functions could be refined following further studies of manual translation workflows. These studies are currently being planned, and their results (including a complete description of the resulting CAT tool) will be the subject of a follow-up paper.

Acknowledgments

This work has been supported by the Austrian Science Fund (FWF) under project M 2625-N31. The Austrian Research Institute for Artificial Intelligence is supported by the Austrian Federal Ministry for Science, Research and Economy.

References

Debra Aarons. 2017. Puns and tacit linguistic knowledge. In Salvatore Attardo, editor, *The Routledge Handbook of Language and Humor*, pages 80–94. Routledge.

Vicent Alabau, Christian Buck, Michael Carl, Francisco Casacuberta, Mercedes García-Martínez, Ulrich Germann, Jesús González-Rubio, Robin Hill, Philipp Koehn, Luis Leiva, Bartolomé Mesa-Lao, Daniel Ortiz-Martínez, Herve Saint-Amand, Germán Sanchis Trilles, and Chara Tsoukala. 2014. CASMACAT: A computer-assisted translation workbench. In *Proceedings of the 14th Conference of the European Chapter of the Association for Computational Linguistics (System Demonstrations)*, pages 25–28.

Keith Alan. 2001. *Natural Language Semantics*. Blackwell, Oxford.

Davide Albanesi, Andrea Bellandi, Giulia Benotto, Gianfranco Di Segni, and Emiliano Giovannetti. 2015. When translation requires interpretation: Collaborative computer–assisted translation of ancient texts. In *Proceedings of the 9th SIGHUM Workshop on Language Technology for Cultural Heritage, Social Sciences, and Humanities*, pages 84–88.

Salvatore Attardo. 1994. *Linguistic Theories of Humor*. Mouton de Gruyter, Berlin.

Salvatore Attardo. 2002. Translation and humour. *The Translator*, 8(2):173–194.

Salvatore Attardo, Christian F. Hempelmann, and Sara Di Maio. 2002. Script oppositions and logical mechanisms: Modeling incongruities and their resolutions. *Humor*, 15:3–46.

Salvatore Attardo and Victor Raskin. 1991. Script theory revis(it)ed: Joke similarity and joke representation model. *Humor*, 4:293–348.

J. L. Austin. 1975. *How to Do Things with Words.* Oxford University Press, Oxford.

Chiara Bucaria. 2017. Audiovisual translation of humor. In Salvatore Attardo, editor, *The Routledge Handbook of Language and Humor*, pages 430–443. Routledge, New York, NY.

Chris Callison-Burch. 2007. *Paraphrasing and Translation.* D.Phil. thesis, University of Edinburgh.

Dirk Delabastita. 1994. Focus on the pun: Wordplay as a special problem in translation studies. *Target*, 6(2):222–243.

Dirk Delabastita. 1996. Introduction to the special issue on wordplay and translation. *The Translator*, 2(2):1–22.

Dirk Delabastita. 1997. Introduction. In Dirk Delabastita, editor, *Traductio: Essays on Punning and Translation*, pages 1–22. St. Jerome, Manchester.

Dirk Delabastita and Jacqueline Henry. 1996. Wordplay and translation: A selective bibliography. *The Translator*, 2(2):347–353.

David Farwell and Stephen Helmreich. 2006. Pragmatics-based MT and the translation of puns. In *Proceedings of the 11th Annual Conference of the European Association for Machine Translation*, pages 187–194.

Marcello Federico, Nicola Bertoldi, Mauro Cettolo, Matteo Negri, Marco Turchi, Marco Trombetti, Alessandro Cattelan, Antonio Farina, Domenico Lupinetti, Andrea Martines, Alberto Massidda, Holger Schwenk, Loïc Barrault, Frederic Blain, Philipp Koehn, Christian Buck, and Ulrich Germann. 2014. The MateCat tool. In *Proceedings of the 25th International Conference on Computational Linguistics (System Demonstrations)*, pages 129–132.

Christiane Fellbaum, editor. 1998. *WordNet: An Electronic Lexical Database.* MIT Press, Cambridge, MA.

Heidi Anne Fleischhacker. 2005. *Similarity in Phonology: Evidence from Reduplication and Loan Adaptation.* Ph.D. thesis, UCLA.

Dmitriy Genzel, Jakob Uszkoreit, and Franz Och. 2010. "Poetic" statistical machine translation: Rhyme and meter. In *Proceedings of the 2010 Conference on Empirical Methods in Natural Language Processing*, pages 158–166.

Yunchao Gong, Qifa Ke, Michael Isard, and Svetlana Lazebnik. 2014. A multi-view embedding space for modeling internet images, tags, and their semantics. *International Journal of Computer Vision*, 106(2):210–233.

Jonathan Michael Gordon. 2014. *Inferential Commonsense Knoweldge from Text.* Ph.D. thesis, University of Rochester.

Erica Greene, Tugba Bodrumlu, and Kevin Knight. 2010. Automatic analysis of rhythmic poetry with applications to generation and translation. In *Proceedings of the 2010 Conference on Empirical Methods in Natural Language Processing*, pages 524–533.

Pierre Guiraud. 1976. *Les jeux de mots.* Presses Universitaires de France, Paris.

Iryna Gurevych, Judith Eckle-Kohler, Silvana Hartmann, Michael Matuschek, Christian M. Meyer, and Christian Wirth. 2012. UBY – A large-scale unified lexical-semantic resource. In *Proceedings of the 13th Conference of the European Chapter of the Association for Computational Linguistics*, pages 580–590.

Silvana Hartmann and Iryna Gurevych. 2013. FrameNet on the way to Babel: Creating a bilingual FrameNet using Wiktionary as interlingual connection. In *Proceedings of the 51st Annual Meeting of the Association for Computational Linguistics*, volume 1, pages 1363–1373.

Christian F. Hempelmann. 2003a. *Paronomasic Puns: Target Recoverability Towards Automatic Generation.* Ph.D. thesis, Purdue University.

Christian F. Hempelmann. 2003b. YPS – The Ynperfect Pun Selector for computational humor. In *Proceedings of the CHI 2003 Workshop on Humor Modeling in the Interface*.

Christian F. Hempelmann. 2004. Script opposition and logical mechanism in punning. *Humor*, 17(4):381–392.

Christian F. Hempelmann. 2010. *Incongruity and Resolution of Medieval Humorous Narratives: Linguistic Humor Theory and the Medieval Bawdry of Rabelais, Boccaccio, and Chaucer.* VDM Verlag Dr. Müller.

Christian F. Hempelmann and Salvatore Attardo. 2011. Resolutions and their incongruities: Further thoughts on logical mechanisms. *Humor*, 24:125–149.

Christian F. Hempelmann and Tristan Miller. 2017. Puns: Taxonomy and phonology. In Salvatore Attardo, editor, *The Routledge Handbook of Language and Humor*, pages 95–108. Routledge, New York, NY.

Jacqueline Henry. 2003. *La traduction des jeux de mots.* Presses Sorbonne Nouvelle, Paris.

Aaron Jaech, Rik Koncel-Kedziorski, and Mari Ostendorf. 2016. Phonological pun-derstanding. In *Proceedings of the 2016 Conference of the North American Chapter of the Association for Computational Linguistics*, pages 654–663.

Justine T. Kao, Roger Levy, and Noah D. Goodman. 2016. A computational model of linguistic humor in puns. *Cognitive Science*, 40(5):1270–1285.

Martin Kay. 1980. The proper place of men and machines in language translation. Working Paper CSL-80-11, Xerox PARC, Palo Alto, CA, USA.

Dorothy Kenny. 2011. Electronic tools and resources for translators. In Kirsten Malmkjær and Kevin Windle, editors, *The Oxford Handbook of Translation Studies*. Oxford University Press, Oxford.

Linnea M. Lagerquist. 1980. Linguistic evidence from paronomasia. In *Papers from the Sixteenth Regional Meeting Chicago Linguistic Society*, pages 185–191.

Xiang Li, Aynaz Taheri, Lifu Tu, and Kevin Gimpel. 2016. Commonsense knowledge base completion. In *Proceedings of the 54th Annual Meeting of the Association for Computational Linguistics*, volume 1, pages 1445–1455.

Peter Alan Low. 2011. Translating jokes and puns. *Perspectives: Studies in Translation Theory and Practice*, 19(1):59–70.

Michael Matuschek. 2014. *Word Sense Alignment of Lexical Resources*. Dr.-Ing. thesis, Technische Universität Darmstadt.

Tristan Miller. 2016. *Adjusting Sense Representations for Word Sense Disambiguation and Automatic Pun Interpretation*. Dr.-Ing. thesis, Technische Universität Darmstadt.

Tristan Miller, Christian F. Hempelmann, and Iryna Gurevych. 2017. SemEval-2017 Task 7: Detection and interpretation of English puns. In *Proceedings of the 11th International Workshop on Semantic Evaluation*, pages 58–68.

Roberto Navigli. 2009. Word sense disambiguation: A survey. *ACM Computing Surveys*, 41(2):10:1–10:69.

Roberto Navigli and Simone Paolo Ponzetto. 2013. An overview of BabelNet and its API for multilingual language processing. In Iryna Gurevych and Jungi Kim, editors, *The People's Web Meets NLP: Collaboratively Constructed Language Resources*, pages 177–197. Springer, Berlin/Heidelberg.

Eugene A. Nida. 1964. *Toward a Science of Translating*. E. J. Brill, Leiden, the Netherlands.

Sergei Nirenburg, Jaime Carbonell, Masaru Tomita, and Kenneth Goodman. 1992. *Machine Translation: A Knowledge-based Approach*. Morgan Kaufmann, San Mateo, CA.

Martha Palmer, Daniel Gildea, and Nianwen Xue. 2010. *Semantic Role Labeling*. Morgan & Claypool, Williston, VT.

Victor Raskin. 1985. *Semantic Mechanisms of Humor*. Springer Netherlands.

Fabio Regattin. 2015. Traduire les jeux de mots: une approche intégrée. *Atelier de traduction*, 23.

Willibald Ruch, Salvatore Attardo, and Victor Raskin. 1993. Towards an empirical verification of the General Theory of Verbal Humor. *Humor*, 6(2):123–136.

Josef Ruppenhofer, Michael Ellsworth, Miriam R. L. Petruck, Christopher R. Johnson, and Jan Scheffczyk. 2016. *FrameNet II: Extended Theory and Practice*. ICSI, Berkeley, CA.

Ferdinand de Saussure. 1995. *Cours de linguistique générale*. Grande Bibliothèque Payot, Paris.

Edwin Simpson, Erik-Lân Do Dinh, Tristan Miller, and Iryna Gurevych. 2019. Predicting humorousness and metaphor novelty with Gaussian process preference learning. In *Proceedings of the 57th Annual Meeting of the Association for Computational Linguistics*.

Manfrede Stede and Dan Tidhar. 1999. Towards a humour switch for machine translation. In *Proceedings of the AISB '99 Symposium on Creative Language: Humour and Stories*.

Benno Stein, Matthias Hagen, and Christof Bräutigam. 2014. Generating acrostics via paraphrasing and heuristic search. In *Proceedings of the 25th International Conference on Computational Linguistics*, pages 2018–2029.

Oscar Täckström, Kuzman Ganchev, and Dipanjan Das. 2015. Efficient inference and structured learning for semantic role labeling. *Transactions of the Association for Computational Linguistics*, 3:29–41.

Jeroen Vandaele. 2011. Wordplay in translation. In Yves Gambier and Luc van Doorslaer, editors, *Handbook of Translation Studies*, volume 2, pages 180–183. John Benjamins.

Oriol Vinyals, Alexander Toshev, Samy Bengio, and Dumitru Erhan. 2017. Show and tell: Lessons learned from the 2015 MSCOCO image captioning challenge. *IEEE Transactions on Pattern Analysis and Machine Intelligence*, 39(4):652–663.

Piek Vossen, editor. 1998. *EuroWordNet: A Multilingual Database with Lexical Semantic Networks*. Springer.

Chris Westbury, Cyrus Shaoul, Gail Moroschan, and Michael Ramscar. 2016. Telling the world's least funny jokes: On the quantification of humor as entropy. *Journal of Memory and Language*, 86:141–156.

Avner Ziv. 1984. *Personality and Sense of Humor*. Springer.

Comparing a Hand-crafted to an Automatically Generated Feature Set for Deep Learning: Pairwise Translation Evaluation

Despoina Mouratidis
Department of Informatics, Ionian University
/ Tsirigoti Squ. 7, 49100 Corfu, Greece
`c12mour@ionio.gr`

Katia Lida Kermanidis
Department of Informatics, Ionian University
/ Tsirigoti Squ. 7, 49100 Corfu, Greece
`kerman@ionio.gr`

Abstract

The automatic evaluation of machine translation (MT) has proven to be a very significant research topic. Most automatic evaluation methods focus on the evaluation of the output of MT as they compute similarity scores that represent translation quality. This work targets on the performance of MT evaluation. We present a general scheme for learning to classify parallel translations, using linguistic information, of two MT model outputs and one human (reference) translation. We present three experiments to this scheme using neural networks (NN). One using string based hand-crafted features (Exp1), the second using automatically trained embeddings from the reference and the two MT outputs (one from a statistical machine translation (SMT) model and the other from a neural machine translation (NMT) model), which are learned using NN (Exp2), and the third experiment (Exp3) that combines information from the other two experiments. The languages involved are English (EN), Greek (GR) and Italian (IT) segments are educational in domain. The proposed language-independent learning scheme which combines information from the two experiments (experiment 3) achieves higher classification accuracy compared with models using BLEU score information as well as other classification approaches, such as Random Forest (RF) and Support Vector Machine (SVM).

1 Introduction

MT systems need to be evaluated in order to assess the degree of reliability of their results, and to facilitate means for improvement as well. Some of the most popular automatic MT evaluation methods are the BLEU score (Papineni et al., 2002), TER (Snover et al., 2006), METEOR (Lavie and Agarwal, 2007) etc. Zechner and Waibel 2000 introduced the word error rate (WER), a lexical similarity metric. WER uses the number of steps required to make the output similar to reference translation. Mouratidis and Kermanidis (2019) used parallel corpora and they showed that string-based features (e.g. length of source (*src*) sentence), similarity based (e.g. the ratio of common suffix of MT outputs and the reference) etc. could improve the performance of MT system. Giménez and Màrquez (2007) used syntactic similarity methods like information from part of speech tagging (POS). Pighin and May (2012) proposed the analysis of an annotated corpus based on automatic translation and user-provided translation corrections gathered through an online MT system. Barrón-Cedeño et al. (2013) used an extension of the corpus of the study by Pighin and May (2012). They introduced new features and they tried different configurations of classifiers. Both papers showed that the quality of an SMT system can be improved.

Word representations (embeddings) are very useful in Natural Language Processing (NLP) applications such as automatic speech recognition and MT (Schwenk, 2007). They can model the semantic and syntactic information of every word in a document (Hill et al., 2014). There are lots of different methods for generating embeddings such as methods based on simple recursive neural networks (RNN) (Cho et al., 2014), convolutional neural networks and RNN using Long short-term memory (LSTM) (Sutskever et al., 2014), count-based methods and others. A big variety of pre-trained embedding models are used in the literature, such as Word2Vec (Mikolov et al., 2014) and GloVe (Pennington et al., 2014).

Temnikova, I, Orăsan, C., Corpas Pastor, G., and Mitkov, R. (eds.) (2019) *Proceedings of the 2nd Workshop on Human-Informed Translation and Interpreting Technology (HiT-IT 2019)*, Varna, Bulgaria, September 5 - 6, pages 66–74.

https://doi.org/10.26615/issn.2683-0078.2019_008

Because of the wide spread development of DL techniques, many researchers have utilized neural networks for MT evaluation. Duh (2008) uses a learning framework for ranking translations in parallel settings, given representations of translation outputs and a reference translation. Duh (2008) used a feature set containing some simple string-based features, like length of the words, but also BLEU score information. He used ranking-specific features and he showed that ranking achieves higher correlation to human judgments. Another important work is presented by Guzmán et al. (2015), (2017) who integrated syntactic and semantic information about the reference and the machine-generated translation as well, by using pre-trained embeddings and the BLEU scores of the translations. They used a multi-layer NN to decide which of the MT outputs is better. Ma et al. (2016) designed metrics based on LSTM, allowing the evaluation of single hypothesis with reference, instead of pairwise situation.

In this paper, we consider the choice of the best translation as a classification problem to be solved using deep learning architectures, by investigating two translation prototypes for our experiments. One is based on SMT and the other on NMT. We present a general learning scheme to classify machine-generated translations, using information from linguistic representations and one reference translation, for two language pairs (EN-GR, EN-IT). Unlike earlier works, the present approach includes the following novelties:

- Automatically extracted embeddings in two languages: GR and IT.

- A learning scheme based on a combination of a hand-crafted feature set (string similarity) and automatically trained embeddings as well.

- The proposed approach is language-independent.

To the author's knowledge, this is the first time that this architecture is used for a classification task using automatically extracted embeddings and hand-crafted features for this particular data genre, and these language pair.

The rest of the paper is organized as follows: Section 2 describes the corpora, the feature set (hand-crafted features), the embeddings, the annotation procedure and the experimental setup. Sec-

tion 3 presents and analyzes our experimental results (including linguistic analysis). Finally, section 4 presents our conclusions and directions for future research.

2 Materials and Methods

2.1 Data

The dataset used in our work is a parallel corpus which is part of the test sets developed in the TraMOOC project (Kordoni et al., 2016). The corpora consist of educational data, lecture subtitle transcriptions etc., with unorthodox syntax, ungrammaticalities etc (i.e. 1.To criticize, 2. Has no objections.). The corpora are described in detail by Mouratidis and Kermanidis (2018), (2019). The EN-GR corpus consists of 2686 sentences, whereas the EN-IT corpus of 2745 sentences. For each sentence, two translations were provided, generated by the Moses phrase-based SMT toolkit (*T1*) (Koehn et al., 2007) and the NMT Nematus toolkit (*T2*) (Sennrich, 2017). Moreover, a professional translation (*Tr*) is provided and used as a reference for each language. Both models are trained on both in- and out- of domain data. Out-of-domain data included corpora e.g., Europarl, WMT News corpora etc. In-domain data included data from TED, Coursera, etc. (Barone et al., 2017). NMT model is trained on additional in-domain data provided via crowdsourcing. More details on the datasets can be found in Sosoni et al. (2018).

2.2 Annotation

We consider the translation evaluation problem as a binary classification task. Two MT outputs *T1* and *T2* and the reference segment (*Tr*) are provided. Two annotators, for each language pair, annotated the corpora, as follows:

$$y = \begin{cases} 0, if\ T1\ is\ worse\ than\ T2 \\ 1, if\ T1\ is\ better\ than\ T2 \end{cases} \quad (1)$$

In order to decide if *T1* is better than *T2*, annotators used the source and reference sentences. The two annotators had an inter-annotator disagreement percentage of 3% for EN-GR and 5% for EN-IT. For the different answers, the annotators discussed and agreed on one class. The ID3 on Table 3 (Appendix) is an example of disagreement for the EN-GR language pair. We observed low annotation value for SMT class (38% EN-GR

/ 43% EN-IT) compared with NMT class (62% EN-GR /57% EN IT).

2.3 Features

We decided to use linguistic features based on string similarity, that involve no morphosyntactic information (no information about word forms and sentence structure), and are language independent. The features used were (i) Simple features (e.g. length in tokens, or some distances), (ii) Noise-Based features (e.g. frequentness of the repeated words) and (iii) Similarity-Based features (e.g. character 3-gram similarity). Each segment pair ($T1,Tr$), ($T2,Tr$) was modeled as a feature-value vector. The features have values between 0 and 1. The feature set was based on the work described in Mouratidis and Kermanidis (2019), with the difference that we used two classes instead of three (one for every MT output). This reduction in the number of classes was performed in order to allow for a more straightforward comparison between the three experiments and related work.

2.4 Word Embeddings

Word embeddings are very important in our model, because they allow us to model the relations between the two translations and the reference. In this work, we created and trained our own embeddings between the two MT outputs, as well as the reference translation for the two target languages (GR and IT). To prepare the input to the embedding layer, we used the bag of words model encoding a one hot function to generate the integer matrix. In order to avoid the inputs having different lengths, we used the pad sequences function, which padded all inputs to have the same length. The size, in number of nodes, of the embedding layer is 64 for both languages. The input dimensions of the embedding layers are in agreement with the vocabulary of each language (taking into account the most frequent words): 400 for EN-GR and 200 for EN-IT. We used the embedding layer provided by Keras (Chollet, 2015) with TensorFlow as backend (Abadi et al., 2016).

2.5 Experimental Setup

Experiment 1: For the first experiment, we used tuples ($T1$, $T2$, Tr), with string based features (the 2D matrix $A[i,j]$). Matrix $A[i,j]$ contains 50 hand-crafted linguistic features (described in sec-

tion 2.3) for every segment based on Mouratidis and Kermanidis (2019), where i represents the number of segments ($T1,T2,Tr$) and j the number of features. In this work, we have used two classification classes (one for the SMT output and the other for the NMT output) instead of three (used in Mouratidis and Kermanidis (2019)). Furthermore, a different network architecture is used, a simple but classic architecture of three Dense (Feed-Forward) layers. Dense layers serve the purpose of doing the classification. We also used a dropout layer to every Dense layer to prevent overfitting. Also a NN API is used instead of the WEKA framework (used in Mouratidis and Kermanidis (2019)). The model architecture used for the first experiment is shown in Fig.1.

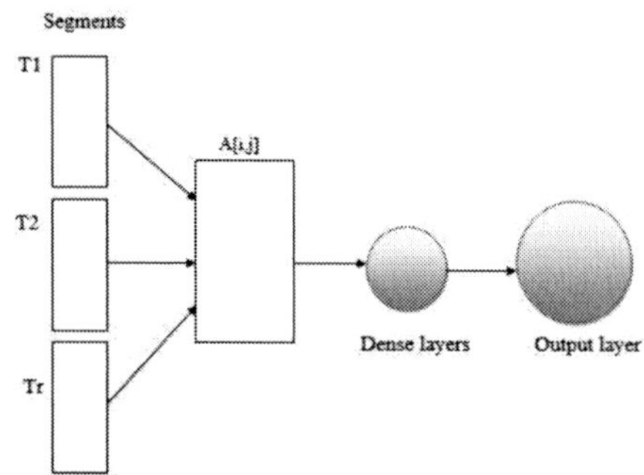

Figure 1: Learning scheme for Exp1.

Experiment 2: Based on the sentences $T1$, $T2$, Tr, we have created word embeddings ($EmbT1$, $EmbT2$, $EmbTr$). We used the word embeddings to find the probability for segment $T1$ to be better than $T2$ and vice-versa, given Tr and y. The probability is a Bernoulli conditional distribution (Krstovski and Blei, 2018).

$$p(y/T1, T2, Tr) = Bernoulli(y/b) \quad (2)$$

The parameter b_y is defined as follows:

$$b_y = \sigma\big(w^T f(T1, T2, Tr)\big) \quad (3)$$

where σ is the sigmoid function, w^T are the rows of a weight matrix W, and function f is the transformation of $T1$, $T2$ and Tr in the hidden layer, i.e. $f(T1,T2,Tr)=[h1,h2,hr]$. The embeddings for every tuple ($T1$, $T2$, Tr) are concatenated in a pairwise fashion, i.e. i. $EmbT1,EmbT2$, ii. $EmbT1,EmbTr$, iii. $EmbT2,EmbTr$. These fixed-length vectors are the input for the evaluation groups $h12$, $h1r$, $h2r$. We have checked if $T1$ and $T2$ are similar to the reference translation Tr

(*h1r, h2r* respectively), but also if *T1* is similar to *T2* (*h12*). This is quite interesting because in many cases we observed a similarity between *T1* and *T2*, but this does not mean that they were the proper translations, when compared to *Tr*. The input to our neural model is represented by concatenating the vector representation of the outputs of these evaluation groups.

The model architecture used for the second and the third experiment is shown in Fig.2.

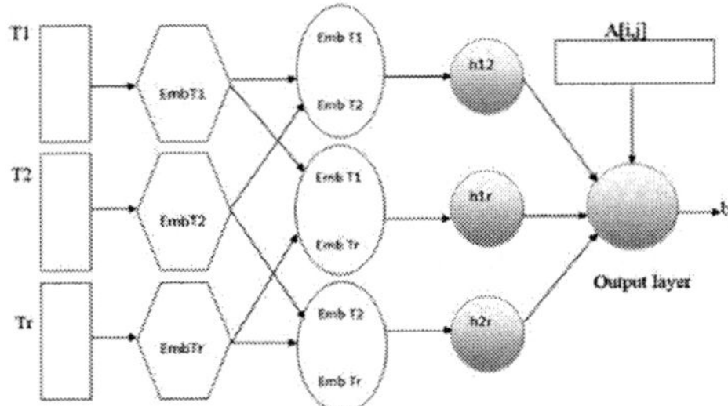

Figure 2: Learning scheme for Exp2 and 3.

Experiment 3: In this experiment, we utilized the tuple (*T1, T2, Tr*) as input to our model and the same configuration with Exp2 as well. We wanted to find out if the hand-crafted features, in combination with the automatically extracted embeddings, can improve classification accuracy of Exp2. For this purpose, as an extra input to our neural model, we utilized the 2D matrix *A[i,j]* with hand-crafted features (string-based), described in the Exp1.

Particularly, the model architecture for the first experiment is defined as follows:

- Size of layers: Dense 1 & 2 with 128 Hidden Units, Dense 3 with 64 Hidden Units

- Output layer: Activation Sigmoid

- Learning rate: 0.001

- Activation Function of Dense Layers: Softmax

- Dropout of Dense Layers: 0.2

- Lossfunction: Binary cross entropy

The architecture for the second and third experiments is a classic architecture of Dense (Feed-Forward) layers. After running multiple tests, we configured our experiments as follows:

- Size of layers: Dense 1, 2 &3 with 128 Hidden Units, (Dense 4 with 64 Hidden Units)

- Activation Function of Dense Layers: Relu

- Dropout of Dense Layers: 0.4

The networks are trained using the stochastic optimizer Adam (Kingma and Lei Ba, 2014) with a learning rate of 0.005. In Table 1, we present the complete set training parameters.

	Exp1	**Exp2**	**Exp3**
Batch size	128	64	256
Epochs	5	30	10

Table 1: Training parameters for Exp2/Exp3.

As a validation option for all the experiments, we used 10 fold cross validation (CV), which is effective for small datasets.

3   Results

In this section, we present the results from our experiments. We utilized the Positive Predictive Value (Precision) and the Sensitivity (Recall), as evaluation metrics, which are commonly used in classification tasks. The first metric shows which proportion of identifications is actually correct, whereas the second metric shows that the proportion of actual positives is correctly identified.

Fig. 3 and Fig. 4 show the accuracy performance of our experiments for both classes (SMT, NMT) for EN-GR and EN-IT respectively.

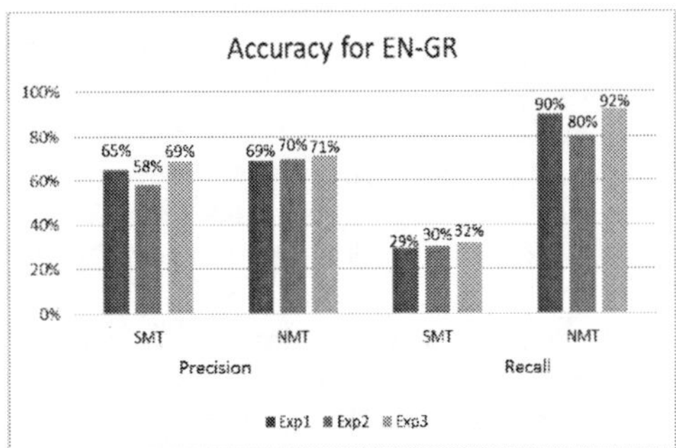

Figure 3: Accuracy for EN-GR.

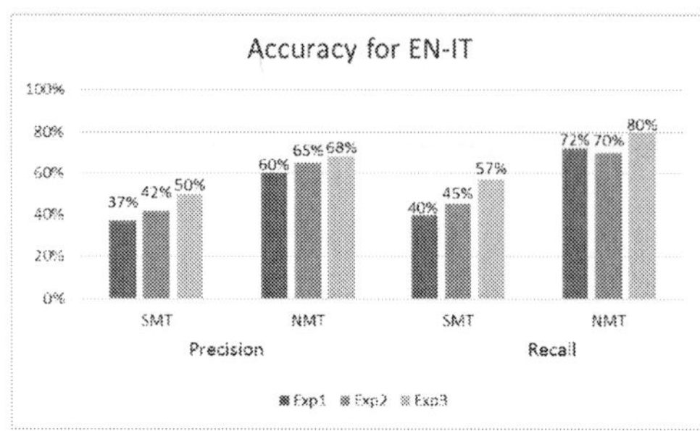

Figure 4: Accuracy for EN-IT.

We observed that the use of hand-crafted features in combination with embeddings have a positive effect on performance for both language pairs. Table 2 shows the accuracy results between our proposed model and the model proposed by Guzmán et al. (2017) which uses information from the MT evaluation metric BLEU score for language pairs EN-GR and EN-IT. The BLEU metric does not distinguish between content and function words and it is a language independent metric. As we are dealing with an uneven class distribution, unbalanced scores between Precision and Recall are observed, we present the F1 Score as well. F1, in statistical analysis of binary classification, is a measure of a test's accuracy. It penalizes classifiers with imbalanced precision and recall scores (Chinchor, 1992). As an averaging method, we used macro average.

Our proposed model (Exp3) achieved better accuracy performance than the model using information from Bleu scores of the MT outputs. A reason for that may be that BLEU attempts to measure the correspondence between an MT output and a human translation. Nevertheless, the hand-crafted feature set provides more information about not only the correspondence but also the correlation between suffixes, word distances and others.

To enable a direct comparison of our experimental results with earlier work (Barrón-Cedeño et al., 2013, Mouratidis and Kermanidis, 2019), we ran additional experiments using the WEKA framework as backend (Singhal and Jena, 2013). Different configurations were experimented with, including SVM and RF for EN-GR (Fig. 5) and EN-IT (Fig. 6).

	AVG Precision	AVG Recall	AVG F1
Language pair EN-GR			
Hand-crafted features + embeddings (Exp3)	69%	69%	65%
Bleu score	63%	63%	60%
Language pair EN-IT			
Hand-crafted features + embeddings (Exp3)	62%	68%	64%
Bleu score	60%	60%	62%

Table 2: Comparison with Bleu score.

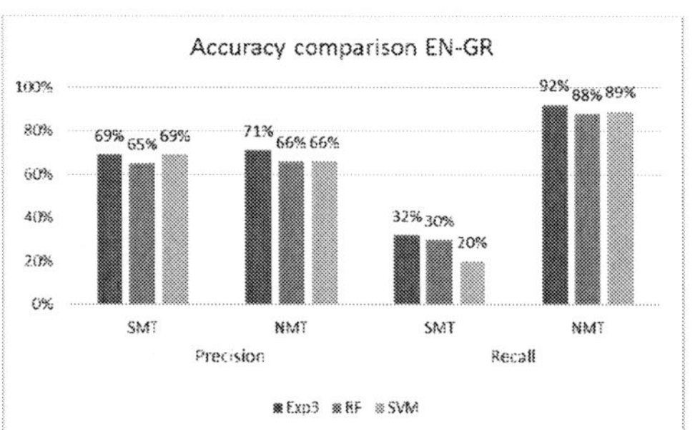

Figure 5: Accuracy comparison with other approaches for EN-GR.

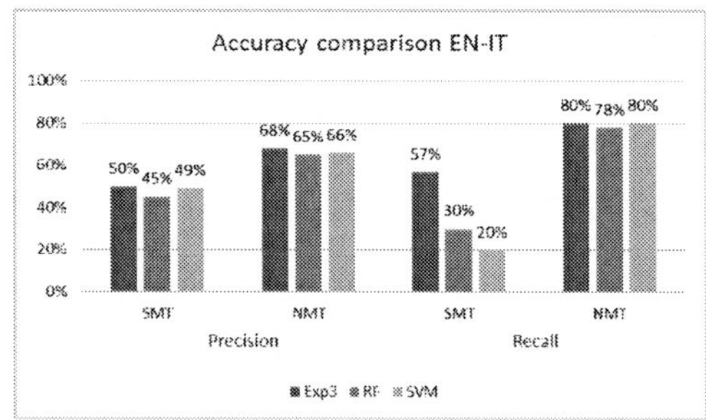

Figure 6: Accuracy comparison with other approaches for EN-IT.

We conclude that all evaluation metrics demonstrated the primacy of the NMT model over the SMT one, which agrees with the annotators' choice.

3.1 Linguistic Analysis

In order to show a part of the linguistic reasons for these accuracy values, we show some segments (*T1, T2, Tr*) from the EN-GR parallel corpus (Table 3, Appendix). ID 3 is an example of annotation disagreement.

For ID1:

•*T2* has erroneously translated the word *hoods* as *κουκκίδες*: *dots*, instead of the correct and most common translation: *κουκούλες*. There is no obvious and understandable reason for this.

•The word *flagella* is a really problem in *T1, T2* and *Tr* sentences. The word is of Latin origin (*flagellum*, diminutive of *flagrum: whip*) and has not been changed in English. In science, there is the bacterial flagellum, translated in Greek as: *μαστίγιο των βακτηρίων*. *T1* did not at all translate it, *T2* translated it as *πλάκες μαστιγίων* (*plates of whips*), but the *Tr* as *βλεφαρίδες* (*eyelashes*).

•*T1* has chosen the most common translation for the word *nodules*: *οζίδια*, but according to the *Tr*, the word has probably the sense of *clots*. On the contrary, *T2* has translated the word as *ακίδες*: *pins, thorns, splinters*.

•*T1* and *T2* have correctly identified the sense of the word *stems* as *κοτσάνια* and *μίσχων* respectively. Nevertheless, these two words are not used in the same contexts. *Κοτσάνι* is a hellenized slavic word, commonly used in oral speech, but *μίσχος* is an hellenistic word, rather used in official texts.

•Neither *T1* nor *T2* correctly translated the idiom: *and what have you*, meaning: *and many other such things, and so on, etc*. They both literally translated this expression as: *και τι έχετε* and *και σε αυτό που έχετε* respectively, meaning: *what you have got*.

In this case, the annotators have chosen T2 as the best translation, whereas Exp3's choice was T1.

For ID2:

•*T1* has correctly translated the title of Michel Foucault' book (*Επιτήρηση και Τιμωρία*). It's obvious that this title is included in *T1*'s "armory". On the contrary, *T2* translated the title in a completely wrong way, especially the second word: *Στην πειθαρχι ? α και στο Πω ? νητο*. The choice of the question marks it is not understandable.

•In *T1*, the author's name and surname haven't been translated into Greek and that is the best choice. In *T2*, these are hellenized, but the surname in a very wrong way: *Φουκούλτ*, instead of: *Φουκώ*. The second syllable of this surname has been wrongly hellenized letter by letter, without being taken into account that, according to its pronunciation, the French suffix *–ault* has been commonly hellenized: *-ω*.

•*T1* has correctly translated the word power as *εξουσίας* and not: *δύναμης*, as *T2* did. *T1* "knew" what is commonly known, that is the word *power* in the phrase: *instrument of power* has the sense of authority.

Both annotators and Exp3 have chosen T1 as the best translation.

For ID3:

Annotator 1 labeled *T1* as the better translation for the following reasons:

•Only *T1* successfully translated the "difficult" word of the text: *sumo*, as it is usually said in Greek: *σούμο*. The difficulty about this word is due to two reasons: i. The word *sumo* isn't an English word, but a Japanese one (meaning: *to compete*). ii. The same word is a paronym of the English common, well known, word: *sum*, (having, of course, a different meaning: *amount, total, aggregate*). On the contrary, *T2* "fell into the trap" of the paronym and translated the word as *a sum* (*αθροίσματος*).

•Only *T1* successfully translated the other "difficult" word of the text: *delicious* as *υπέροχα*. The problem is about the literal (*γευστικός: tasty*) and the figurative (*υπέροχος: wonderful*) sense of the word. In this segment, the word *delicious* has a figurative sense (*wonderful guys*). On the contrary, *T2* wrongly used the literal meaning (*tasty guys!*).

Annotator 2 labeled *T2* as the better translation for the following reasons:

•*T2* was the only one that has successfully translated the personal pronoun *you* (*I would like you to...*).

•*T2* has correctly translated the verb *to get* as *to obtain, to take, to collect*. The verb *to get* is used in a lot of patterns having different meanings. One of them is: *to get*+ direct object= *to obtain*. It's just the case here: *to get fat=to fatten*. On the contrary, *T1* has wrongly translated, in a literal way, the two words (*παίρνει το λίπος: take the suet!*).

After discussion, the annotators finally consented to T1 as the best translation in this case, whereas Exp3 had chosen T2.

4 Conclusion and Future Work

In this paper, we have compared the hand-crafted feature set with the automatically extracted ones, for a pairwise translation evaluation application in a deep learning setting.

In particular, we ran three experiments using hand-crafted string-based features, automatically extracted embeddings and both hand-crafted string-based features and automatically extracted embeddings respectively. The purpose of our work has been to find out whether information of string-based features, in combination with embeddings, affects classification accuracy, in order to train a model which will correctly choose the best translation.

The results showed that the proposed learning scheme improved the classification accuracy when using the vector representation (word embeddings) and the hand-crafted features as well (Exp3). Additionally, we have run experiments using Bleu as extra information, as well as well-known approaches, such as RF and SVM. Our model achieved better accuracy results in all the cases. For a more integrated analysis of the accuracy results, we have also carried out a qualitative linguistic analysis.

In future work, we intend to implement other combinations of NN, layer architectures and sizes, as well as other criteria. We believe that information from the *src* sentence could improve the accuracy scores. We could experiment with other ways for calculating embeddings, for example the utilization of more sophisticated bag of word model encoding, like TF-IDF. Although there are not enough available pre-trained embeddings in languages involved in our experiments, we want to examine if the use of pre-trained embeddings will give better accuracy results. Finally, we state our willingness to improve the text preprocessing phase, as we believe that it will lead to better results.

Acknowledgments

The authors would like to thank the reviewers for their significant suggestions and comments. We would also to thank the TraMOOC project for the corpora used in our experiments.

References

Martín Abadi, Paul Barham, Jianmin Chen, Zhifeng Chen, Andy Davis, Jeffrey Dean, Matthieu Devin, Sanjay Ghemawat, Geoffrey Irving, Michael Isard, Manjunath Kudlur, Josh Levenberg, Rajat Monga, Sherry Moore, Derek G. Murray, Benoit Steiner, Paul Tucker, Vijay Vasudevan, Pete Warden, Martin Wicke, Yuan Yu, and Xiaoqiang Zheng. 2016. Tensorflow: A system for large-scale machine learning. In *Proceedings of 12th USENIX Symposium on Operating Systems Design and Implementation*. USENIX Association, pages 265-283.

Antonio Valerio Miceli Barone, Barry Haddow, Ulrich Germann, and Rico Sennrich. 2017. Regularization techniques for ne-tuning in neural machine translation. *In Proceedings of the 2017 Conference on Empirical Methods in Natural Language Processing (Volume 1: Short Papers)*. Association for Computational Linguistics, pages 1-6. http://arxiv.org/abs/1707.09920.

Alberto Barrón-Cedeño, Lluís Vilodre Màrquez, Carlos Alberto Henríquez Quintana, Lluís Fanals Formiga, Enrique Marino Romero, and Jonathan May. 2013. Identifying useful human correction feedback from an on-line machine translation service. In *Proceedings of 23rd International Joint Conference on Artificial Intelligence*. International Joint Conference on Artificial Intelligence, pages 2057–2063.

Yoshua Bengio, Réjean Ducharme, Pascal Vincent, and Christian Jauvin. 2003. A neural probabilistic language model. *Journal of machine learning research*, 3:1137-1155.

Nancy Chinchor. 1992. MUC-4 Evaluation Metrics. *In Proccedings of the Fourth Message Understanding Conference*, pages 22–29.

Kyunghyun Cho, Bart Van Merrienboer, Caglar Gulcehre, Dzmitry Bahdanau, Fethi Bougares, Holger Schwenk, and Yoshua Bengio. 2014. Learning phrase representations using RNN encoder-decoder for statistical machine translation. In *Proceedings of the 2014 Conference on Empirical Methods in Natural Language Processing (Volume 1)*. Association for Computational Linguistics, pages 1724-1734.

François Chollet. Keras: Deep learning library for theano and tensorflow. 2015. URL: https://keras.io/k 7.8

Kevin Duh. 2008. Ranking vs. regression in machine translation evaluation. In *Proceedings of the Third Workshop on Statistical Machine Translation*. Association for Computational Linguistics, pages 191–194.

Francisco Guzmán, Joty Shafiq, Lluís Màrquez, and Nakov Preslav. 2015. Pairwise neural machine translation evaluation. In *Proceedings of the 53rd Annual Meeting of the Association for Computational Linguistics and the 7th International Joint Conference on Natural Language Processing (Volume 1: Long Papers)*. Association for Computational Linguistics, pages 805-814. doi>10.1162/COLI_a_00298.

Francisco Guzmán, Joty Shafiq, Lluís Màrquez, and Nakov Preslav. 2017. Machine translation evaluation with neural networks. *Computer Speech & Language*, 45: 180-200.

Felix Hill, Kyunghyun Cho, Sebastian Jean, Coline Devin, and Yoshua Bengio. 2015. Embedding word similarity with neural machine translation. *arXiv:1412.6448*, 4: 1-12.

Diederik Kingma, and Jimmy Lei Ba. 2014. Adam: A method for stochastic optimization. *arXiv preprint arXiv:1412.6980*, 9: 1-15.

Philipp Koehn, Hieu Hoang, Alexandra Birch, Chris Callison-Burch, Marcello Federico, Nicola Bertoldi, Chris Dyer, Brooke Cowan, Wade Shen, Christine Moran, Richard Zens, Ondřej Bojar, Alexandra Constantin, and Evan Herbst. 2007. Moses: Open source toolkit for statistical machine translation. In *Proceedings of the 45th Annual Meeting of the ACL on Interactive Poster and Demonstration Sessions*. Association for Computational Linguistics, pages 177-180.

Valia Kordoni, Lexi Birch, Ioanna Buliga, Kostadin Cholakov, Markus Egg, Federico Gaspari, Yota Georgakopoulou, Maria Gialama, Iris Hendrickx, Mitja Jermol, Katia Kermanidis, Joss Moorkens, Davor Orlic, Michael Papadopoulos, Maja Popović, Rico Sennrich, Vilelmini Sosoni, Dimitrios Tsoumakos, Antal van den Bosch, Menno van Zaanen, and Andy Way. 2016. TraMOOC (Translation for Massive Open Online Courses): Providing Reliable MT for MOOCs. In *Proceedings of the 19th annual conference of the European Association for Machine Translation*. European Association for Machine Translation, page 396.

Kriste Krstovski, and David M. Blei. 2018. Equation embeddings. *arXiv preprint arXiv:1803.09123*, 1: 1-12.

Alon Lavie, and Abhaya Agarwal. 2007. METEOR: An Automatic Metric for MT Evaluation with High Levels of Correlation with Human Judgments. In *Proceedings of the Second ACL Workshop on Statistical Machine Translation*. Association for Computational Linguistics, pages 228-231.

Qingsong Ma, Fandong Meng, Daqi Zheng, Mingxuan, Yvette Graham, Wenbin Jiang and Qun Liu. 2016. Maxsd: A neural machine translation evaluation metric optimized by maximizing similarity distance. In *Natural Language Understanding and Intelligent Applications*. Springer, Cham, pages 153-161.

Tomas Mikolov, Ilya Sutskever, Kai Chen, Greg Corrado, & J effrey Dean. 2013. Distributed representations of words and phrases and their compositionality. *In Advances in neural information processing systems* (pp. 3111-3119).

Despoina Mouratidis, and Katia Lida Kermanidis. 2018. Automatic Selection of Parallel Data for Machine Translation. In *IFIP International Conference on Artificial Intelligence Applications and Innovations*. Springer. pages 146-156.

Despoina Mouratidis, and Katia Lida Kermanidis. 2019. Ensemble and Deep Learning for Language-Independent Automatic Selection of Parallel Data. *Algorithms,* 12(1):26. https://doi.org/10.3390/a12010026.

Kishore Papineni, Salim Roukos, Todd Ward, and Wei-Jing Zhu. 2002. BLEU: a method for automatic evaluation of machine translation. In *Proceedings of the 40th Annual Meeting on Association for Computational Linguistics*. Association for Computational Linguistics, pages 311–318. doi>10.3115/1073083.1073135.

Jeffrey Pennington, Richard Socher, and Christopher Manning. 2014. Glove: Global vectors for word representation. In *Proceedings of the 2014 conference on empirical methods in natural language processing*. Empirical Methods in Natural Language Processing, pages 1532-1543.

Daniele Pighin, Lluís Màrquez, and Jonathan May. 2012. An analysis (and an annotated corpus) of user responses to machine translation output. In *Proceedings of the 8th International Conference on Language Resources and Evaluation*. European Language Resources Association, pages 1131-1136.

Holger Schwenk. 2007. Continuous space language models. *Computer Speech and Language*, 21(3): 492-518. doi:10.1016/j.csl.2006.09.003.

Rico Sennrich, Orhan Firat, Kyunghyun Cho, Alexandra Birch-Mayne, Barry Haddow, Julian Hitschler, Marcin Junczys-Dowmunt, Samuel Läubli, Valerio Miceli Barone, Jozef Mokry, and Maria Nădejde. 2017. Nematus: A toolkit for neural machine translation. In *Proceedings of the EACL 2017 Software Demonstrations*. Association for Computational Linguistics, pages 1-4.

Swasti Singhal, and Monika Jena. 2013. A study on WEKA tool for data preprocessing, classification and clustering. *International Journal of Innovative Technology and Exploring Engineering*, 2(6): 250-253.

Matthew Snover, Bonnie Dorr, Richard Schwartz, Linnea Micciulla, and John Makhoul. 2006. A Study of Translation Edit Rate with Targeted Human Annotation. In *Proceedings of the 7th Conference of the Association for Machine Translation in the Americas*. The Association for Machine Translation in the Americas, pages 223-231.

Vilelmini Sosoni, Katia Lida Kermanidis, Maria Stasimioti, Thanasis Naskos, Eirini Takoulidou, Menno van Zaanen, Sheila Castilho, Panayota Georgakopoulou, Valia Kordoni, and Markus Egg. 2018. Translation Crowdsourcing: Creating a Multilingual Corpus of Online Educational Content. In *Proceedings of the 11th International Conference on Language Resources and Evaluation*. European Language Resources Association, pages 479-483.

Ilya Sutskever, Vinyals Oriol, and Le V. Quoc. 2014. Sequence to sequence learning with neural networks. *In Proceedings of the Advances in Neural Information Processing Systems*. NIPS, pages 8–13.

Klaus Zechner, and Alex Waibel. 2000. Minimizing word error rate in textual summaries of spoken language. *1st Meeting of the North American Chapter of the Association for Computational Linguistics*.

Appendix

ID	Src	T1	T2	Tr
1	And so you end up with, you know, hoods and flagella and little nodules on the end of stems and what have you.	Και έτσι καταλήγεις, ξέρετε, κουκούλες και flagella και η μικρή οζίδια στο τέλος του κοτσάνια και τι έχετε.	Και έτσι καταλήγετε με, ξέρετε, κουκκίδες και πλάκες μαστιγίων και μικρές ακίδες στο τέλος των μίσχων και σε αυτό που έχετε.	Και έτσι καταλήγετε με , ξέρετε , κουκούλες και βλεφαρίδες και μικρούς θρόμβους στο τέλος των βλαστών και διάφορα άλλα τέτοια.
2	In Discipline and Punish, Michel Foucault described the Panopticon as the "perfect" instrument of power.	Στο Επιτήρηση και Τιμωρία, Michel Foucault περιέγραψε την Panopticon ως το "τέλειο" όργανο εξουσίας.	Στην πειθαρχι ? α και στο Πω ? νητο, ο Μισέλ Φουκούλτ περιέγραψε το Πανοπτικόν ως το "τέλειο" όργανο δύναμης.	Στο έργο του Επιτήρηση και Τιμωρία, ο Michel Foucault περιέγραψε το Πανοπτικό ως το «τέλειο» όργανο εξουσίας.
3	That's why I would like you to start taking sumo lessons, because... just look at those delicious guys! it's obvious that sumo fighting gets you fat!"	Γι' αυτό θα ήθελα να αρχίσουμε να παίρνουμε μαθήματα σούμο, επειδή... απλά κοιτάξτε αυτά τα υπέροχα παιδιά! Είναι προφανές ότι σούμο μάχες παίρνει το λίπος!	Γι' αυτό θα ήθελα να αρχίσετε να παίρνετε μαθήματα αθροίσματος, γιατί... κοιτάξτε αυτούς τους γευστικότερους τύπους! Είναι προφανές ότι οι μάχες στο sumo σας παχαίνουν!	Γι' αυτό θα ήθελα να αρχίσεις μαθήματα σούμο, γιατί... κοίτα αυτούς τους νόστιμους τύπους! Είναι προφανές ότι το σούμο σε παχαίνει!

Table 3: Linguistic Analysis

Differences between SMT and NMT Output - a Translators' Point of View

Jonathan Mutal[1], **Lise Volkart**[1], **Pierrette Bouillon**[1], **Sabrina Girletti**[1], and **Paula Estrella**[2]

[1]FTI/TIM, University of Geneva, Switzerland
[2]FaMaF y FL, University of Córdoba, Argentina
{Jonathan.Mutal,Lise.Volkart}@unige.ch
{Pierrette.Bouillon,Sabrina.Girletti}@unige.ch
paula.estrella@unc.edu.ar

Abstract

In this study, we compare the output quality of two MT systems, a statistical (SMT) and a neural (NMT) engine, customised for Swiss Post's Language Service using the same training data. We focus on the point of view of professional translators and investigate how they perceive the differences between the MT output and a human reference (namely deletions, substitutions, insertions and word order). Our findings show that translators more frequently consider these differences to be errors in SMT than NMT, and that deletions are the most serious errors in both architectures. We also observe there to be less agreement on differences to be corrected in NMT than SMT, suggesting that errors are easier to identify in SMT. These findings confirm the ability of NMT to produce correct paraphrases, which could also explain why BLEU is often considered to be an inadequate metric to evaluate the performance of NMT systems.

1 Introduction

Some recent studies have investigated the differences between statistical machine translation (SMT) and neural machine translation (NMT) in terms of the quality of the output (Daems and Macken, 2019; Toral and Cartagena, 2017; Bentivogli et al., 2016). In this paper, we focus on the point of view of professional translators and investigate how they perceive the differences in the translations produced by a SMT and a NMT system, both trained on the same data for comparison purposes.

Since we cannot evaluate all the differences, we will only look at divergent cases, that is, where one type of system (SMT or NMT) produces a sentence which is identical or very close to a human reference translation, while the other produces a different translation. We want to answer the following research questions: 1) What are the differences between SMT and NMT in terms of *edits* needed to reach the Post's official reference (namely deletions, substitutions, insertions and word order)?, 2) Would translators post-edit these differences? and, finally, 3) Do the translators agree on this task? Our hypothesis is that the type of edits differs between NMT and SMT and that with NMT, edits will be less often considered as real errors by translators.

In the following sections, we will describe the context of this study, the test data and how we built the SMT and NMT engines. We will then describe the methodology used for the evaluation and the results obtained.

2 Context, MT Engine Training and Test Data

This study is part of a collaboration between the University of Geneva and Swiss Post's in-house Language Service (Bouillon et al., 2018). The Language Service translates a broad range of texts from and into German, French, Italian and English. In the context of testing two MT architectures (SMT and NMT), we are interested in discovering which differences between the MT output and the reference translation are considered by the translators to be errors worth editing.

Our analysis focuses on two customised machine translation engines for the language pair German-to-French, a neural and a statistical one, trained with the same training data. The train-

Temnikova, I, Orăsan, C., Corpas Pastor, G., and Mitkov, R. (eds.) (2019) *Proceedings of the 2nd Workshop on Human-Informed Translation and Interpreting Technology (HiT-IT 2019)*, Varna, Bulgaria, September 5 - 6, pages 75–81.

https://doi.org/10.26615/issn.2683-0078.2019_009

ing data consisted of 2,558,148 translation units from the main translation memory of Swiss Post's Language Service. In order to avoid dealing with different variables that interfere with the real objective of this evaluation, such as pre-processing, post-processing and tune hyper-parameters, we kept the training as simple as possible for both architectures.

SMT engine. We followed the training process (corpus tokenization, language and translation model training, tuning and testing on a disjoint set from training) using the tools provided by Moses[1]. Language models were trained using KenLM (Heafield, 2011) on 4-grams.

NMT engine. We segmented infrequent words into their corresponding sub-word units by applying the byte pair encoding (BPE) approach (Sennrich et al., 2015); an encoder-decoder NMT model, transformer (Vaswani et al., 2017), was then trained using OpenNMT-tf (Klein et al., 2017). For this model, we used default hyper-parameters[2].

Subset	#sentences	#tokens	#vocabulary
Train	2M	36M	618k
Dev	100k	1.6M	112k
Test	1k	23k	4k

Table 1: Number of sentences, tokens and vocabulary for German (source language).

Subset	#sentences	#tokens	#vocabulary
Train	2M	40M	252k
Dev	100k	2.1M	56k
Test	1k	32k	3k

Table 2: Number of sentences, tokens and vocabulary for French (target language).

Test data. In order to evaluate both models, we built a development data set by extracting 5% of the sentence pairs from the training data. The test data consist of 1,736 translation units retrieved from process manuals. Tables 1 and 2 summarise the number of sentences, tokens and vocabulary for each subset in each language.

---

[1] For training processes, see:
http://www.statmt.org/moses/?n=Moses.Baseline

[2] http://opennmt.net/OpenNMT-tf/model.html#catalog

3 Methodology

In order to compare the two architectures and answer our research questions, we performed both an automatic and human evaluation with professional translators from Swiss Post's Language Service. In the literature, many error taxonomies have been used to carry out MT evaluations (Daems et al., 2017; Lommel et al., 2014; Stymne and Ahrenberg, 2012). In this study, we focus instead on type of edits, namely (*i*) word insertions, (*ii*) word deletions, (*iii*) word substitutions, and (*iv*) word order.

3.1 Automatic Evaluation

Two standard MT metrics were used to measure the performance of both architectures on the complete test set: TER (Snover et al., 2006) and BLEU (Papineni et al., 2002). The different types of edits (substitutions, deletions, word order and insertions) were also automatically calculated using TER.

3.2 Human Evaluation

In order to compare the two types of systems (SMT and NMT), we decided to focus on translations that are different in the two architectures and are close to the reference from the translation memory (see Section 2) in one architecture, but more distant in the other. These sentences are interesting since at least one of the systems was able to produce a good translation.

We selected the two sets of data using BLEU. The first (SMT-div) contains all sentences for which NMT obtains a high BLEU score (> 85) and SMT a lower score (< 85) (353 sentences). The second (NMT-div) includes sentences with a high BLEU score in SMT (> 85) and a lower one in NMT (< 85) (77 sentences).

For this human evaluation, we decided to manually identify the edits (insertions, substitutions, etc.) in order to group successive edits in one single edit, for example the two insertions ("sont autorisés") and the substitution ("peuvent" by "à") were grouped in an single substitution " sont autorisés à", as illustrated in Table 3. In that way, we identified 143 edits in the test set NMT-div and 675 in the SMT-div. As we were conducting a qualitative study and due to time constraint for the human evaluation, we decided to evaluate the same number of edits for both systems. We randomly extracted 143 edits from SMT-div to build the final test sets. In each test set, the edits were

TER	MT output	Human annotation	Type
Substitution Deletion (forces de)	evénements dus aux éléments naturels (tremblements de de terre, inondations, etc.)	evénements dus aux éléments naturels (tremblements de de terre, inondations, etc.)	Substitution
Reference: *événements dus aux forces de la nature (tremblement de terre, inondation, etc.)*			
Insertion Substitution	les filiales sont autorisées à vérifier certains groupes de marchandises plus souvent. les filiales sont autorisées à vérifier certains groupes de marchandises plus souvent.	les filiales sont autorisées à vérifier certains groupes de marchandises plus souvent.	Substitution
Reference: *les filiales peuvent vérifier certains groupes de marchandises plus souvent.*			

Table 3: Examples of grouping multiple edits into a single edit.

Source	MT Output	Edits
der Abholer ist persönlich bekannt:	la personne qui vient retirer l'envoi est connue personnellement:	Insertion
Reference: *cette personne est connue personnellement:*		
immer die Adresse der Filiale aufführen, nicht diejenige des Hauptsitzes.	toujours indiquer l'adresse de la filiale, et non celle du siège principal.	Substitution
Reference: *toujours mentionner l'adresse de la filiale, et non celle du siège principal.*		
mit einer Zustellliste XXX werden mehrere Sendungen auf einer Liste zusammengeführt.	plusieurs envois sont regroupés sur une liste avec une feuille de distribution XXX.	Word order
Reference: *avec une feuille de distribution XXX, plusieurs envois sont regroupés sur une liste.*		

Table 4: Examples of sentences with edits in colour

highlighted in red. In order to evaluate the edits individually, we duplicated the sentences containing more than one edit, and we marked only one edit at a time. Three translators from Swiss Post's Language Service received these target sentences in a spreadsheet along with the source sentences. For each edit, they had to state if they would modify the red part during a full post-editing task. They were not asked to post-edit the sentences, but only to indicate if they would change the highlighted part or not. Table 4 shows three different sentences with edits marked in red (as presented to the evaluators), as well as the corresponding reference translations. During the evaluation task, the evaluators did not have access to the reference translation and had no information about the type of system used to produced the output.

Results were collected. We calculated 1) how many differences post-editors would change in both systems, 2) the corresponding type of edit and 3) the inter-rater agreement.

4 Results

4.1 Automatic Evaluation

The two systems obtained high BLEU scores on the test set (1,736 sentences), 0.68 for NMT and 0.59 for SMT, and low TER scores of 19.96 and 30.05, showing that both systems produce good quality translations according to automatic evaluation.

Table 5 shows the number of substitutions, insertions, deletions and word order differences in both architectures. The total number of edits is higher for SMT than NMT, with a total of 10,399 and 7,327 edits respectively.

For both systems, the most frequent type of edits are substitutions, followed by deletions, insertions and word order. However, the proportion of deletions is higher for SMT than NMT (36% vs 27%), whereas the proportion of substitutions is higher for NMT (47% vs 37%).

Table 6 shows the number of edits in the output

Edit	SMT	NMT
Insertions	1,869 (18%)	1,305 (18%)
Deletions	3,754 (36%)	1,995 (27%)
Substitutions	3,881 (37%)	3,470 (47%)
Word order	895 (9%)	557 (8%)
Total	10,399 (100%)	7,327 (100%)

Table 5: Number of edits and percentage per edit in SMT vs NMT for language pair German-to-French.

sentences for items where SMT obtained a higher BLEU score than NMT (396 sentences). Table 7 shows the number of edits in the reverse situation (1,003 sentences). For the 424 remaining sentences, the translations by both systems obtained identical BLEU scores (100 BLEU point).

Edit	SMT	NMT
Insertions	342	547
Deletions	758	820
Substitutions	670	1333
Word order	144	252

Table 6: Number of edits in sentences where SMT has a higher BLEU score than NMT (396 sentences).

Edit	SMT	NMT
Insertions	1461	690
Deletions	2911	1092
Substitutions	3044	1837
Word order	1467	289

Table 7: Number of edits in sentence output where NMT has a higher BLEU score than SMT (1003 sentences).

It can be observed that when SMT has a higher BLEU, NMT almost doubles the number of substitutions (by 1.95) and word order (by 1.75) compared to SMT, whereas when NMT is better, all types of edits double, with word order edits being multiplied by 5.07. This means that when NMT is good, SMT produces more word order difference, as shown in example (Table 8).

Overall, the most common edit is substitution for both systems. However, if we compare the percentage of edits in both architectures, the number of substitutions is much higher in NMT (47.34%), which can be explained by the well-known ability

of NMT to paraphrase (Mallinson et al., 2017). We can see a clear example in Table 9. On the other hand, SMT had more deletions (36.09%). For the other types of edits, there is not much difference between the two systems.

4.2 Human Evaluation

The aim of the human evaluation is to shed light on how translators perceive edits in the output of each system, namely whether they would edit them or not. We also wanted to determine which types of edits would be post-edited more often by translators.

For each sentence, we considered the majority judgement (at least 2 judges agree) and we computed the results for both test subsets (143 edits per system). Figure 1 shows the percentages of edits that a majority of judges would change, per system and per type of edit.

If we consider all edits together, the evaluators would have post-edited the SMT output more than the NMT output: 68.53% of the edits would have been modified by a majority of judges in SMT versus 14.69% in NMT. This confirms our hypothesis that the edits in NMT are more often considered to be non-significant in the post-editing task.

For both systems, the edit type most frequently marked by the translators as something they would modify was deletions, which is not surprising since an omission in the output will very likely affect the quality of the translation. As for substitutions, which was the most frequent edit in both systems (see Tables 5 and 10), the majority of judges would modify more than half of them (62.82%) in SMT output vs only 14.81% in NMT. This illustrates the ability of neural systems to paraphrase and use correct synonyms. Finally, we can see that word order differences, which increase in SMT when NMT is better (Table 7), were mostly considered to be mistakes in SMT, which reflects the well-known fact that SMT has problems dealing with word order differences.

We also looked at the agreement between judges on this task. We computed Light's Kappa (Light, 1971) for the SMT and NMT evaluation. For SMT overall, we obtained a Kappa of 0.332 with a high statistical significance of evidence (p-value of 0.6%), corresponding to a fair agreement. For NMT overall, however, we obtained a Kappa of 0.166 which represents a slight agreement (Landis and Koch, 1977), but with a low statistical

Source	SMT output
suchen Sie die Räumlichkeiten und die Umgebung der Filiale bis zum Eintreffen der Polizei nach verdächtigen Gegenständen ab.	fouillez les locaux et les environs de la filiale jusqu'à l'arrivée de la police après d'objets suspects.
Reference: *fouillez les locaux et les environs de la filiale à la recherche d'objets suspects jusqu'à l'arrivée de la police.*	

Table 8: An example of word order error for SMT.

Source	NMT output
der zuständige Geschäftsbereich übernimmt die interne Information und leitet bei Bedarf Massnahmen ein.	l'unité d'affaires compétente prend en charge l'information interne et prend des mesures si nécessaire.
Reference: *l'unité d'affaires compétente assure l'information interne et met en œuvre des mesures en cas de besoin.*	

Table 9: An example of substitution for NMT.

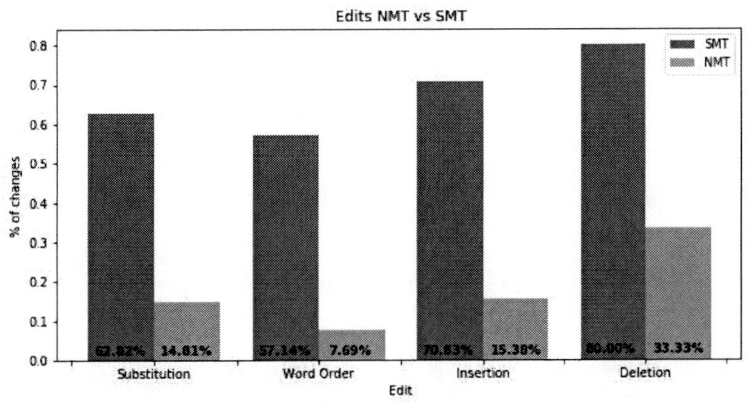

Figure 1: % of edits the translators would modify for SMT and NMT (by at least two judges).

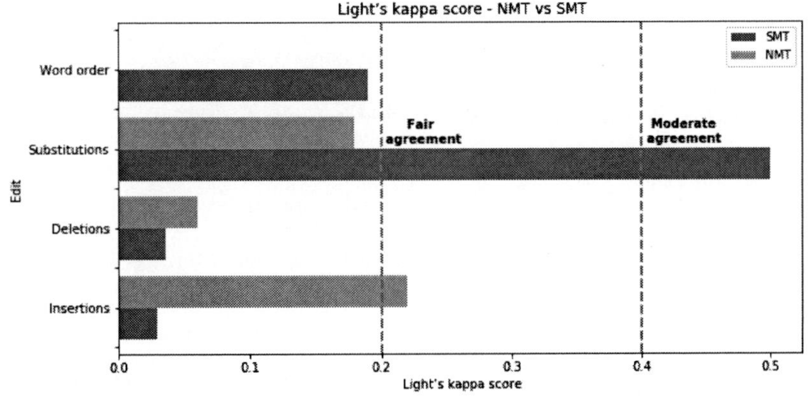

Figure 2: Agreement for each type of edit.

Edit	SMT	NMT
Insertions	16.78%	10%
Deletions	17.48%	4.19%
Substitutions	54.54%	75.52%
Word order	11.18%	10%

Table 10: %edit type in 143 edits extracted from each model.

significance (p-value 34%).

Figure 2 illustrates individual Light's kappa scores computed for each edit type. These scores show that judges do not strongly agree on the divergences that would need post-editing, particularly with NMT output. In particular, evaluators disagree on the word order category for NMT output, where the Light's kappa score obtained is negative. Translators moderately agreed (K=0.50) on substitutions in SMT (p-value<0.0011) and fairly on insertions (K=0.22) in NMT (p-value>0.62) (see Figure 1). This suggests that in NMT, translators have more difficulties clearly stating whether a sentence has to be modified or not.

5   Conclusion and Future Work

In this paper, we presented an innovative methodology to compare SMT and NMT based on differences with an official reference. We showed that (*i*) the most common edits are substitutions, with respectively 37.32% and 47.34% for NMT and SMT, and deletions with 27% and 36.09%; (*ii*) the most significant difference from a translator's point of view is deletions, in particular in SMT, with 80% of changes in SMT but only 33.33% in NMT; (*iii*) NMT edits are more often considered to be non-significant from a post-editing point of view (14.68%), as opposed to SMT edits (68.53%); (*iv*) translators have more difficulties stating whether a sentence has to be modified with NMT than with SMT.

This study has several limitations: three judges were not enough to obtain a good inter-agreement score. It will be interesting to test the same methodology with the different languages of the Post (Italian and English) in order to see if there are cross-lingual differences, as well as with translators trained for post-editing. We also would like to see if differences considered to be wrong by translators are related to specific types of errors.

However, despite its limitations, the paper provides interesting perspectives. Firstly, the fact that NMT produces correct paraphrases of the reference confirms a common hypothesis that BLEU is not an adequate metric for evaluating the performance of NMT (Shterionov et al., 2017, 2018; Volkart et al., 2018). From a broader perspective, the collected data, which focus on different types of individual edits, could also be used to train translators on how to distinguish between essential vs non essential changes.

Acknowledgement

We would like to thank the translators who kindly accepted to participate in this study, as well as Martina Bellodi and the whole Swiss Post's Language Service.

References

Luisa Bentivogli, Arianna Bisazza, Mauro Cettolo, and Marcello Federico. 2016. Neural versus phrase-based machine translation quality: a case study. In *Proceedings of the 2016 Conference on Empirical Methods in Natural Language Processing*. Association for Computational Linguistics, Austin, Texas, pages 257–267. https://doi.org/10.18653/v1/D16-1025.

Pierrette Bouillon, Paula Estrella, Sabrina Girletti, Jonathan Mutal, Martina Bellodi, and Beatrice Bircher. 2018. *Integrating MT at Swiss Post's Language Service: preliminary results*, pages 281–286. Proceedings of the 21st Annual Conference of the European Association for Machine Translation. ID: unige:105252. https://archive-ouverte.unige.ch/unige:105252.

Joke Daems and Lieve Macken. 2019. Interactive adaptive smt versus interactive adaptive nmt: a user experience evaluation. *Machine Translation* 33(1):117–134. https://doi.org/10.1007/s10590-019-09230-z.

Joke Daems, Sonia Vandepitte, Robert Hartsuiker, and Lieve Macken. 2017. Identifying the machine translation error types with the greatest impact on post-editing effort. *Frontiers in Psychology* 8:1282. https://doi.org/10.3389/fpsyg.2017.01282.

Kenneth Heafield. 2011. KenLM: Faster and smaller language model queries. In *Proceedings of the Sixth Workshop on Statistical Machine Translation*. Association for Computational Linguistics, Edinburgh, Scotland, pages 187–197. https://www.aclweb.org/anthology/W11-2123.

J. Richard Landis and Gary G. Koch. 1977. The measurement of observer agreement for categorical data. *Biometrics* 33(1).

Richard Light. 1971. Measures of response agreement for qualitative data: Some generalizations and alternatives. *Psychological Bulletin* 76:365–377.

Arle Lommel, Aljoscha Burchardt, Maja Popovic, Kim Harris, Eleftherios Avramidis, and Hans Uszkoreit. 2014. Using a new analytic measure for the annotation and analysis of mt errors on real data. pages 165–172.

Jonathan Mallinson, Rico Sennrich, and Mirella Lapata. 2017. Paraphrasing revisited with neural machine translation. In *Proceedings of the 15th Conference of the European Chapter of the Association for Computational Linguistics: Volume 1, Long Papers*. Association for Computational Linguistics, Valencia, Spain, pages 881–893. https://www.aclweb.org/anthology/E17-1083.

Kishore Papineni, Salim Roukos, Todd Ward, and Wei-Jing Zhu. 2002. Bleu: A method for automatic evaluation of machine translation. In *Proceedings of the 40th Annual Meeting on Association for Computational Linguistics*. Association for Computational Linguistics, Stroudsburg, PA, USA, ACL '02, pages 311–318. https://doi.org/10.3115/1073083.1073135.

Rico Sennrich, Barry Haddow, and Alexandra Birch. 2015. Neural machine translation of rare words with subword units. *CoRR* abs/1508.07909. http://arxiv.org/abs/1508.07909.

Dimitar Shterionov, Pat Nagle, Laura Casanellas, Riccardo Superbo, and Tony O'Dowd. 2017. Empirical evaluation of nmt and pbsmt quality for large-scale translation production.

Dimitar Shterionov, Riccardo Superbo, Pat Nagle, Laura Casanellas, Tony O'dowd, and Andy Way. 2018. Human versus automatic quality evaluation of nmt and pbsmt. *Machine Translation* 32(3):217–235. https://doi.org/10.1007/s10590-018-9220-z.

Matthew Snover, Bonnie Dorr, Richard Schwartz, Linnea Micciulla, and John Makhoul. 2006. A study of translation edit rate with targeted human annotation. In *In Proceedings of Association for Machine Translation in the Americas*. pages 223–231.

Sara Stymne and Lars Ahrenberg. 2012. On the practice of error analysis for machine translation evaluation. In *Proceedings of the Eighth International Conference on Language Resources and Evaluation (LREC-2012)*. European Languages Resources Association (ELRA), Istanbul, Turkey, pages 1785–1790. http://www.lrec-conf.org/proceedings/lrec2012/pdf/717_paper.pdf.

Antonio Toral and Víctor Cartagena. 2017. A multi-faceted evaluation of neural versus phrase-based machine translation for 9 language directions. pages 1063–1073. https://doi.org/10.18653/v1/E17-1100.

Ashish Vaswani, Noam Shazeer, Niki Parmar, Jakob Uszkoreit, Llion Jones, Aidan N. Gomez, Lukasz Kaiser, and Illia Polosukhin. 2017. Attention is all you need. *CoRR* abs/1706.03762. http://arxiv.org/abs/1706.03762.

Lise Volkart, Pierrette Bouillon, and Sabrina Girletti. 2018. *Statistical vs. Neural Machine Translation: A Comparison of MTH and DeepL at Swiss Post's Language Service*, pages 145–150. Proceedings of the 40th Conference Translating and the Computer. ID: unige:111777. https://archive-ouverte.unige.ch/unige:111777.

The Chinese/English Political Interpreting Corpus (CEPIC): A New Electronic Resource for Translators and Interpreters

Jun Pan

Hong Kong Baptist University / 224 Waterloo Road, Kowloon Tong, Hong Kong SAR, China
janicepan@hkbu.edu.hk

Abstract

The Chinese/English Political Interpreting Corpus (CEPIC) is a new electronic and open access resource developed for translators and interpreters, especially those working with political text types. Over 6 million word tokens in size, the online corpus consists of transcripts of Chinese (Cantonese & Putonghua) / English political speeches and their translated and interpreted texts. It includes rich metadata and is POS-tagged and annotated with prosodic and paralinguistic features that are of concern to spoken language and interpreting. The online platform of the CEPIC features main functions including Keyword Search, Word Collocation and Expanded Keyword in Context, which are illustrated in the paper. The CEPIC can shed light on online translation and interpreting corpora development in the future.

1 Introduction

1.1 Rationale

The Chinese/English Political Interpreting Corpus (CEPIC) is a new electronic and open access resource developed for translators and interpreters, especially those working with political text types.

The rationale for developing the CEPIC is multifold. One of the reasons is the understudied challenges involved in political interpreting, as illustrated by Buri (2015):

> Both interpreters and translators are under continuous scrutiny in diplomatic settings. Notetakers or other members of the delegation at meetings, round tables, bilateral talks and negotiations are

always ready to provide another solution claiming it is more pertinent. Moreover, interpreters and translators may be easily transformed into scapegoats especially when there are misunderstandings or friction between parties – straightforwardly attributed to misinterpretation.

Pan (2007) also identified cases of interpreters failing to capture the source text or mistakenly using the source language instead of the target language due to stress involved in interpreting for presidential speeches. Yet the cases were sporadically identified ones and could not reveal any pattern. Therefore, a corpus that collects political speeches and their interpreting, especially one that is annotated with specific interpreting and spoken language features/issues (such as code-mixing/code-switching as stated above), will benefit greatly the study of the "problematic patterns", apart from offering rich examples of interpreting and translation done by professional practitioners.

1.2 Related Work

Despite the significance of Corpus-based Interpreting Studies (CIS), there are still very few open access interpreting corpora (Shlesinger, 1998; Bendazzoli and Sandrelli, 2009; Setton, 2011; Straniero Sergio and Falbo, 2012; Russo et al., 2018), mainly due to the difficulties of data collection, transcription and annotation (Bendazzoli, 2018; Bernardini et al., 2018) .

Among the few number of existing (and publicly accessible) interpreting corpora, the EPTIC (European Parliament Translation and Interpreting Corpus; `https://corpora.dipintra.it/eptic/`) is very relevant to the CEPIC as both covered official translations and transcribed interpreted texts of speeches delivered in

Temnikova, I, Orăsan, C., Corpas Pastor, G., and Mitkov, R. (eds.) (2019) *Proceedings of the 2nd Workshop on Human-Informed Translation and Interpreting Technology (HiT-IT 2019)*, Varna, Bulgaria, September 5 - 6, pages 82–88.

https://doi.org/10.26615/issn.2683-0078.2019_010

political settings. In particular, the EPIC (European Parliament Interpretation Corpus; http://catalog.elra.info/en-us/ repository/browse/ELRA-S0323/) also included annotation of paralinguistic features, which are of interest to interpreting researchers. The EPTIC and the CEPIC are very similar to a great extent since both included simultaneous interpreting of parliamentary speeches, yet the CEPIC also collected data of consecutive interpreting, which is often employed at bilateral meetings or questions and answers at press conferences in political settings. In addition, the EPTIC only included languages translated and interpreted at the European Parliament, while a comparison with those translated and interpreted in other regions/continents would provide interesting perspectives on political translation/interpreting at large.

In this regard, the WAW corpus (http://alt.qcri.org/resources/wawcorpus/) provides a very interesting perspective by covering conference interpreting between English and Arabic in Qatar. However, the data were collected from international conferences rather than from political settings.

Many other corpora that involve the Chinese and English language interpreting in similar settings, including the CEIPPC (Chinese-English Interpreting for Premier Press Conferences, see Wang (2012); also introduced by Setton (2011) and Bendazzoli (2018)) and the CECIC (Chinese-English Conference Interpreting Corpus, see Hu (2013); also introduced by Setton (2011) and Bendazzoli (2018)), are unfortunately not open to public access. In addition, although Cantonese to Putonghua and English simultaneous interpreting has been performed at the Legislative Council (LegCo) of Hong Kong SAR for over two decades, there has seen no existing publicly available corpus designed specifically for the study of interpreting of such speeches, especially one that included paralinguistic features such as the EPIC, although part of the official transcripts are archived regularly online (on government or LegCo websites).

The CEPIC, therefore, aims to provide an open access corpus covering Chinese and English language political interpreting, also in the hope of offering a possible solution to future collection of interpreting corpora by providing templates of metadata collection and solutions to spoken data

Language subsets	Word tokens	Types
Chinese	2,578,911	83,312
Cantonese	*1,072,368*	*61,837*
Putonghua	*1,506,541*	*30,320*
English	3,815,083	32,748
Total	6.393,994	116,060

Table 1: The composition of the CEPIC by language.

transcription and annotation, especially for interpreting with the language combination of Chinese (Cantonese and Putonghua) and English.

2 About the CEPIC[1]

2.1 General Information

The CEPIC is currently over 6 million word tokens in size. It consists of transcripts of speeches delivered by top political figures (e.g. government leaders) from Hong Kong, Beijing, Washington DC and London, as well as their translated/interpreted texts[2]. The speeches were delivered by native speakers (otherwise coded as code-mixing) and interpreted into the B language of the interpreters (usually government interpreters), a phenomenon common in political setting at which the Chinese and English languages are concerned (Pan and Wong, forthcoming). Both directions of Chinese-English and English-Chinese interpreting were covered. Table 1 shows some basic statistics of the CEPIC.

The main speech types of CEPIC include the reading of government reports such as policy addresses and budget speeches, questions and answers at press conferences, parliamentary debates, as well as remarks delivered at bilateral meetings, most of which were done and collected on a yearly basis, except for remarks at bilateral meetings when it depends on if such meetings were held in a specific year. Some of the speeches were interpreted in a consecutive mode, and some in simultaneous, which were coded in the metadata.

In particular, speeches in the Hong Kong subset were mainly interpreted from Cantonese into Putonghua and English, and those in the Beijing subset from Putonghua to English. The other two

---

[1]Some of the information in this section is also accessible via the CEPIC website (Pan, 2019).

[2]Speeches collected in the corpus, in particular those provided on the official government websites, are considered translations instead of interpreting, as they are translated before interpreting or revised based on the interpreted version, which, with spoken language features (e.g. spoken words and particles) deleted, read more like written language.

subsets, i.e. Washington DC and London, mainly included English speeches delivered in similar settings (which can be regarded as monolingual reference subsets to the interpreted English speeches) and whenever applicable, their interpreted versions in Chinese (usually only at bilateral meetings or joint press conferences).

2.2 POS Tagging

The CEPIC is POS tagged with the assistance of Stanford CoreNLP 3.9.2 (Manning et al., 2014). The English taggers used were based on the Part-of-Speech Tagging Guidelines for the Penn Treebank Project (Santorini, 1990), and the Chinese (both Putonghua and Cantonese) on the Part-Of-Speech Tagging Guide-lines for the Penn Chinese Treebank (3.0) (Xia, 2000).

A semi-automatic process was employed to enhance the accuracy rate of machine tagging, in which all taggers were checked and revised based on subsets of manually checked testing data that consisted of about 30 percent of the entire corpus. The process is documented by Pan et al. (forthcoming).

2.3 Speech Transcription & Annotation

Data of CEPIC were collected in two ways:

- Speech transcripts and their translations collected from government websites (Raw);

- A revised or newly transcribed version (when there are no readily available transcripts) of these speeches and their interpreted texts based on audios/videos collected from government websites and TV programme archives (Annotated). In particular, the annotated version of the CEPIC was transcribed and annotated in a way that reflects features of spoken language data.

Texts of the CEPIC were manually revised or transcribed based on audios/videos with the speeches and their interpreting, if any. Whenever possible, existing official transcripts provided on government websites and transcripts generated by voice recognition software were used as basis for transcription to help speed up the process. The transcription of CEPIC follows a standardised process and aims to represent the spoken text as close as it was delivered. In addition, all Cantonese texts were transcribed in a way to capture spoken Cantonese features (including particles that are usually omitted in official transcripts provided on government websites). Text and audio/video links were also included at the end of each text for those who may be interested in the sources of the speeches (Figure 1).

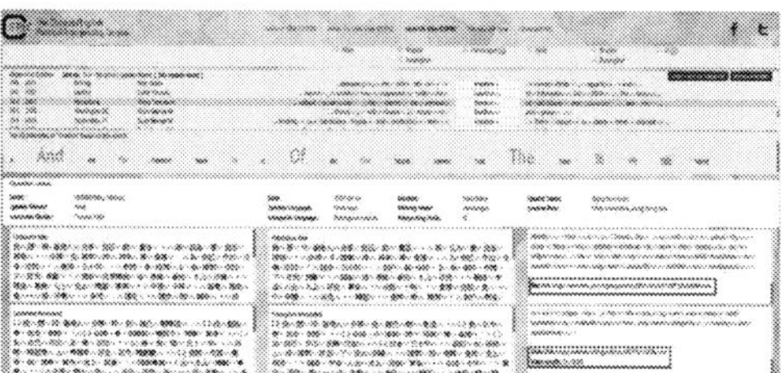

Figure 1: An image of the CEPIC texts with audio/video links and text information

The following examples shows the differences between the raw and annotated data:

- English Raw: So that is the big difference in our approach and the approach that I think might have been debated about. (Press Conference of US Budget Speech, 1997-02-06),

- English Annotated: [er] So [that] that is the big difference [er] in our approach and the approach [er] that [er] I think [er] might have been debated about. (Press Conference of US Budget Speech, 1997-02-06)

As can be seen from the above examples, the annotated version features annotations of different prosodic and paralinguistic features (e.g. fillers, repetitions and self-repair, etc.) that are of concern to the study of spoken language as well as interpreting.

3 Main Functions of the CEPIC[3]

The CEPIC features a user-friendly interface with three main functions.[4]

3.1 Keyword Search

Users can input a keyword in English or (Simplified/Traditional) Chinese in the corpus. The corpus has a lexical associative function. Therefore, when characters/letters are keyed in the search box, the associative results will automatically display beneath the search box.

---

[3]A full user manual including graphics of examples can be accessed from the CEPIC website (Pan, 2019).

[4]Examples and data listed in this paper were generated using the CEPIC online search engine (Pan, 2019).

Parameters	Value
{Keyword}	Interesting
{Speaker Role}	Member of Parliament (UK)
{Time}	1997 to 2017
{Subset}	Annotated

Table 2: Parameters used for a sample Keyword Search.

A prosodic/paralinguistic feature can also be searched when choosing the annotated version of the corpus.

Apart from choosing either the raw or annotated subset of the corpus for searching, users can adjust parameters including Part of Speech, Location, Speaker Name, Speaker Role, Speaker Gender, Speaker Language, Delivery Mode, Interpreter Gender, Interpreter Language, Interpreting Mode, and Time Span, to refine a search.

The search results can be arranged by Year, Location, or Speaker Name, and downloaded in excel format.

For instance, if the parameters listed in Table 2 are selected, a total of 8 instances can be found in the CEPIC (Figure 2).

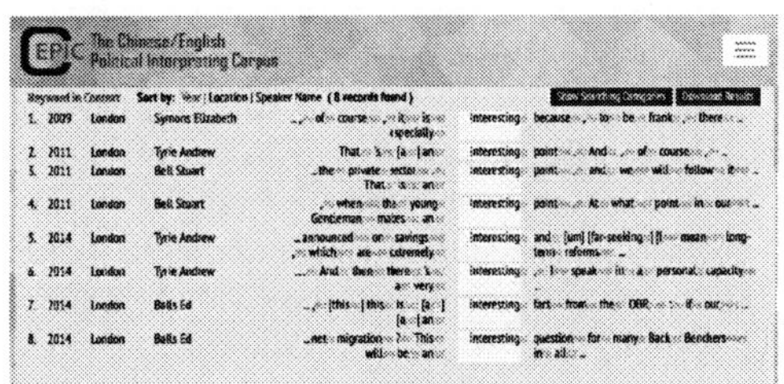

Figure 2: Results of a Keyword Search of "interesting"(1)

Among the 8 instances, Tyrie Andrew appeared 3 times, showing a possible speaker feature in this case. In addition, all of the instances fell in the time period of 2009-2014, showing a possible trend of using the word among Members of the Parliament in the UK during this specific period of time. Such information may help interpreters and translators acquire knowledge relating to words used by certain speakers or in specific time periods.

3.2 Word Collocation

Users can automatically obtain a list of the top 20 collocates of the queried word token in the form of a word cloud. The collocation range is set as 7 words before and after the search term.

Parameters	Value
{Keyword}	Interesting
{Location}	Hong Kong
{Time}	1997 to 2017
{Subset}	Raw

Table 3: Parameters used for a sample Expanded Keyword in Context.

If users click on one of the collocates, the concordance lines that included both the search term and the collocate will appear under Keyword in Context.

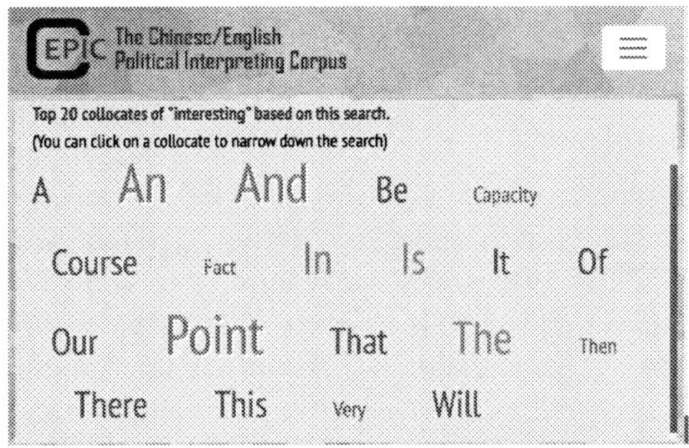

Figure 3: Word Collocation of "interesting"

Using the same search of "interesting" in the previous section, we can find "an", "and" and "point" as the three most frequent collocates of "interesting" (Figure 3). Such information can benefit greatly anticipation (e.g. of linguistic structures or contextual meaning) in interpreting or translation, in particular in the case of simultaneous interpreting or when a speedy translation service is required (Gile, 1991).

3.3 Expanded Keyword in Context

Users can further click a keyword to obtain an Expanded Context, with the respective sub-corpora aligned at the paragraph-level.

The Expanded Context includes the detailed information about the selected Keyword, which also features six windows that display the same speech segment in different languages and versions at paragraph level. For every paragraph, there is a link that redirects to the original text (for the Raw version) or its audio/video (for the Annotated version; including information of the audio/video length).

Again, using "interesting" as a keyword with the parameters set in Table 3, 2 instances can be found (Figure 4).

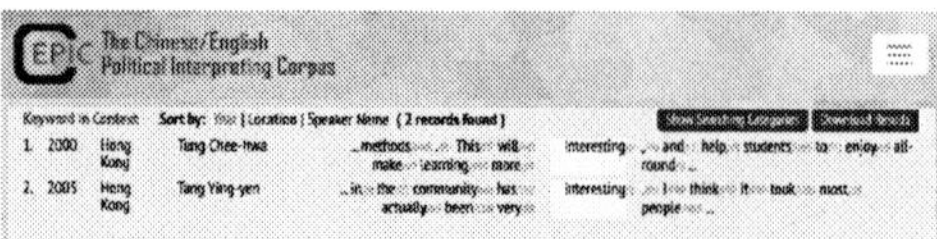

Figure 4: Results of a Keyword Search of "interesting" (2)

The corresponding words of the first "interesting" in the source text in Cantonese and the interpreted/translated versions in Putonghua are the same nouns, i.e. "hing3ceoi3" (in Cantonese Raw) and "xing4qu4" (in both Putonghua Raw and Annotated; both meaning "interest") (Figure 5). The correspondences of the second "interesting" are, however, "jau5ceoi3" in Cantonese Annotated and "you3yi4si1" in Putonghua Annotated (both meaning "interesting", though the former refers to something funnier), but "qiang2lie4" in Putonghua Raw (meaning "intensive") (Figure 6). These renditions indicate certain strategies employed by the speaker or interpreter/translator, i.e. normalisation (in the cases of "hing3ceoi3" and "xing4qu4") and explicitation (in the case of "qiang2lie4").

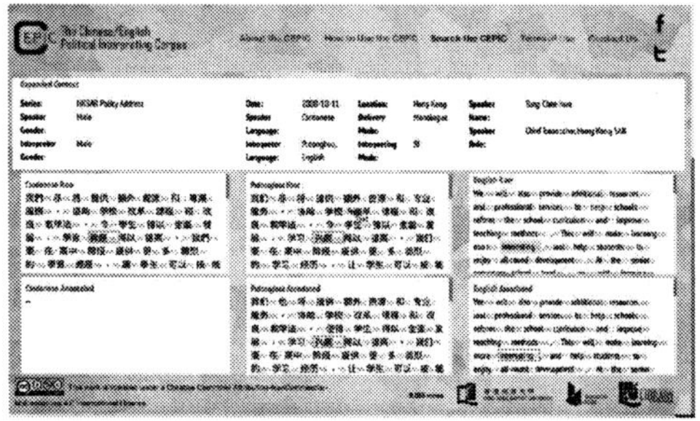

Figure 5: Expanded Keyword in Context of "interesting" (1)

With the help of the detailed information of the Expanded Context, translators/interpreters can then find out how a term is translated/interpreted among Cantonese, Putonghua and English. They can study in detail how the words and their contexts were rendered in spoken and written contexts, or even find out how self-corrections were rendered in a different language, especially in the case of simultaneous interpreting.

Since users can search the CEPIC easily online, interpreters and translators can get timely support not only at the preparation stage, but also during

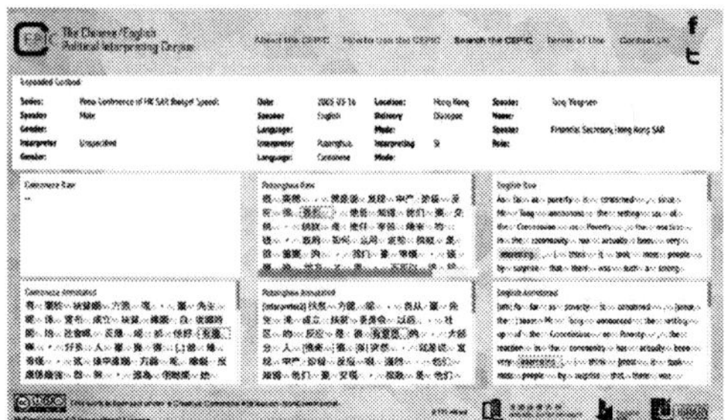

Figure 6: Expanded Keyword in Context of "interesting" (2)

the process of translation and interpreting. In addition, the CEPIC can benefit language learners, who can make use of the video links to study the pronunciation of certain terms.

4 The Way Forward

The CEPIC, as discussed in the previous sections, offers a new online and open access resource for translators and interpreters, with its collection of rich annotated corpora data. It can, as illustrated in the previous section, be used for the preparation of translation and interpreting tasks, and provide online support to interpreters and translators during interpreting/translation. Apart from acquiring knowledge about the use of certain words in political language and interpretation, users can benefit much from exploring the CEPIC in different ways, including finding possible solutions for certain words that are difficult to translate and/or do not have a one-to-one equivalence in the target language.

The CEPIC will provide a good basis for further research on many different topics in interpreting research. The corpus itself will be further expanded and the online platform continuously enhanced to meet various research and education purposes.

In addition, the CEPIC can shed light on future collection and annotation of translation and interpreting corpora, especially the latter, with its systematic annotation scheme, rich metadata information, and unique display and alignment of different language versions.

With its large amount of transcribed interpreting and spoken data of political texts, the CEPIC will also lead to the development of possible tools for computer-assisted interpreting, semi-automatic transcription and alignment, and semi-automatic POS enhancement (especially for Cantonese). In particular, its data can be used to train machine translation systems (for political texts) or automatic speech recognition and speech-to-text transcription systems (of English, Cantonese and Putonghua).

Acknowledgements

The CEPIC is developed with the funding and support of the Early Career Scheme (ECS) of Hong Kong SAR's Research Grants Council (Project No.: 22608716), and the Digital Scholarship Grant and the Faculty Research Grant of the Hong Kong Baptist University (Project No.: FRG2/17-18/046).

I would like to thank my colleagues Dr. Billy Tak Ming WONG and Ms. Rebekah WONG for their support and advice, and all the research assistants, student helpers and library colleagues who contributed to the project. Please refer to `https://digital.lib.hkbu.edu.hk/cepic/about.php#project` for a list of the team members.

References

Claudio Bendazzoli. 2018. Corpus-based interpreting studies: Past, present and future developments of a (wired) cottage industry. In *Making Way in Corpus-based Interpreting Studies (New Frontiers in Translation Studies Series)*. Singapore: Springer, pages 1–19.

Claudio Bendazzoli and Annalisa Sandrelli. 2009. Corpus-based interpreting studies: Early work and future prospects. *Revista Tradumtica: L'aplicaci dels corpus lingstics a la traducci* (7). https://revistes.uab.cat/tradumatica.

Silvia Bernardini, Adriano Ferraresi, Mariachiara Russo, Camille Collard, and Bart Defrancq. 2018. Building interpreting and intermodal corpora: A how-to for a formidable task. In *Making Way in Corpus-based Interpreting Studies (New Frontiers in Translation Studies Series)*. Singapore: Springer, pages 21–42.

Maria Rosaria Buri. 2015. Interpreting in diplomatic settings. https://aiic.net/page/7349/interpreting-in-diplomatic-settings/lang/.

Daniel Gile. 1991. A communication-oriented analysis of quality in nonliterary translation and interpretation. In *Translation: Theory and Practice, Tension and Interdependence*. Amsterdam: John Benjamins Publishing Company, pages 188–200.

Kaibao Hu and Qing Tao. 2013. The chinese-english conference interpreting corpus: Uses and limitations. *Meta* 58(3):626–642.

Christopher D. Manning, Mihai Surdeanu, John Bauer, Jenny Finkel, Steven J. Bethard, and David McClosky. 2014. The stanford corenlp natural language processing toolkit. In *Proceedings of the 52nd Annual Meeting of the Association for Computational Linguistics: System Demonstrations.*. Baltimore, Maryland: Association for Computational Linguistics, pages 55–60. https://aclweb.org/anthology/papers/P/P14-5010/.

Jun Pan. 2007. Two styles of interpretation: Reflection on the influence of oriental and western thought patterns on the relationship between the speaker and the interpreter. *Foreign Language and Culture Studies,* 6:677–688.

Jun Pan. 2019. *The Chinese/English Political Interpreting Corpus (CEPIC)*. Hong Kong Baptist University Library [Retrieved on 19 June 2019]. https://digital.lib.hkbu.edu.hk/cepic.

Jun Pan, Fernando Gabarron Barrios, and Haoshen He. forthcoming. Part-of-speech (pos) tagging enhancement for the chinese/english political interpreting corpus (cepic). In *Translation Studies in East Asia: Tradition, Translation and Transcendence*. http://www.cbs.polyu.edu.hk/2019east/index.php.

Jun Pan and Billy T.M. Wong. forthcoming. Pragmatic competence in chineseenglish retour interpreting of political speeches: A corpus-driven exploratory study of pragmatic markers. *Intralinea* https://www.intralinea.org.

Mariachiara Russo, Claudio Bendazzoli, and Bart Defrancq (Eds.). 2018. *Making Way in Corpus-based Interpreting Studies*. Singapore: Springer.

Beatrice Santorini. 1990. *Part-of-Speech Tagging Guidelines for the Penn Treebank Project (3rd revision, 2nd printing)*. Department of Linguistics, University of Pennsylvania. https://catalog.ldc.upenn.edu/docs/LDC99T42/tagguid1.pdf.

Robin Setton. 2011. Corpus-based interpreting studies (cis): Overview and prospects. In *Corpus-based Translation Studies. Research and Applications*. London: Continuum, pages 33–75.

Miriam Shlesinger. 1998. Corpus-based interpreting studies as an offshoot of corpus-based translation studies. *Meta: Journal des traducteurs* 43(4):486–493. https://doi.org/10.7202/004136ar.

Francesco Straniero Sergio and Caterina Falbo. 2012. *Breaking Ground in Corpus-based Interpreting Studies*. Bern: Peter Lang.

Binhua Wang. 2012. A descriptive study of norms in interpreting : based on the chinese-english consecutive interpreting corpus of chinese premier press conferences. *Meta* 57(1):198–212.

Fei Xia. 2000. The part-of-speech tagging guidelines for the penn chinese treebank (3.0). *RCS Technical Reports Series* (38). http://repository.upenn.edu/ircs$_r$eports/38.

A Supplemental Material

Examples and data listed in this paper are generated using the CEPIC online search engine, which should be cited as:

- Pan, Jun. (2019). The Chinese/English Political Interpreting Corpus (CEPIC). Hong Kong Baptist University Library, [Retrieved on 19 July 2019], Accessed from https://digital.lib.hkbu.edu.hk/cepic/

The following are links related to the CEPIC:

- Link to the CEPIC search engine: https://digital.lib.hkbu.edu.hk/cepic/search.php

- A Google Site page of the CEPIC: https://sites.google.com/a/hkbu.edu.hk/cepic-the-chinese-english-political-interpreting-corpus/

Translation Quality Assessment Tools and Processes in Relation to CAT Tools

Viktoriya Petrova

Institute for Bulgarian Language -Bulgarian
Academy of Sciences
v.k.petrova@abv.bg

Abstract

Modern translation QA tools are the latest attempt to overcome the inevitable subjective component of human revisers. This paper analyzes the current situation in the translation industry in respect to those tools and their relationship with CAT tools. The adoption of international standards has set the basic frame that defines "quality". Because of the clear impossibility to develop a universal QA tool, all of the existing ones have in common a wide variety of settings for the user to choose from. A brief comparison is made between most popular standalone QA tools. In order to verify their results in practice, QA outputs from two of those tools have been compared. Polls that cover a period of 12 years have been collected. Their participants explained what practices they adopted in order to guarantee quality.

1. Introduction

There is no single ideal translation for a given text, but a variety of translations are possible. All of them serve different purposes for different fields. For example, a legal translation will have very distinct requirements in terms of accuracy and adherence to locale-specific norms than that of an advertisement or a user instruction manual. CAT tools are adapted for texts such as contracts, technical texts and others that have in common a standardized and repetitive pattern. In the last 20 years the use of CAT tools increased and overturned human perceptions about the way those texts are processed and worked.

CAT assists human translators during their work by optimizing and managing the translation projects. They include a wide range of features, such as the possibility to work with different types of documents without needing to convert the text to a different format.

Another factor that overturned human perceptions about time and achievability is machine translation. Its improvements (in particular NMT in the last years) and the use of plug-ins allowed its effective use in the CAT environment.

The result was a substantial reduction of delivery times and decrease in budgets, which forced participants in the industry to change their workflows. Consequently, those changes reflected directly on the speed of translation evaluation. Previously an additional difficulty was that translation quality assessment was carried out by humans, thus the subjective component of the "human factor" was even more pronounced (Zehnalová, 2013). QA tools and quality assessment processes are the latest attempt to overcome those limitations. According to their creators, they are able to detect spelling errors, inconsistencies and all sorts of mismatches in an extremely short period. Since there are many such tools, it might be useful to distinguish them as built-in, cloud-based and standalone QA tools. In this paper, the focus will be on the last group because they represent, at least at the time of writing, the most used ones. Probably the advantage of standalone programs is that they can work with different types of files, whereas the others are limited by the format of the program. Section four shows sample output reports from two of those tools and how they behave. This paper analyzes the quality assessment tools that are being adopted by the translation industry. The first section shows the current situation in the industry and use of CAT tools in combination with their help tools (translation memories and terminology bases). The second section traces the adoption of international standards and regulations that every participant in the work chain has to follow. The third section describes the most popular standalone

Temnikova, I, Orăsan, C., Corpas Pastor, G., and Mitkov, R. (eds.) (2019) *Proceedings of the 2nd Workshop on Human-Informed Translation and Interpreting Technology (HiT-IT 2019)*, Varna, Bulgaria, September 5 - 6, pages 89–97.

https://doi.org/10.26615/issn.2683-0078.2019_011

"QA tools" with their common characteristics, results and reliability. The fourth section shows examples of two different QA reports with real examples of the detected issues. The last chapter presents polls on the practices adopted by the translation industry's participants that cover a period of 12 years.

2. CAT Tools and Their Help Tools

The main help tools in a CAT tool are translation memory and term bases. The second one is crucial when a translation quality assessment is performed.

Translation memory or TM is "…a database of previous translations, usually on a sentence-by-sentence basis, looking for anything similar enough to the current sentence to be translated" (Somers, 2003). This explains why standardized texts are very much in use and make quite a good combination with CAT tools.

The help tool that deserves more attention for the purpose of this paper is the term base. A term base is a list of specialized terms (related to the fields of engineering, physics, law, medicine etc.)
Practice shows that usually they are prepared in-house and sent to the translation agency or the freelancer to use them during their work. For one thing, this practice saves time for the translator, so they do not have to research the specific term. Moreover, clients may have preferences for one specific term instead of another. Here is also the place to mention the so-called "DNTs" or Do Not Translate lists (mostly brand names that have to remain the same as in the source language). By using terminology tools, translators ensure greater consistency in the use of terminology, which not only makes documents easier to read and understand, but also prevents miscommunication.

This is of great importance at QA stage. A properly-defined term-base will allow the QA tool to identify unfollowed terminology. As this paper later describes, unfollowed terminology is the main reason for sending back a translation and asking to change it.

3. International Standards

There are a number of international standards related to the definition of quality and what may affect it: The final product quality, the skills necessary for the translator to have, the quality of the final revision procedure and the quality of the processes for selecting translators or subcontracting, as well as the management of the whole translation process.

- **EN 15038:** Defines the translation process where quality is guaranteed not only by the translation itself (it is just one phase of the entire process), but by the fact that the translation text is reviewed by a person other than the translator. On a second level, this standard specifies the professional competences of each of the participants in the translation process. This is important especially for new professions such as "Quality Assurance Specialist". This standard was withdrawn in 2015[1].

- **ISO 17100:** Provides requirements for the processes, resources, and all other aspects that are necessary for the delivery of a quality translation service. It also provides the means by which a translation service provider can demonstrate the capability to deliver a translation service that will meet the client's requirements (as well as those of the TSP itself, and of any relevant industry codes)[2]. Later in the paper examples are given of why it is so important to follow clients' requirements.

- **ISO 9000:** Defines the Quality Management Systems (QMS) and the necessary procedures and practices for organizations to be more efficient and improve customer satisfaction. Lather becomes ISO 9001[3].

---

[1] Bulgarian Institute for Standardization (BDS) - БДС EN 15038:2006 http://www.bds-bg.org/standard/?national_standard_id=51617

[2] Bulgarian Institute for Standardization (BDS) БДС EN ISO 17100:2015

http://www.bds-bg.org/standard/?national_standard_id=90404

[3] Bulgarian Institute for Standardization - БДС EN ISO 9000:2015 http://www.bds-bg.org/bg/standard/?natstandard_document_id=76231

- **SAE J2450:** This standard is used for assessing the quality of automotive service translations[4].

4. Translation Quality Measurement

Translation Quality Assessment in professional translation is a long-debated issue that is still not settled today partly due to the wide range of possible approaches. Given the elusive nature of the quality concept first it must be defined from a multifaceted and all-embracing viewpoint (Mateo, 2016). Simultaneously and from a textual perspective, the quality notion must be defined as a notion of relative (and not absolute) adequacy with respect to a framework previously agreed on by petitioner and translator. Since the target text (TT) will never be the ideal equivalence of the source text (ST) because of the nature of human languages, and the translation needs to be targeted for a specific situation, purpose and audience, translation quality evaluation needs to be targeted in the same way: For a specific situation, a specific purpose and a specific audience. This is where translation standards set some rules that are to be followed by everyone is the sector.

The question of how the quality of a translation can be measured is a very difficult one. Because of the clear impossibility to develop a universal QA tool, the "7 EAGLES steps"[5] has been developed. It is a personalized QA that suggests 7 major steps necessary to carry out a successful evaluation of language technology systems or components:

1. Why is the evaluation being done?
2. Elaborate a task model (all relevant role agents).
3. Define top level quality characteristics.
4. Produce detailed requirements for the system under evaluation (on basis of 2. and 3.).
5. Devise the metrics to be applied to the systems for the requirements (produced under 4.).
6. Design the execution of the evaluation (test metrics to support the testing).
7. Execute the evaluation.

4.1 Translation Quality Assurance Tools

The main issue associated with the evaluation of translations is undoubtedly the subjectivity of evaluation. In order to find a solution to this, various software programs for determining translation quality have been developed and adopted in the last decade.

Quality Assurance (QA) is one of the final steps in the translation workflow. In general, its goal is to finalize the quality of the text by performing a check on consistency and proper use of terminology. The type of errors that a Quality Assurance specialist should track are errors in language register, punctuation, mistakes in numerical values and in Internet links (Debove, 2012). This paragraph is dedicated to the QA tools and the advantages they bring. It should be noted that only standalone tools will be analyzed. It is highly probable that new-generation tools will be cloud-based (one example is the recent lixiQA), however, based on the author's knowledge, standalone QA tools are currently the most preferred, and in particular those listed here.

The following tools are among the most widespread across the industry: QA Distiller, Xbench, Verifika, ErrorSpy and Ltb. They are the most frequently listed in blogs, companies' websites and translation forums, and this is why they are included here.

In the early stages of their development, translation quality assurance tasks were grouped into two categories: Grammar and formatting. Grammar was related to correct spelling, punctuation and target language fluency. Formatting - detecting unnecessary double spaces, redundant full stops at the end of a sentence, glossary inconsistencies, and numerous other tasks, which do not require working knowledge of the target language. If required from the user and properly set, all detected errors are included in a report, which allows convenient correction without the use of external software. A crucial turnover for the industry was that, thanks to those tools, such issues regarding terminology and consistency were immediately detected and marked differently into the reports. Some of them offer the possibility to create checklists that can be used for a specific client, in order to minimize risk of omissions.

---

[4] https://www.sae.org/standardsdev/j2450p1.htm

[5] https://www.issco.unige.ch/en/research/projects/eagles/ewg99/7steps.html

Xbench[6]

Xbench is a multi-dictionary tool rather than a QA tool in the true sense of the word. It provides the possibility to import different file types simultaneously, which can then be used as glossaries. Another very important feature is the possibility to convert a term base into different formats. Its functionalities are related to the options of checking consistency of the translated text, numbers, omissions, tag verifier, spacing, punctuation and regular expressions. It has a plugin for SDL Trados Studio.

Verifika[7]

Verifika is another tool that locates and resolves formal errors in bilingual translation files and translation memories. As in the previous tool, this one detects formatting, consistency, terminology, grammar and spelling errors in the targeted language. In addition, Verifika features an internal editor for reviewing and amending translations. For many error types, Verifika also offers an auto-correction feature. It has a plugin for SDL Trados Studio.

ErrorSpy[8]

ErrorSpy is the first commercial quality assurance software for translations. As the other two, in this one the reviser receives a list of errors and can either edit the translation or send the error report to the translator. The evaluation is based on metrics from standard SAE J 2450.

Ltb[9]

Ltb (i.e Linguistic ToolBox) provides automated pre-processing and post-processing work documents prior to and after translation, allowing the user to easily perform QA tasks on files. Some of its features include: Batch spell check over multiple files, translation vs. revision comparison, inconsistency and under-translation checks.

QA Distiller[10]

QA Distiller detects common errors like double spaces, missing brackets, wrong number formats. It supports omissions, source and target language inconsistencies, language-independent formatting, language-dependent formatting, terminology, search and regular expressions.

As shown in these brief descriptions and the table below, these tools have a lot of common features. For example, all of them can detect URL mismatches, alphanumeric mismatches, unfollowed terminology, tag mismatch, the possibility to create and export a report covering inconsistencies in both the source and target.

Advanced settings, such as change report or the option to use profiles, are not common to all the tools.

	Xbench	Verifika	ErrorSpy	Ltb	QA Distiller
Empty segments	X	X	X	X	X
Target text matches the source text*	X	X	X	X	X
Tag mismatch	X	X	X	X	X
Number mismatch	X	X	X	X	X
Grammar		X		X	
URL mismatch	X	X	X	X	X
Spelling	X	X	X	X	X
Alphanumeric mismatch	X	X	X	X	X
Unpaired symbols**	X	X	X	X	X
Partial translation***	X	X		X	X
Double blanks	X	X		X	X
Repeated words	X	X	X	X	
Source consistency	X	X	X	X	X

---

[6] https://www.xbench.net/

[7] http://help.e-verifika.com/

[8] https://www.dog-gmbh.de/en/products/errorspy/

[9] http://autoupdate.lionbridge.com/LTB3/

[10] http://www.qa-distiller.com/en

Target consistency	X	X	X	X	X
Change report				X	
Multiple files	X	X		X	X
CamelCase	X	X	X	X	X
Terminology	X	X	X	X	X
Checklists	X	X			X
PowerSearch* ***	X	X	X		X
Profiles*****		X		X	X
Report	X	X	X	X	X
Command line******					X
DNT List	X	X	X	X	X

* Potentially untranslated text
** I.e. unpaired parentheses, square brackets, or braces
*** Setting with minimum number of untranslated consecutive words
****Searching modes: Simple, Regular Expressions, and MS Word Wildcards.
***** "Profiles" are custom QA and language settings that are selected for a specific customer
****** It allows to automate the QA tool without processing files via the graphical user interface

Even though those tools have many similar settings, some of them are preferable to others.
As has been described in the ISO 17100 standard, client requirements are determined before the start of a translation project. The following files are usually requested at the time of delivery:
"Deliverables:
1. Cleaned files
2. _______ QA report with commented issues"
The blank space usually signifies which type of report if required. "Commented issues" relates to all false positives that are inevitably detected. A few such examples are given below.

5. QA Tools Output Comparison

As already established, those tools have many common characteristics, but also a lot of different ones. Some of them can be connected to a CAT tool, while others cannot. They all verify terminology, inconsistency, numbers, tags, links, and create an exportable report (mostly in excel format), which can then be verified by a QA specialist, or sent to the translator, who worked on the project. This last step depend on what practices have been adopted by the participants in the project. Although those tools provide an excellent quality when used for the verification of formal characteristics of a translation, they are not perfect. False-positive errors can be a difference in spacing rules from SL to TT, difference in length from source to target, the word forms, instruction regarding numbers. Each specific QA tool is better at detecting something than the rest. For example, in English, a number and its unit measures are written without a space in-between, while for Norwegian it is mandatory to write the number separated by a space. In an Ltb report, this will be indicated as an error. Another false-positive issue is the difference in length from source to target. When the target is 20% longer, Verifika indicates it as a possible error, even though languages have distinct semantic and morphological structures. Xbench is unable to detect linguistic differences as well. In order to achieve the best possible outputs, it is mandatory to set specific settings for every project by installing the proper language and settings.

Below are listed examples from exported reports from Xbench and Ltb. Since they have a lot of common features, it will be interesting to verify how they behave with identical settings.

In addition, it is important to briefly touch upon privacy restrictions. As quality notion is previously agreed upon by petitioner and translator, so are confidentiality agreements. Texts are not to be shared or inserted into machine translation engines under any circumstances. For the needs of this paper, and only with a previously corrected text, that would not contain any sort of references about the client, it was possible to use parts of the hereby-listed examples.

Further down are a few examples of how those tools detect possible errors and visualize them. An identical text has been imported in Xbench and Ltb. Only their general settings are activated. This is due to the fact that each translation project is characterized by specific settings related to the client's requirement and instructions. The translation is from English to Bulgarian.

EN	Ltb	Xbench
Dear Mr/Mrs [NAME],	Уважаема г-жо/г-не <x id="213" mmq78catalogvalue="<nts value="[NAME]"/>" mmq78shortcatalogvalue="nts" />,	Уважаема г-жо/г-не [ИМЕ],

Table 1: Link visualization.

Both tools have identified that between the parentheses there is a link, but have visualized it in a different way. In the Ltb report it is far more difficult to see where the issue is.

EN	Ltb	Xbench
xxx@123456group.com	xxx@123456group.com	xxx@123456group.com
<g id="383">2B. </g>		<g id="383">2B. </g>

Table 2. Segment not translated

While both tools have identified that the email addresses have not been translated, only Xbench has identified the other segment as untranslated.

EN	Ltb	Xbench
NA		Неприложимо

Table 3. Uppercase mismatch

This issue has been detected only in the Xbench and not in the Ltb.

EN	Ltb	Xbench
Please answer any incomplete (red) questions before trying to submit.	Отговорете на всички **непопълнени** (в червено) въпроси преди изпращане.	

Table 4: Difference in error detection.

It frequently occurs that a tool will determine something as a potential error, which another tool will not. An example is the Bulgarian word "непопълнени". The file is less than a 100 words. Xbanch has detected no errors, while the Ltb has registered a possible spelling error. Even though here we have only a few examples, it is enough to see that Ltb is better at spelling, while Xbench verifies more possible errors on a segment level.

All of the above are false positives. In a real work situation, those issues will be declared "False" or marked "Ignore" before delivering them to the client. A QA specialist or an experienced translator will immediately understand which of those warnings are real and which are not. Nevertheless these tools help visualize quickly what can be wrong with a text, especially when the settings for the specific project are set correctly.

6. Polls

Over the years many researchers have attempted to determine what the current state of affairs is within the translation industry. Julia Makoushina describes in her article (2007), among other things, awareness of existing QA automation tools, the distinct approaches to quality assurance, the types of QA checks performed, the readiness to automate QA checks, and the reasons not to. According to her survey, 86.5% of QA tool users represented translation/localization service provider companies, while a few were on the service buyer side, and 2 were software developer representatives. 1/3 reported that they applied quality assurance procedures at the end of each translation. Small companies applied QA before delivery. 30% of respondents applied QA procedures to source files as well as to final ones. Over 5% of respondent companies, mostly large ones, didn't apply any QA procedures in-house and outsourced them. Other QA methods (selected by

4.62% of the respondents) included spot-check of final files and terminology check, while the most popular response in this category was "it depends on a project". The least popular check for that period was word-level consistency, which is often one of the most important checks, but on the other hand is very difficult and time consuming. The most popular QA automation tools were those built into the TM tools - Trados and SDLX. Almost 17% of large companies indicated they used their own QA automation tools. Other tools specified by respondents included Ando tools, Microsoft Word spell-checker and SDL's ToolProof and HTML QA. Also SAE J2450 standard and LISA12 QA model were mentioned which are not in fact QA automation tools, but metrics.

In 2013, QTLaunchPad[11] analyzes which models are being used to assess translation quality. Nearly 500 respondents indicated to use more than one TQA model. This happens because in certain cases, the models depend on the area of application. Such shortcomings lead to the use of internal or modified models in addition to the above. Internal models were by far the most dominant at 45%. The QA options included in a CAT tool, were also popular at 32%. The most widely used external standard was EN 15038 followed (30%), followed closely by ISO 9000 series models (27%). Others had no formal model (17%), and 16% employed the LISA QA. To the question which QA tools are being used, most respondents use a built-in QA tool functionality of their existing CAT tools (48%) or their own in-house quality evaluation tools (39%). Here too, in some cases, more than one tool is used. Particularly popular choices were ApSIC XBench (30%) and Yamagata QA Distiller (12%), yet 22% state they do not use QA tools at all.

The situation has not changed much, as can be seen from a poll from few years ago from SDL Trados[12]. The poll is based on the responses from the Translation Technology Insights Research 2016[13]. One of the key findings of the research is the overriding importance of translation quality (it has been pointed as 2.5X more important than speed and 6X more important than cost). At the same time, 64% of the polled have to rework their projects. Terminology is the top challenge. Those who face rework have to deal with 'Inconsistencies in the use of terminology' - almost 48%. Another fact is that quality assessment is largely subjective. 59% of respondents are not measuring it at all or using ill-defined or purely qualitative criteria. Only 4% are relying entirely on formal, standardized metrics for quality assessment. This result is echoed in a question asking about feedback received: Twice as many receive subjective feedback as getting objective feedback. 59% either don't measure translation quality at all, or use ill-defined or purely qualitative assessment. In details, 35% have no measures or have ill-defined ones. 24% rely on qualitative feedback, 37% have adopted mixed measures and only 4% of respondents have adopted standardized assessment procedures.

According to the same poll, in order to improve translation quality, it is necessary to prioritize terminology management (as terminology inconsistencies are the top cause of rework), participants should familiarize themselves with existing international standards and adopt formal objective approach to measuring quality.

7. Conclusion

Translation quality assurance is a crucial stage of the working process. QA tools are convenient when it comes to both the economical aspect and time-consumption of the work process. Their adoption has helped to create new professions in the industry.

Although the examples that have been shown are mostly false issues, this does not mean that those tools are not able to detect real errors in a text, be it source or target. QA tools are valuable when there is necessity to verify if the right terminology has been followed, and that there are no inconsistencies in the translated text. The last one was previously not considered as important.

---

[11] QTLaunchPad is a two-year European Commission-funded collaborative research initiative dedicated to identifying quality barriers in translation and language technologies and preparing steps for overcoming them. http://www.qt21.eu/

[12] https://www.sdltrados.com/download/the-pursuit-of-perfection-in-translation/99851/

[13] https://www.sdl.com/software-and-services/translation-software/research/

References

Antonia Debove, Sabrina Furlan and Ilse Depreatere. 2012. *"Five automated QA tools (QA Distiller 6.5.8, Xbench 2.8, ErrorSpy 5.0, SDL Trados 2007 QA Checker 2.0 and SDLX 2007 SP2 QA Check)"-* Prespectives on translation quality
https://books.google.bg/books?hl=en&lr=&id=KAmIx MyFfeAC&oi=fnd&pg=PA161&dq=translation+QA+t ools&ots=xpMe0j-cer&sig=bS0WEjNWI6p_XI068NpS5e6-yhc&redir_esc=y#v=onepage&q&f=false

"Benjamins Translation Library", Computers and Translation, A translator's guide,Chapter 4, "Terminology tools for translators" Lynne Brwker, University of Ottawa, Canada, 2003
https://books.google.bg/books?hl=en&lr=&id=-WU9AAAAQBAJ&oi=fnd&pg=PA31&dq=translation +memory&ots=7sq2g4unoS&sig=vveWdiX5SZHOFC oA6wnkjMyCzLM&redir_esc=y#v=onepage&q=transl ation%20memory&f=false

Bulgarian Institute for Standardization (BDS) - БДС EN 15038:2006
http://www.bds-bg.org/standard/?national_standard_id=51617

Bulgarian Institute for Standardization - БДС EN ISO 9000:2015
http://www.bds-bg.org/bg/standard/?natstandard_document_id=76231

Bulgarian Institute for Standardization - БДС EN ISO 17100:2015
http://www.bds-bg.org/standard/?national_standard_id=90404

Doherty, S. Gaspari, F. Groves, D., van Genabith, J., Specia, L., Burchardt, A., Lommel, A., Uszkoreit, H. 2013. *"Mapping the Industry I: Findings on Translation Technoloogies and Quality Assessment"-* Funded by the European Commission – Grant Number: 296347
http://doras.dcu.ie/19474/1/Version_Participants_Final.pdf

ErrorSpy
https://www.dog-gmbh.de/en/products/errorspy/

Harold Somers. 2003. *"Benjamins Translation Library", Computers and Translation, A translator's guide, Chapter 3, "Translation memory systems",* UMIST, Manchester, England
https://books.google.bg/books?hl=en&lr=&id=-WU9AAAAQBAJ&oi=fnd&pg=PA31&dq=translation +memory&ots=7sq1f2vnhP&sig=C3fzF4zADUOsj4jG yJOxfJZBBP8&redir_esc=y#v=onepage&q=translatio n%20memory&f=false

Ilse Depreatere (Ed.). 2007. *"Perspectives on Translation Quality"* - A contrastive analysis of Antonia Debove, Sabrina Furlan and Ilse Depreatere

Jitka Zehnalová. 2013. „Tradition and Trends in Translation Quality Assessment"
Palacký University, Philosophical Faculty, Department of English and American Studies, Křížkovského 10, 771 80 Olomouc, Czech Republic
https://www.researchgate.net/publication/294260655_T radition_and_Trends_in_Translation_Quality_assessme nt

Julia Makoushina. 2007. *"Translation Quality Assurance Tools: Current State and Future Approaches"*
[Translating and the Computer 29, November 2007]
Palex Languages and Software
Tomsk, Russia
julia@palex.ru
http://citeseerx.ist.psu.edu/viewdoc/download?doi=10.1.1.464.453&rep=rep1&type=pdf

Lynne Brwker. 2003. *"Benjamins Translation Library", Computers and Translation, A translator's guide,Chapter 4, "Terminology tools for translators",* University of Ottawa, Canada
https://books.google.bg/books?hl=en&lr=&id=-WU9AAAAQBAJ&oi=fnd&pg=PA31&dq=translation +memory&ots=7sq2g4unoS&sig=vveWdiX5SZHOFC oA6wnkjMyCzLM&redir_esc=y#v=onepage&q=transl ation%20memory&f=false

QTLaunchPad
http://www.qt21.eu/

Roberto Martinez Mateo. 2016. *Aligning qualitative and quantitative approaches in professional translation quality assessment,* University of Castilla La Mancha
https://ebuah.uah.es/dspace/handle/10017/30326

SAE J2450 Translation Quality Metric Task Force
https://www.sae.org/standardsdev/j2450p1.htm

SDL Research Study 2016: Translation Technology Insights
https://www.sdl.com/software-and-services/translation-software/research/

"SDL Translation Technology Insights. Quality"
https://www.sdltrados.com/download/the-pursuit-of-perfection-in-translation/99851/

Xbench
https://www.xbench.net/

Verifika
http://help.e-verifika.com

Corpus Linguistics, Translation and Error Analysis

Maria Stambolieva

Centre for Computational and Applied Linguistics & Laboratory for Language Technology

New Bulgarian University

Abstract

The paper presents a study of the French *Imparfait* and its functional equivalents in Bulgarian and English in view of applications in (machine) translation, foreign language teaching and error analysis. The aims of the study are: 1/ based on the analysis of a corpus of text, to validate/revise earlier research on the values of the French *Imparfait*, 2/ to define the contextual factors pointing to the realisation of one or another value of the forms, 3/ based on the analysis of aligned translations, to identify the translation equivalents of these values, 4/ to formulate translation rules, 5/ based on the analysis of the translation rules, to refine the annotation modules of the environment used – the NBU E-Platform for language teaching and research.

1 Context

The paper presents work in progress, partly based on an earlier investigation by the same author (Stambolieva 2004), aiming 1/ to define the Tense-and-Aspect values of French sentences/clauses containing a verb marked for the *Imparfait*; 2/ to describe the linguistic markers linked to each value; 3/ to link these markers to translation equivalents in the two target languages: Bulgarian and English.

The software environment is the NBU E-Platform for teaching and research.

The corpora used are the electronic versions of Antoine de Saint-Exupéry's *Le Petit Prince*[1] and its translations in Bulgarian[2] and English[3].

The following procedure was used:

1/ The source text was annotated (POS-tagged and tagged for *Imparfait*-marked forms) in the grammatical analysis module of the E-Platform.

2/ The source text was aligned with the texts in the target languages.

3/ With the respective E-Platform module, two virtual corpora were derived – files with lists of sentences containing a specific annotation value. In this case the corpora contain lists of sentences with *Imparfait*-marked verbal forms and their translation equivalents in the two target languages.

For the analysis of the French sentences in the virtual corpus, the theoretical model proposed by J.-P. Desclés (Desclés 1985, 1990) was adopted – a system organising four main elements: 1/ a system of grammatical forms, 2/ a system of values, 3/ a system of correspondences between 1/ and 2/, 4/ a system of strategies for context analysis. Important studies of the French *Imparfait* and its equivalents in Bulgarian have been published by Zlatka Guentcheva-Desclés (Guentcheva 1990,

---

[1] https://www.ebooksgratuits.com/html/st_exupery_le_petit_prince.html

[2] http://old.ppslaveikov.com/Roditeli/knigi%20Lqto/anton.sent.ekzuperi-makiat.princ.pdf

[3] http://verse.aasemoon.com/images/f/f5/The_Little_Prince.pdf

Temnikova, I, Orăsan, C., Corpas Pastor, G., and Mitkov, R. (eds.) (2019) *Proceedings of the 2nd Workshop on Human-Informed Translation and Interpreting Technology (HiT-IT 2019)*, Varna, Bulgaria, September 5 - 6, pages 98–104.

https://doi.org/10.26615/issn.2683-0078.2019_012

Guentcheva 1997). A study of the French *Imparfai*t by M. Maire-Reppert (Maire-Reppert 1991) was found to be very useful for some of the values of the forms set out, the rich corpus of examples an the excellent attempt at formalization of the contextual markers of the values of the *Imparfait*. Danchev and Alexieva 1974 and Stambolieva 1987, 1998 and 2008 are contrastive corpus-based studies of contextual markers of tense and aspect in English and their Bulgarian functional equivalents. [4] A pioneering work on the compositionality of aspect in English is Verkuyl 1993.

The rules linking values to forms and context contain the following information:

1/ text element under investigation (indicator) – in our investigation, French verbal lexemes to which the morpheme of the *Imparfait* is attached;

2/ scope of the context where the contextual markers (indices) are found;

3/ contextual markers (indices) – elements of the immediate context which resolve the ambiguity of the indicator;

4/ values attributed to the combined indicator and indices;

5/ pairing of the values to functional equivalents in the target languages.

Thus, on a monolingual plane, we derive value indices of the indicators – the French verbal forms marked for the *Imparfait*. On a bilingual plane, indicators and indices are linked to translation equivalents in the target languages of the investigation.

The software environment of the project is that of the NBU e-Platform for language teaching and research (PLT&R)

2 The NBU E-Platform for Language Teaching and Research

The NBU E-Platform, a recent project of the NBU Laboratory for Language Technology[5], was initially developed as a tool for language teaching/learning: a generator of online training exercises from annotated corpora, with exports to Moodle or other educational platforms. It has since been extended with modules and functionalities allowing research in translation and error analysis and supporting lexicographic projects.

The E-Platform integrates: 1/ an environment for creating, organising and maintaining electronic text archives and extracting text corpora; 2/ modules for linguistic analysis: a lemmatiser, a POS analyser; a term analyser; a morphological analyser, a syntactic analyser; an analyser of multiple word units (MWU – including complex terms, analytical forms, phraseological units); a parallel text aligner; a concordancer; 3/ a linguistic database allowing corpus manipulation without loss of information; 4/ modules for the generation and editing of online training exercises. The environment for the maintenance of the electronic text archive organises a variety of metadata which can, individually or in combinations, form the basis for the extraction of text corpora. Following linguistic analysis, secondary ("virtual") corpora can be extracted – lists of sentences containing a particular unit – a lemma (e.g. *it, dislike*), a word form (e.g. *begins*), a MWU (e.g. *has been writing, put off*), a tag (e.g. <intransitive verb>, <comparative degree>, <present perfect progressive tense>, <imparfait>), or a combination of tags. The architecture allows the parallel use of several systems of preprocessing and the comparison of their results for the purpose of making an intelligent choice – which can turn it into an environment for experimentation and research.[6]

---

[4] Functional equivalence finding is the process, where the translator understands the concept in the source language and finds a way to express the same concept in the target language in the way, in which the **equivalent** conveys the same meaning and intent as the original. (Wikipedia)

[5] NBU CFSR-funded project:
https://projects.nbu.bg/projects_inner.asp?pid=642

[6] Cf Stambolieva, Ivanova, Raykova 2018

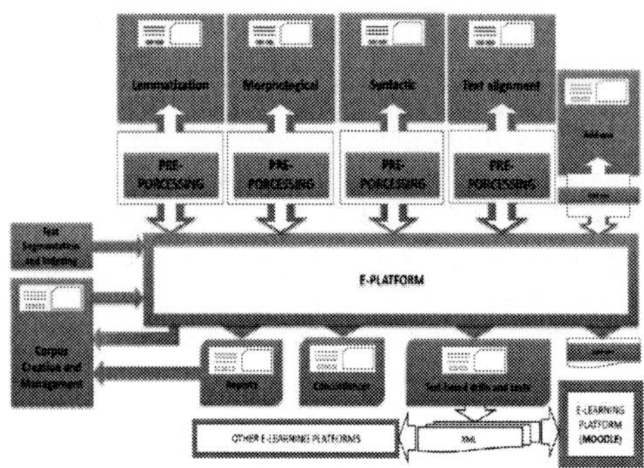

Table 1. Architecture of the E-Platform[7]

The following modules of the platform were extended for the purpose of the project:

- The Text & Corpus organizer
- The annotation modules: Lemmatiser, POS-tagger, Morphological and Syntactic tagger
- The Aligner
- The Virtual Corpus generator.

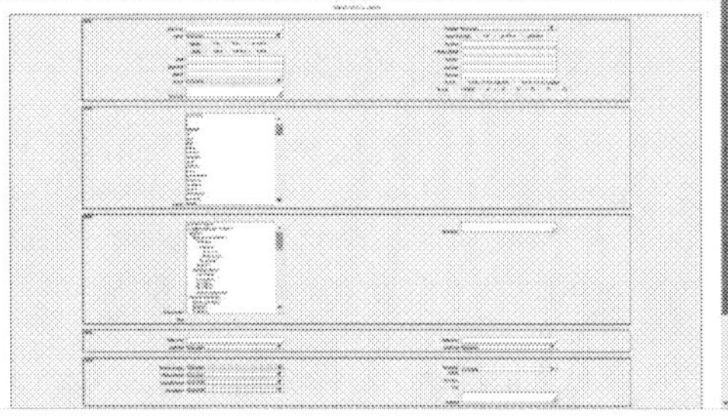

Table 2. The Virtual Corpus generator

A new module combining annotation and alignment was developed as an extension of the Virtual Corpus generator – a generator of virtual corpora coupled with aligned translation equivalents.

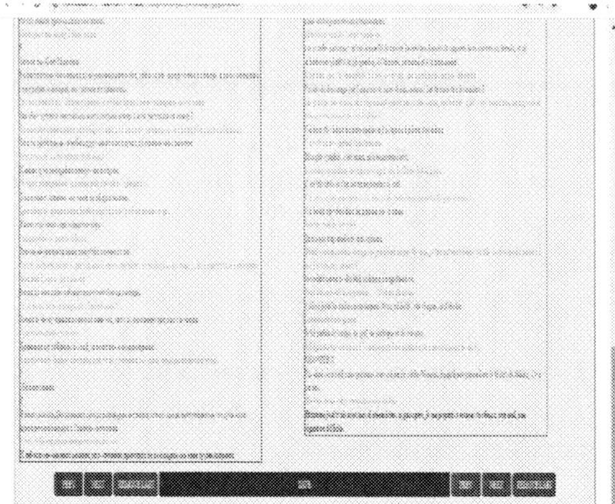

Table 3. Aligning with the E-Platform

3 Values of the *Imparfait* and Its Translation Equivalents in Bulgarian and English

The dominant translation equivalents of the *Imparfait* in our corpus are *The Simple Past Tense* (for English) and *The Past Imperfect* of Imperfective Aspect verbs (for Bulgarian).

> **Rule 1:**
>
> Given an instance X marked by the morpheme of the Imparfait,
>
> and if X is a member of the set of verbs of a stative archetype,
>
> then the value of the Imparfait is that of "descriptive state"
>
> The Bulgarian translation contains a form of an Imperfective Aspect verb marked for The Past Imperfect
>
> The English translation contains a stative verb marked for The Simple Past Tense.

However, other tense-aspect equivalents also appear: *The Past Continuous Tense* (for English) and *The Present Tense*, *The Past Indefinite Tense* and *The Past Perfect Tense* of Perfective Aspect verbs, *The Future in the Past Tense* (for Bulgarian)

---

[7] The E-Platform was initially developed by the Central Institute for Informatics and Computer Engineering of the. For its architecture, regular support and update we are indebted to our colleagues from the Informatics department of New Bulgarian University Dr. Mariyana Raykova.and Dr. Valentina Ivanova.

– hence the necessity to identify the different values of the *Imparfait* and their contextual markers. Maire-Reppert (Maire-Reppert, op. cit.) proposes a very fine-grained set of values of the French *Imparfait* for situation types and for registers, including seven subtypes of states,[8] three subtypes of processes, events, iterative situations, conditions and formulae of politeness. Based on her findings and an analysis of our corpus, we have arrived at a set of rules (94 in all), the general form of which is presented with the following simple rule for **Descriptive States**:

Ex. 1 *Il représentait un serpent boa qui digérait un éléphant. – Тя изобразяваше змия боа, която смила слон. – It was a picture of a boa constrictor digesting an elephant.*

Rule 1 indicates the necessity to extend the annotation module with subcategories/subtypes of verbal lexemes. For the description of the values of the *Imparfait*, six lists of verbal subtypes were drawn up: 1. Stative locative verbs, 2. *Verba dicendi*, 3. Stative link verbs, 4. Stative full verbs, 5. Change of State verbs 6. Dynamic full verbs with a closed right-hand bound (so-called "conclusives" – e.g. *perdre, mourir, comprendre).*

Along with the lists of verbs, 15 more lists were drawn up: of adverbial expressions of frequency or place; of nouns belonging to the semantic subgroups 'characteristic feature', or 'item of clothing'; 'taking'expressions, as e.g. *se servir de, utiliser, employer*, etc.

A similar rule, with non-stative verbs, has been formulated for **Processes in Development**. The Bulgarian translations contain a Past Imperfect form of an Imperfective Aspect verb. The English equivalents can appear in both the Past Continuous Tense and the Past Simple Tense (which is the unmarked member of the opposition).

Ex. 2 *Comme le petit prince s'endormait, je le pris dans mes bras, et me remis en route. – Малкият принц заспиваше, аз го взех на ръце и отново тръгнах. – As the little prince dropped off to sleep,* *I took him in my arms and set out walking once more.*

The following main **triggers of asymmetry** in the translation equivalents were identified:

1/ **The Sequence of Tenses** is part of the grammatical systems of French and English, but not of Bulgarian:

Ex. 3 *J'avais ainsi appris une seconde chose très importante: c'est que sa planète d'origine était à peine plus grande qu'une maison ! – Така узнах второ, много важно нещо: че неговата родна планета е малко по-голяма от къща! – I had thus learned a second fact of great importance: this was that the planet the little prince came from was scarcely any larger than a house!*

Rule 2 relies on syntactic annotation – it involves marking sentences as Simple, Compound and Complex Sentences, and clauses (at least) as Main and Subordinate.

2/ **New State** is typically marked by a verb of dynamic archetype (although French source sentences can also appear with the verb *être* in the *Imparfait*). The English translations contain a *Simple Past* tense form of the verb (including *to be*), while a verb of dynamic archetype (of Perfective Aspect) must appear in the Bulgarian translations, marked for *The Past Perfect Tense*. The contextual markers defining the situation as non-descriptive are adverbial expressions appearing in Change-of-State lists, as well as adverbial expressions which do not appear in lists of expressions marking processes in development – such as *pendant, pendant que, tandis que, alors que*. etc.

Rule 3.

Given an instance X marked by the morpheme of the *Imparfait*

and if X has a dynamic archetype

and if X is in a list of verbs of the Conclusive type

---

[8] (Descriptive (état descriptif), Resultant, (état résultant), Inferential (état à valeur inférentielle), of Acquired experience (état à valeur d'expérience), Passive (état passif), New (nouvel état) or Permanent state (état permanent)).

> and it there is, in the same clause, a phrase belonging to list of temporal expressions
>
> then the value of X is that of "new state"
>
> The Bulgarian translation contains a form of a verb marked for *The Past Perfect of Perfective Aspect verbs*
>
> The English verb contains a verb in *The Past Simple Tense.*

Ex. 4 *Le premier ministre arrivait. On entra en conférence.* (Corpus of M.-Reppert)

> **Rule 2**
>
> Given an instance X marked by the morpheme of the *Passé Composé* or *Passé Simple* ,
>
> and if X is in the list of verb 'Verba dicendi',
>
> and given an instance of a verb Y marked by the morpheme of the *Imparfait* within a Subordinate Clause introduced by the Conjunction *que*
>
> then the value of the *Imparfait* is that of "permanent state"
>
> The Bulgarian translation contains a form of a verb marked for *The Present.*
>
> The English verb contains a verb in *The Past Simple, The Past Continuous* or *The Perfect Perfect Tense*.

For the New State translation rules, the Bulgarian forms must be tagged for Aspect. The values of this category are part of the POS-tagger of the e-Platform.

Rule 3 is one of the 9 New State rules formulated for New States and their translations.

3/ Real Conditions. French verbs appearing in the Subordinate Clause of Real Conditions introduced by the conjunction *si* often appear in the *Imparfait*. The English tense form in the translation equivalent is in most cases in the *Simple Present Tense*; the Bulgarian one is in the *Present Tense*.

Ex. 5 *Elle serait bien vexée, se dit-il, si elle voyait ça. – Ако види това – каза си той, -- ще бъде обидена. – If she sees that, he thought, she will be hurt.*

4/ Iterative situations. For this value, the data from the two corpora have been described in 19 rules; the cases of asymmetry are restricted to predictable, structure-induced cross-language transformations. The general rule is presented below:

> **Rule 5.**
>
> Given an instance X marked by the morpheme of the *Imparfait*
>
> and if an element, member of a list of adverbs of frequency (*parfois, quelquefois, plusieurs fois*, etc.), appears in the same clause,
>
> then the value of X is that of "Iterative Situation".
>
> The Bulgarian translation contains a form of a verb marked for *The Past Imperfect Tense*
>
> The English verb contains a verb in *The Past Simple Tense* OR *Past Continuous Tense* OR *a would/used to + Infinitive* structure.

5/ Expression of Politeness. This value of the *Imparfait* allows the speakers to grant their interlocutors – as a sign of politeness or reserve – the option to oppose, as it were, the process:

> **Rule 6.**
>
> Given an instance X marked by the morpheme of the *Imparfait*
>
> and if the clause contains a *verbum dicendi*,
>
> and if the main clause contains a personal pronoun in the first or second person singular or plural or a nominal syntagm from a list of polite forms of address,

then the value of X is that of "Expression of Politeness"

The Bulgarian translation contains a form of a verb marked for *The Past Imperfect Tense*

The English verb contains a verb in *The Past Simple Tense*. OR *a modal form*, e.g. *would like + to-infinitive.*

Ex. 6 *Je voulais vous dire que je ne pourrai pas venir demain.# Je venais dire à Madame que le déjeuner était servi.*

> **Rule 4.**
>
> Given an instance X marked by the morpheme of the *Imparfait*
>
> and if X appears in a Subordinate Clause introduced by the Conjunction *si*
>
> and if the main clause contains a verbal form marked for the *Conditionnel,*
>
> then "Real Condition" can be the value of X.
>
> The Bulgarian translations contain a form of a verb marked for *The Present Tense*
>
> The English translations contain a verb in *The Present Simple Tense.*

Contextual markers for this value of the Imparfait are: 1/ the presence of *verba dicendi*, 2/ personal pronouns for the first and second person singular or plural in the same clause, or a nominal syntagm from a list including *Madame, Mademoiselle, Monsieur*. The Bulgarian translations appear in the Present Tense, the English translations − in the Present Simple tense.

6/ **The Non-Evidential mood** [9] in Bulgarian. The contextual factors triggering this type of French &

---

[9] The (Non)Evidential Mood is an epistemic grammatical mood. It indicates that the utterance is based on what the speaker has/has not seen with their own eyes, or heard with their own ears.

English vs Bulgarian asymmetry are yet to be analyzed before the formulation of the translation rules.

4 Conclusions

The analysis of the corpus indicates that the formulation of translation rules for the French *Imparfait* involves lexical, morphological and syntactic annotation of the micro context of the tense marker (the verbal lexeme) and of the macrocontext of the sentence/clause.

The verbal lexemes forming the microcontext of the *Imparfait* marker fall into several subclasses, which have been added to the tagsets in the annotation modules of the e-Platform. The macrocontext of the verbal forms, i.e. their left and right hand environment, must be syntactically tagged for sentence type and clause status and function, along with the standard parts-of-the sentence and POS-tagging. These values were added to the annotation set of the syntactic module.

Our findings also indicate that simple identification of WHEN-type adverbial modification [10] is not sufficient to define the temporal values of the French *Imparfait*. They confirm the need to include frequency expressions − as proposed in the guidelines and methods formulated by I. Mani et al (Mani et al, 2001) and J.-P. Desclés (Desclés 1997).

An extended set of annotation values was found to be necessary for the description of those values of the *Imparfait*-marked sentences/ clauses where the morpheme does not mark temporality.

5 Applications

The analysis of the contextual and translation rules of the French *Imparfait* is part of a larger task − the development of a multilingual annotated corpus of

---

[10] As e.g. in Vazov 1999

Tense and Aspect with rules for value identification and translation. As our examples and rules indicate, the corpus of aligned translations can be used not only to derive monolingual contextual rules (with or without rules for translation equivalence in a target language), but also to assign possible values in the source language based on translation equivalents.

The rules formulated by analyzing the aligned corpora of text will be tested in a system of automatic tense-and-aspect translation. The types of cross-language asymmetry can be integrated both in machine translation applications and in the test generating modules of the E-Platform. Student translations in the target language will be automatically tested against the target language equivalents of the corpus for appropriateness of tense-and-aspect values.

Our final objective in developing the corpora and providing input rules is to create an automatic or machine-assisted training system allowing:

1/ the choice between alternative values given an input of contextual markers;

2/ the proposal of contextual markers given an input of values;

3/ the choice between alternative target language Tense/Aspect values based on source text context analysis;

4/ the choice between source text values based on markers in the target text;

5/ error analysis and assessment of machine or student generated target texts.

References

Danchev & Alexieva 1974. Izborat mejdu minalo svarsheno i minalo nesvarsheno vreme pri prevoda na past simple tense ot angliyski na balgarski ezik. In : Yearbook of Sofia University, Faculty of classical and modern languages, vol. LXVII, 1, pp 249-329

Desclés 1985. J.-P, Desclés. Représentation des connaissances : archétypes cognitifs, schèmes conceptuels et schémas grammaticaux. Actes sémiotiques VII ; No 69-70

Desclés 1990 : J.-P, Desclés. The concepts of state, process, event and topology. General Linguistics, vol. 29, No 3. The Pennsylvania State University Press. University Park and London, 159-200

Desclés et al. 1997. J.-P, Desclés, E. Cartier, A. Jackiewicz, J.-L. Minel. Textual processing and contextual exploration method. In : CONTEXT'97, pp 189-197, Brasil, Rio de Janeiro

Guentcheva 1990. Zlatka Guentcheva. Temps et aspect: exemple du bulgare contemporain. CNRS, Paris

Guentcheva 1997. Imparfait, aoriste et passé simple : confrontation de leurs emplois dans des textes bulgares et français. In : J.-P. Desclés et al. 1997. Textual processing and contextual exploration method. In CONTEXT'97, pp 189-197, Brasil, Rio de Janeiro

Maire-Reppert 1991. Danièle Maire-Reppert. Les temps de m'indicatif du français en vue d'un traitement informatique: Imparfait. CNRS, Paris

Mani et al. 2001. I. Mani, L. Ferro, B. Sanheim, G. Wilson. Guidelines for annotating temporal information. In: Notebook Proceedings of Human Language Technology Conference 2001, pp 299-302, San Diego, California

Stambolieva 1997. TO BE and SAM in the systems of English and Bulgarian. PhD Dissertation, Sofia University Sv. Kliment Ohridski

Stambolieva 1998. "Context in Translation". Proceedings of the Third European Seminar "Translation Equivalence". Montecatini Terme, Italy, October 16-18 1997. The TELRI Association. Institut fur deutsche Sprache, Mannheim & The Tuscan Word Centre, pp. 197-204

Stambolieva 2008. Maria Stambolieva. Building Up Aspect. Peter Lang Academic Publishers

Stambolieva, Ivanova, Raykova 2018. M. Stambolieva, V. Ivanova, M. Raykova. A Platform for Language Teaching and Research (PLT & R). CLARIN annual conference, Pisa 2018

Vazov 1999. N. Vazov. Context-scanning strategy in temporal reasoning. In: Modeling and Using Context, CONTEXT Conference 1999, Springer-Verlag

Verkuyl 1993. Henk Verkuyl. A Theory of Aspectuality. The interaction between temporal and atemporal structure. Cambridge Studies in Liguistics. Cambridge University Press

Human-Informed Speakers and Interpreters Analysis in the WAW Corpus and an Automatic Method for Calculating Interpreters' Décalage

Irina Temnikova[1], Ahmed Abdelali[2], Souhila Djabri[3] and Samy Hedaya[4]
[1]Freelancer, Sofia, Bulgaria
[2]Qatar Computing Research Institute, HBKU, Doha, Qatar
[3]University of Alicante, Spain
[4]Translation and Interpretation Institute, HBKU, Doha, Qatar

[1]`irina.temnikova@gmail.com`, [2]`aabdelali@hbku.edu.qa`,
[3]`sd89@alu.ua.es`, [4]`SHedaya@hbku.edu.qa`

Abstract

This article presents a multi-faceted analysis of a subset of interpreted conference speeches from the WAW corpus for the English-Arabic language pair. We analyze several speakers and interpreters variables via manual annotation and automatic methods. We propose a new automatic method for calculating interpreters' décalage (ear-voice span) based on Automatic Speech Recognition (ASR) and automatic alignment of named entities and content words between speaker and interpreter. The method is evaluated by two human annotators who have expertise in interpreting and Interpreting Studies and shows highly satisfactory results, accompanied with a high inter-annotator agreement. We provide insights about the relations of speakers' variables, interpreters' variables and décalage and discuss them from Interpreting Studies and interpreting practice point of view. We had interesting findings about interpreters behavior which need to be extended to a large number of conference sessions in our future research.

1 Introduction

A key characteristics which speech-to-speech machine translation systems strive to have is a good trade-off between accuracy of translation and low latency (Waibel and Fuegen, 2012; Bangalore et al., 2012). **Latency** is defined as the delay between the input speech and the delivered translation (Niehues et al., 2016) and roughly corresponds to interpreter's **décalage** in human interpreting.

While a number of engineering approaches are being proposed to reduce latency by in the same time maintaining good automatic speech translation quality (Waibel and Fuegen, 2012; Bangalore et al., 2012; Sridhar et al., 2013b; Schmid and Garside, 2005), few approaches are getting explicitly inspired by human interpreting, by learning from the strategies which interpreters employ in order to produce good quality translation (Niehues et al., 2016; He et al., 2015; Sridhar et al., 2013a).

In line with this area of research, starting with an initial objective to boost a speech machine translation system working with English/Arabic language pair (Dalvi et al., 2017) we conduct experiments on a subset of sessions from the WAW corpus (Abdelali et al., 2018) - a corpus of simultaneously interpreted conference speeches, to get informed about interpreters' behaviour and learn which strategies interpreters employ to maintain good output accuracy while in the same time not exceeding their delay from the speaker. Our task is complex, as we want to find a way in which human expertise in interpreting can boost the performance of speech machine translation systems.

With this article, we are enriching our previous research (Temnikova et al., 2017; Abdelali et al., 2018) and run an extensive multilateral analysis on a subset of WAW corpus interpreted sessions, before extending to a large number of sessions. The aim of this article is to test how much and what information we can extract by a combined manual (expert) and automatic analysis and also to propose a new automatic method for décalage calculation. We present the results of a manual evaluation run by two human experts on the points of reference generated by our décalage method.

Knowing that the strategies applied by interpreters and their décalage (including décalage as a sign of cognitive challenges and as a strategy) depend on source input characteristics, and that décalage can subsequently influence other interpreters' variables (Lee, 2002), we analyze: 1)

Temnikova, I, Orăsan, C., Corpas Pastor, G., and Mitkov, R. (eds.) (2019) *Proceedings of the 2nd Workshop on Human-Informed Translation and Interpreting Technology (HiT-IT 2019)*, Varna, Bulgaria, September 5 - 6, pages 105–115.
https://doi.org/10.26615/issn.2683-0078.2019_013

the source speech characteristics of several conference sessions (including the presence of noise and other interruptions), 2) several output variables of interpreters (such as décalage, average interpreters' output speed, number of hesitations, repetitions and false starts) and we interpret our findings using the rich knowledge of a practitioner interpreter with background in Interpreting Studies. We address all these issues with a combination of automatic methods and manual (expert) annotations of both speech recordings and speakers' and interpreters' transcripts. We link our new findings with the manually annotated interpreting strategies in the same subset of conference sessions by two human annotators (Abdelali et al., 2018; Temnikova et al., 2017), see Section 3.

The rest of the article is structured as follows: Section 2 presents some of the relevant related work; Section 3 introduces the data and the general methodology; Sections 4 and 5 present the analysis of source speeches (both manual annotation and automatic analysis of fluency indicators and external conditions tags); Sections 6 and 8 discuss the analysis of interpreter variables (décalage and fluency indicators) and present our automatic décalage calculation method; Section 7 shows an approximate analysis of speakers input rate and interpreters delivery rate (speaking speed). Section 9 provides the overall results discussion and Section 10 concludes the article.

2   Related Work

Interpreting corpora are used as a resource for research in both Interpreting Studies (IS) (Bendazzoli and Sandrelli, 2009; Russo et al., 2018; Defrancq, 2015) and in Machine Translation (MT) (Paulik and Waibel, 2009; Shimizu et al., 2013; Sridhar et al., 2013a). Due to the different aims and available tools, the methods used for research in these two fields are somewhat different. As we come from the MT research perspective (but get inspired by IS), the related works which are the closest to us are He et al. (2016) and Sridhar et al. (2013a). He et al. (2016) run a corpus analysis on a parallel corpus of translated and simultaneously interpreted text for the Japanese-English language pair. They use a machine learning classifier (differently from us) in order to classify interpreters' strategies in the text. The strategies that they examine are segmentation, passivization, generalization, and summarization

(similar to us). Sridhar et al. (2013a) performs a corpus analysis of the EPIC corpus (Bendazzoli and Sandrelli, 2005) investigating interpreters strategies and behaviour for the English-Spanish language pair. They analyze features such as décalage, compression (somewhat corresponding to our *summarizing* and *omissions*), hesitations, some discourse features (e.g. analysis of the use of pronouns). Their paper makes an overview of the whole corpus for these features, without linking the features as potentially causing one another and without entering in details and analyzing specific sessions, as our paper does.

Calculation of Décalage Most of the Interpreting Studies approaches for calculating interpreters décalage involve manual input: there can be manual adding of tags while using software to display aligned segments and play speaker's and interpreter's recordings (Defrancq, 2015; Lee, 2002). Some researchers use the EXMARaLDA platform[1]. Although humans can usually make deeper choices than machines, manual methods take a lot of efforts. The automatic approaches include Sridhar et al. (2013a) and Ono et al. (2008).

The most important issue in calculating interpreters décalage is deciding on the measurement units and points of reference (Defrancq, 2015; Timarová et al., 2011). Measuring units can be words or seconds. The points of reference vary: e.g. end of a speaker's and start of interpreter's content word (Ono et al., 2008), words with literal translation (Oléron and Nanpon, 1965), every 5 seconds, beginning of segments where at least one interpreter omitted more than 15 words, beginning of sentence, units of meaning (Podhajská, 2008) and "segments correspondence based on content, instead only on simple lexical equivalence" (Barik, 1973). Our measurement units are seconds, and reference points are selected aligned words (see Section 6.1). Our method differs from Sridhar et al. (2013a) as we removed the stop words and used content words and Named Entities (for NEs we also differ from Ono et al., 2008). We also differ from both approaches as we run evaluation of our décalage method reference points alignment with two expert human annotators.

3   General Methodology

Data Selection - The WAW Corpus: For all experiments and analysis we used the recordings

---

[1] https://exmaralda.org

and transcripts of conference speeches and of interpreters from the WAW corpus for the source language English and target Arabic. **The WAW corpus** is a conference interpreting corpus collected from three conferences which took place in Qatar in 2013-2014: WISE 2013 (World Innovation Summit for Education), ARC'14 (Qatar Foundation's Annual Research and Development Conference), and WISH 2013 (World Innovation Summit for Health). Most speeches (133) have as source language English, target Arabic, with very few (7) having source language Arabic and target English. The WAW corpus was collected in order to train the QCRI's[2] speech-to-speech machine translation system. It is composed of the recordings of both the conference speeches and interpreters (collected from interpreters' booths), their transcripts (obtained from transcription agencies), and the translations of the transcripts into the opposite language. The transcripts were manually annotated with tags[3]. For more details see Abdelali et al. (2018). The WAW corpus currently contains information such as: recordings length in seconds, interpreters' gender, topics, length of transcripts in words, number of tags in each transcript (both for speakers and interpreters). The corpus does not contain the names, nor any personal information about speakers and interpreters, the number of speakers or interpreters per session, prosody annotation. It has not been Part-of-Speech (POS) tagged nor syntactically parsed. We do not also know any details about the way conference interpreting was organized, e.g. if interpreters were given the speeches to get prepared before interpreting took place. In total there were 12 interpreters, some of which interpreted more than one speech. See Figure 1 for number of speeches per interpreter and average session duration.

In Abdelali et al. (2018) and Temnikova et al. (2017) a subset of source and target transcripts were manually annotated for some interpreting strategies (as sequences of words): additions, omissions, self-corrections, and summarizing. The results were showing omissions as highest number of strategies (Korpal, 2012), followed by additions (see Figure 5).

Data Selection - Speeches Used in this Paper: The interpreted conference sessions analyzed in this paper are all for the English-Arabic language

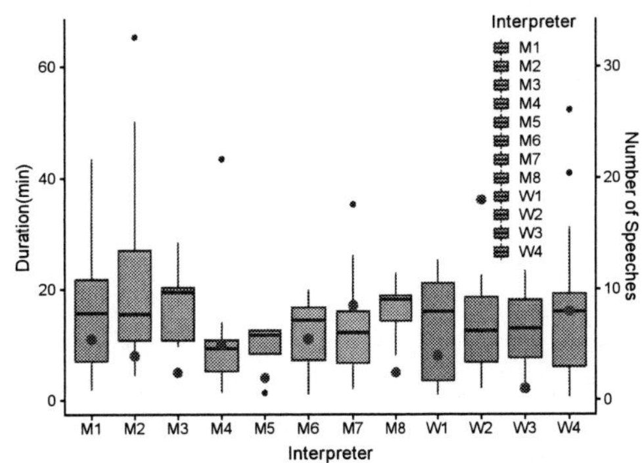

Figure 1: Average session length and number of speeches (●) per interpreter in the WAW Corpus.

direction. The majority of experiments (except for the speed comparison for the whole corpus) analyze **five** interpreted conference sessions, which were a subset of the sessions which we used in our previous research (Abdelali et al., 2018; Temnikova et al., 2017). Out of the 5 sessions two were from the same male interpreter (M7) and three from two female interpreters (W2 and W4). Male and female interpreters were selected in order to be able to analyze potential gender differences. Table 2 shows the duration in minutes of these sessions and the speakers and interpreters transcripts lengths in words. The selection criteria were the following:

1. M7, W2, and W4 were the interpreters, which had the highest numbers of sessions interpreted (see the blue dots in Figure 1).

2. There was a large difference in the number of annotated interpreting strategies in these transcripts (see Figure 5): in M7-T2 the interpreter employed the highest number of strategies, compared to all interpreter-transcript pairs, while in M7-T1 the interpreter employed the lowest number of strategies.

3. Similarly, W2-T2 had the lowest strategies employed by a female interpreter, while W4-T1 had the highest total number of strategies. W2-T1 was added to create a comparison between two very different sessions of the same interpreter as for M7.

The topics and conferences of the five selected recordings were: education conference WISE'14 (interpreter M7 and W4), topics - general edu-

---

[2]Qatar Computing Research Institute (QCRI).

[3]Transcription instructions with tags definition: http://tiny.cc/WAWTranscriptionTags.

cation (M7-T1), MOOCs (M7-T2), online education (W4-T1) and the general conference ARC'14 (W2, topics: W2-T2 - energy and environment, W2-T1 - traffic road accident).

Human Annotators: In Sections 4 (manual analysis of source speeches) and 6.1 (manual evaluation of décalage) we have relied on two annotators (A1 and A2), who both had research experience in Interpreting Studies. In addition, A1 completed studies in translation strategies and A2 has practitioner experience as a simultaneous interpreter and a degree in Interpreting Studies. Both annotators have advanced knowledge of English and native Arabic. We also consulted A3, who is a practitioner conference interpreter in Qatar with English and Arabic as source languages.

Methods Overview: The **source speech characteristics that we analyze are:** 1) environment conditions: noise, music, quality of sound 2) speakers variables: number of speakers, topics, speech intelligibility, (dis)fluency, accent, input rate, technicality of the topic. We have selected these variables in line with the IS state-of-the-art research, e.g. (Moser-Mercer, 1996; Pio, 2003; Plevoets and Defrancq, 2016; Fernández, 2015; Cecot, 2001). The **interpreters variables which we analyze are:** number of hesitations, false starts, repetitions, strategies used, delivery rate, décalage.

We use automatic methods for calculating the number of tags in the transcripts, to compute the speaking speed of speakers and interpreters, and for computing décalage. We use manual methods for evaluating the clarity and challenges in source recordings, for expert feedback on interpreters behaviour, and for manual evaluation of the décalage method. We compare all these new findings with our previous results of manual annotation of interpreting strategies (see Figure 5 from our previous article).

4 Analysis of Source Speeches - Manual Analysis

Method and Settings: The manual analysis of source speeches consisted in both annotators listening to the five recordings and entering values for several criteria and free text comments in an Excel spreadsheet form. The criteria (with available values) included sound quality (*very good, good, bad*), speech intelligibility (*clear, medium, difficult to understand*), (dis-)fluency (*fluent, not*

fluent), number of topics, speakers' accent (*strong foreign accent, accent, no accent*), speakers' speed (*normal, fast, slow* - as perceived by the annotator), number of speakers, topic technicality of the source recording (*very technical, somewhat technical, very few technical words, not technical*).

Results: The manual analysis results are available online [4]. The cells in green show the points in which both annotators agreed. As we are aware that some of these criteria are not concretely defined, we run an objective automatic analysis (see Section 5). The feedback of A1 and A2 was that: M7-T1 and W2-T2 consisted in a conference presentation (with or without the session chair recorded), and W2-T1, W4-T1, and M7-T2 were panels; W2 were two women interpreters, who changed; in M7-T1 the speaker was reading and the interpreter was prepared; in W2-T2 the interpreter applied anticipation. As it can be seen from the online form, there is difference between the two annotators. What they mostly agree about is speech intelligibility, (dis)fluency, number of topics, number of speakers, topic technicality of the source speech, and a bit on speaker's speed. Specifically, M7-T1 had 1 speaker, M7-T2 was a panel with 8 speakers, W2-T1 had 6 or 7 speakers, W2-T2 had 2 speakers (one moderator), and W4-T1 had 6 speakers and was the only speech recording to have 3-4 topics.

5 Analysis of Source Speeches - Tags Analysis

Method and Settings: In order to complement the analysis in Section 4 with more objective numerical results, we counted the number of tags in the source recordings transcripts which were manually annotated by professional transcribers. In order to make the results comparable, we normalized the tags numbers per transcript length (divided per number of words) and then multiplied by 1000 to get a higher (but still comparable) numbers. Table 1 shows the tags and their definitions.

Our hypothesis is, as described by state-of-the-art research, that the presence of at least some of these tags may create challenges for interpreters (e.g. if the speakers make false starts [FALSE], hesitate [HES], repeat or correct themselves [REP] or if there is noise and music). *Unidentifiable* is an important tag, as if a word or phrase is not under-

---

[4]A1 and A2 manual speakers analysis is available at: http://tiny.cc/WAWManualSpeakerAnalysis

Tag	[FALSE]	[REP]	[INTER]	[HES]	[INTERJ]	[BREATH]
Meaning	False start	Repetition or Correction	Interruption	Hesitation	Interjection	Breathing
Tag	[LAUGH]	[APPLAUSE]	[MUSIC]	[NOISE]	[NE]	[UNK]
Meaning	Laugh	Applause	Music	Noise	Named Entity	Unidentifiable

Table 1: Tags annotated in WAW transcripts.

standable by transcribers it may also be such for interpreters. We also counted the Named Entities (NEs), as they correspond to names of people, locations and organizations and interpreters are usually supposed to render them correctly.

Results: We displayed only those tags whose value is above 0. Figure 2 shows the amount of tags per source recording which interpreters had to deal with (here we refer to recordings as "interpreter-transcript pair" for consistency). As it can be seen, the source recording with most tags was interpreted by W2 (W2-T1), the second one was M7-T2, while the source recording corresponding to W4-T1 had nearly no source speech tags at all.

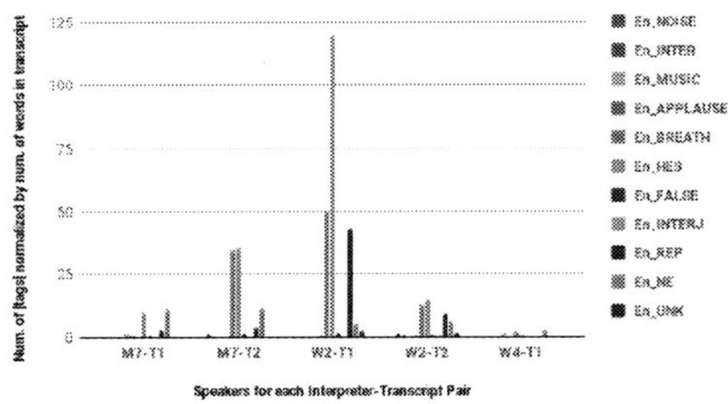

Figure 2: Number of transcription tags for the source speech of each session (normalized by number of words in the source transcript).

6 Analysis of Interpreters Décalage

In this section we propose a new automatic method for calculating the décalage of interpreter from speaker(s).

Gillies (2018) defines décalage as *"the time difference between what the speaker says and its reproduction by the interpreter in the target language"*.

We want to be able to access interpreters' décalage in the WAW corpus for two reasons: 1) to determine when and how often in our data longer décalage is used as a strategy (Cecot, 2001; Moser-Mercer, 1997) and 2) to take it into account when analyzing the potential cognitive difficulties of in-

terpreters. In fact longer décalage is generally to be avoided by interpreters as they should then keep more information in short-term memory and accuracy may significantly decrease (Lee, 2002). This is especially valid for interpreting between languages with highly different syntactic structures (Lee, 2002; Barik, 1975; Gile, 1997) such as English and Arabic (Bassam et al., 2014; Badr et al., 2009). Thus keeping décalage short can also be considered as an interpreting strategy.

Although décalage is an important feature and we wanted to implement it previously, we had a number of obstacles before being able to build this method. The biggest challenges were related to aligning source speech transcripts and interpreters transcripts. In fact interpreters transfer meaning and can completely restructure speaker's speech, make omissions, add words, and use completely different words than the standard translation equivalents.

Also, the alignment needed to be done at word level, which turned out to be very cumbersome and tedious to be performed manually; hence resorting to automatic alignment methods was a better option. This task had to include building or acquiring Automatic Speech Recognition (ASR) systems for both English and Arabic languages, to be able to automatically recognize words and mark them with their appropriate time-stamps.

6.1 Analysis of Interpreters: Décalage - Method and Evaluation

Transcripts alignment: The source speech and interpreters' transcripts were aligned by time and words-anchors were extracted using a bilingual dictionary. The anchors are Named Entities (NEs) and words that carry meaning (content words) - as opposed to frequent and functional words. We obtained the content words and NEs from the output of the part-of-speech (POS) taggers. To carry the alignment, we force-aligned the transcripts using our in-house ASR system (Khurana and Ali, 2016). The result of this process produced a transcript where each word is tagged with its offset time and duration.

POS tagging: Next, we used the part-of-speech tagger module of Farasa (Darwish et al., 2017) to POS tag the Arabic transcripts, and the Stanford POS tagger (Toutanova et al., 2003) for English. Additionally, we acquired a bilingual dictionary that was used for the alignment. The dictionary contains around 20k entries.

Computation of décalage: We compute décalage as the time between when the speaker pronounces a specific named entity (NE) or a content word and when the interpreter pronounces it (or its correspondent) using the onset reference. This time difference reflects the delay between when the interpreter hears a concept and when he is able to produce its correspondence in the target language.

Limitations of the Automatic Décalage Estimation Method: There might be instances in which the approach would not capture this lapse and the availability of these indicators could vary, based on the strategies that the interpreter choose to use. For example, the interpreter might choose to use a pronoun to replace a NE or a concept that was mentioned earlier (e.g. in cases of *summarizing* or *omission*). This will impact the number of anchors that are available for assessment and their alignment. Another inherent issue related to the source and target language pair is when the sentences are reordered differently between the source and target languages. We hypothesize that this would not be a major concern as this additional décalage could be shared across all transcripts/interpreters with the same language pair; but it might impact the comparison with other language pairs.

Décalage Method Evaluation: In order to test if our décalage calculation method is giving correct results, we run manual evaluation with our two annotators A1 and A2. Décalage was run on 16 interpreter-transcript pairs (two per interpreter, with two male interpreters - M7 and M1 and two female interpreters - W2 and W4), resulting in a total of 874 aligned décalage anchor word pairs. We selected semi-randomly from them 20 snippets of 10 consecutive lines (a total of 199). The snippets contained a representative variety of issues: named entities (person names, organizations, countries), content words (nouns, adjectives, verbs, adverbs), function words (like determiners and pronouns), several words which speakers repeated. The annotators had to label each aligned

word pair by providing a label among: *Valid, Invalid, Somewhat valid* and *I don't know*. Annotators were informed to not look for correct word translations only (as interpreters transfer sense), but to also check if the two words are equivalent in terms of being a part of groups of words, in which the speaker and interpreter talk about the same. We then compared their results and run inter-annotator agreement comparison. The evaluation showed that A1 marked **193 (96.98%) pairs as Valid**, 0 as Invalid, 3 as Somewhat valid, and 3 as "I don't know". A2 labeled **185 (92.96%) pairs as Valid**, 14 as Invalid, 0 as Somewhat valid and 0 as "I don't know". In terms of inter-annotator agreement, **the annotators agreed on <u>182</u> out of 199 pairs (both labeled as *Valid*)**; 11 had the combination Invalid (A2)-Valid (A1); 3 were Invalid (A2)-Somewhat valid (A1) and 3 - Valid (A2)-"I don't know" (A1) [5].

6.2 Analysis of Interpreters: Décalage - Results

Figure 3 shows the anchor-based décalages for the two sessions of the male interpreter M7, while Figure 4 - for the female interpreters W2 and W4. The dots are the single décalages per anchored pair, the line is the average décalage over time, and the width of the grey shaded area indicates the variation.

It is clear from Figure 3 that the décalages in M7-T1 are mostly small – Median of 3.630 secs and Mean of 4.235 secs (in light green); while in M7-T2 (in light blue) the dots are much more spread around and there are many more instances in which the décalage (delay) is high and has a Median of 5.250 secs and a Mean of 5.838 secs.

Figure 4, shows one session of interpreter W4 (W4-T1) and the two sessions of interpreter W2 (W2-T1 and W2-T2). While W2's décalage in T2 looks consistent (constant) across the whole session with a Median of 3.880 secs and a Mean of 4.874 secs (light blue line), W4 starts with a lower décalage but there is a significant increase in the delay as time passes (pink line). Something similar with a much steeper increase in Figure 4 can be observed for W2 in T1 (W2-T1, light green line), for which the ending décalage is approximately 14 seconds vs 2 seconds in the beginning.

---

[5]We run Cohen's kappa, but received a surprisingly low IAA (0.132), despite an agreement of 93% between the annotators. This result turned out to be a Cohen's kappa known paradox (Yarnold, 2016).

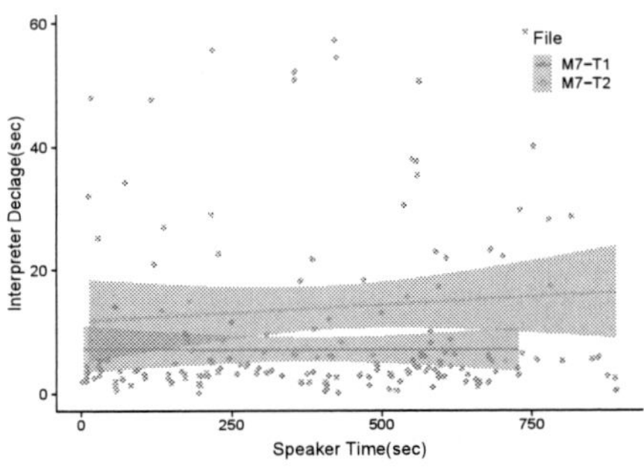

Figure 3: Comparison of interpreter's décalage between the two sessions of male interpreter (M7).

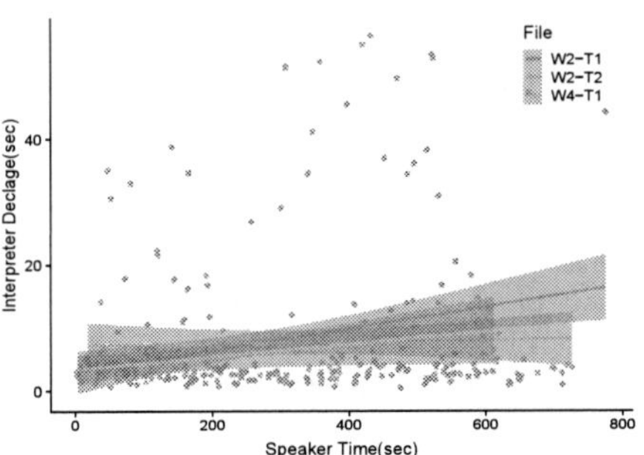

Figure 4: Comparison of interpreter's décalage between the sessions of female interpreters.

As shown above, while the process can be fully automated, challenges that are related to the domain and the availability of an ASR system that can provide the feeds are a major issue. Additionally, the accuracy of the lexicons is the weakest link of the proposed approach. The availability of this type of resource is strictly dependent on the language pair as well as on the domain. On the other hand, efforts by volunteers carrying the task of manually curating these resources and expanding them is a solution and a warranty for the approach.

7 Analysis of Speakers' and Interpreters' Speaking Speed

Method and Settings: As the manual annotation of speakers' speed in source recordings in Section 4 did not show much agreement between annotators (also because no objective definition was given), we wanted to complement our analysis with a more objective numerical approach. In this section we present an approximative calculation of average speaking speed per session of both

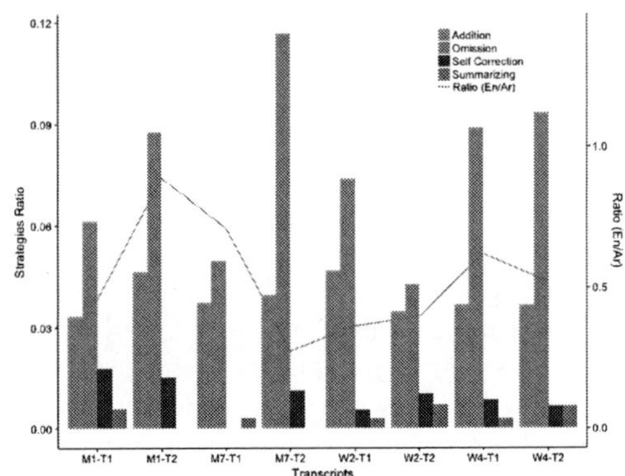

Figure 5: Annotated Strategies normalized by the transcript length in words for each session.

speakers (input rate) in source language recordings and interpreters. We do that by dividing the number of words in each transcript by the length of recordings in minutes. We do this first for the five speeches under consideration, and then in order to validate our approach and get general observations - for all the WAW corpus En-Ar speeches.

We realize that this is an approximative measure, as 1) speaking speed could vary during the session and 2) there are sessions with several speakers and/or interpreters. In future work we will use décalage's anchor points to calculate speaking speed in a more accurate way.

Results: Table 2 shows the results for the 5 sessions. The highest conference speakers' input rates (see column "En (words)") are in descending order for M7-T2, W4-T1, and W2-T2 (which were also indicated by A1 as *fast* speakers). The source speed of W2-T1 is nearly the same as for W2-T2, and M7-T1 is clearly the lowest speed. For matters of conformity with related work, we have converted the source input rate (speakers speed) into words/minute. According to (Pochhacker, 2015), an input rate of 100-120 words per minute is considered as "comfortable speech rate" (Pochhacker, 2015) and 150-180 words per minute is too high. Thus, the source input rates in M7-T2 and W4-T1 were exceptionally high, while in M7-T1 - near the ideal range. In terms of interpreters (see column "Ar (words)") M7-T2 has the lowest average speed and M7-T1 - the highest. This shows large variability of the same interpreter (M7). In addition to this, M7-T1 and M7-T2 exhibit the opposite correlation between speaker's and interpreter's speed: among the 5 speeches M7-T1 has the lowest speaker's speed and the highest interpreter's speed (also close to speaker's speed); M7-T2 has the highest speaker's speed and the lowest interpreter's speed. In terms of difference between speakers' speed and interpreter's speed M7-T2 has the highest value of 108.94 and the lowest difference value is 2.2 for M7-T1 (which means that in average the interpreter is moving almost at the same speed as speaker). It can be also seen that in M7-T1 speaker's (En) and interpreter's (Ar) number of words is nearly the same (differently from the other 4 recordings). According to A2's feedback in Section 4 in M7-T1 the speaker is reading (no spontaneous speech element) and the interpreter seems well prepared (according to both annotators the interpreter rendered correctly all statistical details), and thus most probably had the speech beforehand.

In order to have a wider picture of what our approximate speed calculation method generates, Figure 6 shows the approximate speaking speed results for all source and interpreters recordings in the WAW corpus for the interpreting direction En-Ar. Clearly there is a repeated general tendency across all speeches with the speed of interpreters being generally lower (around 1/2 from the speed of the source language speaker(s)).

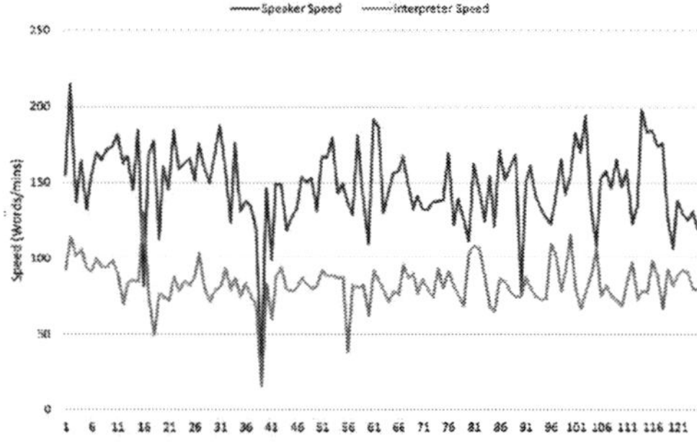

Figure 6: Speakers and Interpreters average speed for English into Arabic.

8 Analysis of Interpreters - Tags

Method and Settings: Similarly to speakers, we counted the number of tags in the interpreters (target language) recordings transcripts which were manually annotated by professional transcribers during transcription. We applied exactly the same method which we used for speakers (described in Section 5). We analyzed the same tags as in Table 1. We base our analysis on the assumption that hesitations, repetitions and false starts in interpreters' transcripts may show that the interpreter is challenged (Cecot, 2001). For example, it is known that hesitation pauses and other disfluencies of interpreters can be caused by difficulties in syntactic and lexical planning of discourse (Cecot, 2001). For matters of consistency we analyze all the available tags.

Results: Figure 7 shows the distribution of tags per interpreter-transcript pair. As in Figure 2, only existing tags are displayed. Clearly W2-T1 and W4-T1 have the highest number of tags. W2-T1 has an exceptionally high number of hesitations and W4-T1 has an exceptionally high number of breathing annotated. The lowest number is for M7-T2 which has only some [NOISE] tags.

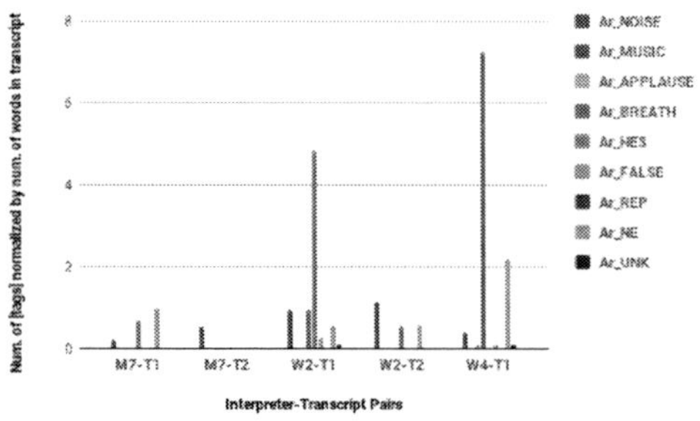

Figure 7: Number of transcription tags for the interpreter's output for each session (normalized by number of words in the interpreter's transcript).

9 Discussion

Analysis of interpreters: W2 interpreted the highest number of sessions (see Figure 1). Next are M7 and W4. The average session length for W4 is higher than of M7 and slightly higher than W2. In M7-T1 and M7-T2, speaker's input rate and interpreter's speaking speed confirm the large difference in strategies used by M7 (see Figure 5). Also, the highest input rates in M7-T2 and W4-T1 could explain the largest number of omissions in these two interpreters' sessions.

Analysis of speaker-interpreter combinations:

<u>M7-T1</u> - 1 speaker (speaker reading and interpreter prepared), second shortest duration. Had a low number of annotated strategies (additions, omissions and summarizing), constant décalage from speaker of in average 3-4 seconds.

<u>M7-T2</u> - panel. Had a relatively high number of

	Duration (sec)	En (words)	Ar (words)	En words/min	Ar words/min	Diff.
M7-T1	742.2	1341	1315	108.4	106.2	<u>2.2</u>
M7-T2	907.8	2656	1007	**175.54**	66.6	**108.94**
W2-T1	859.2	1959	1448	136.79	100.8	35.99
W2-T2	731.8	1678	1137	137.58	93	44.58
W4-T1	1043.5	2737	1423	157.37	81.6	75.77

Table 2: Speakers and interpreters speed (rounded) in the 5 analyzed speeches.

speakers' [BREATH] and [HES]. Interpreter had no tags, except for some [NOISE]. Had the highest number of annotated omissions (see Figure 5) and had also additions and self-corrections. This is the session with highest input rate and the interpreter with lowest speed. Interpreter must have skipped a lot (and used some generalizations according to A1) to maintain low speed. As we have seen in Figure 3 his décalage is higher and is increasing with the duration of the session. According to A2 the interpreter seems to be using silence and pauses to keep décalage lower.

W2-T1 - panel (2 interpreters), the speaker had a high number of hesitations [HES], breathing [BREATH] and repetitions [REP] (see Figure 2). The interpreter had a relatively high number of [HES]. So, there was a high number of hesitations in both speakers and interpreter (compare Figures 2 and 7). Had a much higher number of omissions and higher number of additions than W2-T2. We see a steep increase in décalage which ends with over 14 seconds.

W2-T2 1 speaker (2 interpreters), shortest recording duration. Interpreter applied anticipation. Very technical speech, speakers talked with lower voice. The lowest number of strategies (but all 4 are used). Had a nearly constant décalage (a bit increasing towards the end) of in average 3-4 seconds.

W4-T1 - panel, longest duration. The interpreter had a high number of [BREATH] and the highest number of NEs, which visibly does not correspond to the number of NEs in the speakers' transcript. Further analysis of the [NE] tag is necessary. Has a large number of omissions annotated. Décalage is also increasing, but not so steep as for W2-T1. Also here, the speakers' average input rate (according to our calculations) is high.

10 Conclusions and Future Research

Our aim was to test what amount and quality of insights we can gather from the WAW corpus with our new methods - a combination of automatic approaches and interpreters expertise. We presented an automatic décalage method which was tested on the English-Arabic language pair and showed to have high evaluation results from two expert human annotators.

We analyzed in detail five conference sessions (as they had interpreting strategies manually annotated) and provided general observations about multiple interpreters. We discovered that the dependence between speakers' variables (e.g. input rate and hesitations) and interpreters variables (e.g. décalage and strategies used) is very complex.

We found that: 1) manual expert analysis of an experienced researcher with interpreting and Interpreting Studies background enormously enriches automatic analysis findings; 2) the data existing in our corpus, accompanied by the new automatic décalage method provides rich insights.

Our analysis showed that among the issues that create challenges for interpreters and may generate increasing décalage and a higher amount of used strategies are: 1) large number of speakers; 2) spontaneous speech (as in question-answering sessions and panels vs prepared presentations or reading); 3) speakers' hesitations and repetitions; 4) high speakers input rate (see especially W4-T1 and M7-T2). We also found out that interpreters have much lower speaking speed than speakers' input rate, which adds to our previous and current observations that interpreters usually generate much fewer words.

As future work we need to run our experiments on a larger number of conference sessions to get general observations, to deepen our analysis of input rate and interpreters' delivery rate and test our methods on other corpora and language pairs.

11 Acknowledgements

We would like to thank the HIT-IT 2019 reviewers for their comments and Katsiaryna Panasuyk (A3) for her feedback.

References

Ahmed Abdelali, Irina Temnikova, Samy Hedaya, and Stephan Vogel. 2018. The WAW Corpus: The First Corpus of Interpreted Speeches and their Translations for English and Arabic. In LREC 2018. (ELRA), Miyazaki, Japan.

Ibrahim Badr, Rabih Zbib, and James Glass. 2009. Syntactic phrase reordering for english-to-arabic statistical machine translation. In Proceedings of the 12th Conference of the European Chapter of the Association for Computational Linguistics. Association for Computational Linguistics, pages 86–93.

Srinivas Bangalore, Vivek Kumar Rangarajan Sridhar, Prakash Kolan, Ladan Golipour, and Aura Jimenez. 2012. Real-time incremental speech-to-speech translation of dialogs. In Proceedings of the 2012 Conference of the North American Chapter of the Association for Computational Linguistics: Human Language Technologies. Association for Computational Linguistics, pages 437–445.

Henri C Barik. 1973. Simultaneous interpretation: Temporal and quantitative data. Language and speech 16(3):237–270.

Henri C Barik. 1975. Simultaneous interpretation: Qualitative and linguistic data. Language and speech 18(3):272–297.

Hammo Bassam, Moubaiddin Asma, Obeid Nadim, and Tuffaha Abeer. 2014. Formal description of arabic syntactic structure in the framework of the government and binding theory. Computación y Sistemas 18(3):611–625.

Claudio Bendazzoli and Annalisa Sandrelli. 2005. An approach to corpus-based interpreting studies: Developing EPIC (european parliament interpreting corpus). In MuTra 2005–Challenges of Multidimensional Translation: Conference Proceedings. pages 1–12.

Claudio Bendazzoli and Annalisa Sandrelli. 2009. Corpus-based interpreting studies: Early work and future prospects. Tradumàtica: traducció i tecnologies de la informació i la comunicació 1(7).

Michela Cecot. 2001. Pauses in simultaneous interpretation: A contrastive analysis of professional interpreters performances. The interpreters newsletter 11:63–85.

Fahim Dalvi, Yifan Zhang, Sameer Khurana, Nadir Durrani, Hassan Sajjad, Ahmed Abdelali, Hamdy Mubarak, Ahmed Ali, and Stephan Vogel. 2017. QCRI live speech translation system. EACL 2017 page 61.

Kareem Darwish, Hamdy Mubarak, Ahmed Abdelali, and Mohamed Eldesouki. 2017. Arabic pos tagging: Dont abandon feature engineering just yet. In Proceedings of the Third Arabic Natural Language Processing Workshop. pages 130–137.

Bart Defrancq. 2015. Corpus-based research into the presumed effects of short EVS. Interpreting 17(1):26–45.

Emilia Iglesias Fernández. 2015. Making sense of interpreting difficulty through corpus-based observation. Interpreting Quality: A Look Around and Ahead 19:35.

Daniel Gile. 1997. Conference interpreting as a cognitive management problem. Applied Psychology-London-Sage- 3:196–214.

Andrew Gillies. 2018. Conference Interpreting: A Students Practice Book. Routledge.

He He, Jordan L Boyd-Graber, and Hal Daumé III. 2016. Interpretese vs. translationese: The uniqueness of human strategies in simultaneous interpretation. In HLT-NAACL. pages 971–976.

He He, Alvin Grissom II, John Morgan, Jordan Boyd-Graber, and Hal Daumé III. 2015. Syntax-based rewriting for simultaneous machine translation. In Proceedings of the 2015 Conference on Empirical Methods in Natural Language Processing. pages 55–64.

Sameer Khurana and Ahmed Ali. 2016. QCRI advanced transcription system (QATS) for the Arabic multi-dialect broadcast media recognition: MGB-2 challenge. In Spoken Language Technology Workshop (SLT), 2016 IEEE.

Paweł Korpal. 2012. Omission in simultaneous interpreting as a deliberate act, Intercultural Studies Group Universitat Rovira i Virgili, chapter 9, pages 103–111.

Tae-Hyung Lee. 2002. Ear voice span in english into korean simultaneous interpretation. Meta: Journal des traducteurs/Meta: Translators' Journal 47(4):596–606.

Barbara Moser-Mercer. 1996. Quality in interpreting: Some methodological issues. LINT.

Barbara Moser-Mercer. 1997. Beyond curiosity: Can interpreting research meet the challenge? In G.M. Fountain J.H. Danks, G.M. Shreve and M.K. McBeath, editors, Cognitive Processes in Translation and Interpreting. Sage Publications, London, pages 176–195.

Jan Niehues, Thai Son Nguyen, Eunah Cho, Thanh-Le Ha, Kevin Kilgour, Markus Müller, Matthias Sperber, Sebastian Stüker, and Alex Waibel. 2016. Dynamic transcription for low-latency speech translation. In Interspeech. pages 2513–2517.

Pierre Oléron and Hubert Nanpon. 1965. Recherches sur la traduction simultanée. Journal de psychologie normale et pathologique .

Takahiro Ono, Hitomi Tohyama, and Shigeki Matsubara. 2008. Construction and analysis of word-level time-aligned simultaneous interpretation corpus. In LREC 2008.

Matthias Paulik and Alex Waibel. 2009. Automatic translation from parallel speech: Simultaneous interpretation as mt training data. In Automatic Speech Recognition & Understanding, 2009. ASRU 2009. IEEE Workshop on. IEEE, pages 496–501.

Sonia Pio. 2003. The relation between st delivery rate and quality in simultaneous interpretation. The Interpreters Newsletter 12:69–100.

Koen Plevoets and Bart Defrancq. 2016. The effect of informational load on disfluencies in interpreting. Translation and Interpreting Studies. The Journal of the American Translation and Interpreting Studies Association 11(2):202–224.

Franz Pochhacker. 2015. Routledge encyclopedia of interpreting studies. Routledge.

Květa Podhajská. 2008. Time lag in simultaneous interpretation from english into czech and its dependence on text type. Folia Translatologica 10:87–110.

Mariachiara Russo, Claudio Bendazzoli, Bart Defrancq, et al. 2018. Making way in corpus-based interpreting studies. Springer.

Philipp H Schmid and Adrian Garside. 2005. Method and apparatus for reducing latency in speech-based applications. US Patent 6,961,694.

Hiroaki Shimizu, Graham Neubig, Sakriani Sakti, Tomoki Toda, and Satoshi Nakamura. 2013. Constructing a speech translation system using simultaneous interpretation data. In Proceedings of International Workshop on Spoken Language Translation (IWSLT).

Vivek Kumar Rangarajan Sridhar, John Chen, and Srinivas Bangalore. 2013a. Corpus analysis of simultaneous interpretation data for improving real time speech translation. In INTERSPEECH. pages 3468–3472.

Vivek Kumar Rangarajan Sridhar, John Chen, Srinivas Bangalore, Andrej Ljolje, and Rathinavelu Chengalvarayan. 2013b. Segmentation strategies for streaming speech translation. In Proceedings of the 2013 Conference of the North American Chapter of the Association for Computational Linguistics: Human Language Technologies. pages 230–238.

Irina Temnikova, Ahmed Abdelali, Samy Hedaya, Stephan Vogel, and Aishah Al Daher. 2017. Interpreting strategies annotation in the waw corpus. RANLP 2017 page 36.

Sárka Timarová, Barbara Dragsted, and Inge G Hansen. 2011. Time lag in translation and interpreting: A methodological exploration. Methods and strategies in process research: Integrative approaches in translation studies pages 121–146.

Kristina Toutanova, Dan Klein, Christopher D Manning, and Yoram Singer. 2003. Feature-rich part-of-speech tagging with a cyclic dependency network. In Proceedings of the 2003 Conference of the North American Chapter of the Association for Computational Linguistics on Human Language Technology-Volume 1. Association for computational Linguistics, pages 173–180.

Alexander Waibel and Christian Fuegen. 2012. Simultaneous translation of open domain lectures and speeches. US Patent 8,090,570.

Paul R Yarnold. 2016. Oda vs. π and κ: paradoxes of kappa. chance (PAC; 0= no inter-rater agreement, 100= perfect agreement) 2:7.

Towards a Proactive MWE Terminological Platform for

Cross-Lingual Mediation in the Age of Big Data

Benjamin K. Tsou
City University of Hong Kong
Hong Kong University of Science and
Technology
Chilin (HK) Ltd
btsou99@gmail.com

Junru Nie
Hong Kong University of Science and
Technology
Chilin (HK) Ltd
ulricanie@gmail.com

Kapo Chow
Chilin (HK) Ltd
kapo.rclis@gmail.com

Yuan Yuan
Hong Kong University of Science and
Technology
Chilin (HK) Ltd
belleyuan26@gmail.com

Abstract

The emergence of China as a global economic power in the 21st Century has brought about surging needs for cross-lingual and cross-cultural mediation, typically performed by translators. Advances in Artificial Intelligence and Language Engineering have been bolstered by Machine learning and suitable Big Data cultivation. They have helped to meet some of the translator's needs, though the technical specialists have not kept pace with the practical and expanding requirements in language mediation. One major technical and linguistic hurdle involves words outside the vocabulary of the translator or the lexical database he/she consults, especially Multi-Word Expressions (Compound Words) in technical subjects. A further problem lies in the multiplicity of renditions of a term in the target language.

This paper discusses a proactive approach following the successful extraction and application of sizable bilingual Multi-Word Expressions (Compound Words) for language mediation in technical subjects, which do not fall within the expertise of typical translators, who have inadequate appreciation of the range of new technical tools available to help him/her. Our approach draws on the personal reflections of translators and teachers of translation and is based on the prior R&D efforts relating to 300,000 comparable Chinese-English patents. The subsequent protocol we have developed aims to be proactive in meeting four identified practical challenges in technical translation (e.g. patents). It has broader economic implication in the Age of Big Data (Tsou et al, 2015) and Trade War, as the workload, if not, the challenges, increasingly cannot be met by currently available front-line translators. We shall demonstrate how new tools can be harnessed to spearhead the application of language technology not only in language mediation but also in the "teaching" and "learning" of translation. It shows how a better appreciation of their needs may enhance the contributions of the technical specialists, and thus enhance the resultant synergetic benefits.

1 Two Converging Paths in Cross-Language Mediation

Translation and cross-lingual mediation are no longer exclusively human efforts but draw on many indispensable tools and resources which have resulted from successful and fruitful research and development efforts in natural language processing (Bowker and Pastor, 2015). We highlight four major stages in the translator's workflow, in which distinct technical efforts could enhance productivity (Zaretskaya et al., 2015).

1.1 From the Perspective of Translators

The translator's workflow consists of four major stages. When working with a technical document, even if he/she has excellent command of the languages concerned, it is inevitable that there will be unfamiliar terms outside his/her active vocabulary.

Temnikova, I, Orăsan, C., Corpas Pastor, G., and Mitkov, R. (eds.) (2019) *Proceedings of the 2nd Workshop on Human-Informed Translation and Interpreting Technology (HiT-IT 2019)*, Varna, Bulgaria, September 5 - 6, pages 116–121.

https://doi.org/10.26615/issn.2683-0078.2019_014

A. To cope with these challenges, appropriate lexical resources and other reference materials have to be consulted. Therefore, he/she needs to have convenient access to useful and easily manageable databases. The major challenge is the *Accessibility* of suitable reference materials.

B. Quite often dictionaries provide multiple renditions of given terms appropriate to only some appropriate domains. He/she has to adjust his/her selection for the translation task at hand. The major hurdle at this stage is *Adjustability* in selecting the suitable subset of renditions within the right domain.

C. Having access to the multiple renditions is not sufficient, and access to authentic examples on the use of the alternate renditions would be helpful for making his/her selection. The issue of *Accountability* of the lexical variations is a major requirement at this stage.

D. For self-improvement, the conscientious translator or the student of translation would find it useful to be able to browse through a new relevant lexical database in serendipity search so as to uncover related and associated terms and renditions. This may be seen as a desirable feature of *Adaptability* of the database whereby the user may advance his/her lexical knowledge.

1.2 From the Perspective of the Computer Scientist

To help to cope with the four A issues: ***Accessibly, Adjustability, Accountability*** and ***Adaptability*** concerning the lexical hurdles of the translator, the computer scientist's concern would be to provide a suitable database which would contain the relevant terms and translation tools for the translator. He/she would need to focus on several distinct tasks (Sections 1.1 and 1.2 are cross-referenced):

A. To **secure** the best database in order to produce the best lexical resources for the translator. He/she would be concerned with the identification and access a suitable textual corpus and the use of the best algorithms to accomplish the matching of bilingual terms.

Objective indices such as Precision and Recall, F measures which are purely statistically based, would be upmost on his/her mind (Mitkov, 2016, 2017). As he/she is in most cases unlikely to be knowledgeable with wide-ranging linguistic issues in both languages, he/she would be using the *"Happy Majority Approach"* whereby meeting the statistically significant requirements of the majority would be happily acceptable under normal circumstances. The professional translator demands much more just as his/her demands are incrementally met.

B. The ideal one-to-one matching of the terms and their meanings fall by the wayside very readily and the computer scientist has to deal with the "one-to-how many" problems. It is a major challenge to determine the full range of alternate target renditions and to uncover and select the subset of the results to suit the needs of the users. For example, a common term "multiplication" in arithmetic refers to specifically the number of times an item or a sum is replicated (乘法). However, in biological sciences, it refers to reproductive generation (繁殖，衍生) without the precision required in arithmetic, and must be translated accordingly. The average individual would have the arithmetic sense foregrounded in his/her mind, and only when bilingual texts in English and Chinese are contrasted would the additional sense of reproduction be likely brought to mind. This provision of the multiple alternate renditions is very much appreciated by the translators.

C. In the longer term a necessary feature would be an updated database of terms with representative authentic examples from authoritative technical document (Lu et al., 2011). Such a database would be welcome by the translators as a dynamically maintained thesaurus.

D. The provision of knowledge graph and semantic network on the basis of large textual databases has made considerable advances.

E. It is especially useful for the translator and language mediator who, for self-improvement, is keen to search beyond a single target word to explore related and associated words.

2 Pairing Cross-Lingual Terms

Based on the bilingual MWE database, we have constructed a cross-lingual search MWE platform – PatentLex (Tsou et al., 2017). The following are some examples of search results. Based on the meta information of each patent, we are able to provide insightful statistics through the searchquery function, as can be seen in Table1.

Matched Term （English）	Renditions (Chinese)
heat pump	1. 热泵(98.97%) heat-pump 2. 加热泵(0.67%) add-heat-pump 3. 供热泵(0.28%) supply-heat-pump 4. 受热泵(0.07%) receive-heat-pump
absorption heat pump	吸收式热泵(100%)
air conditioners and heat pumps	1. 空调和热泵(66.66%) 2. 空气调节器和热泵(33.33%)
bernoulli heat pump	1. 柏努利热泵(59.25%) 2. 伯努利热泵(40.74%)
bernoulli heat pumps	伯努利热泵(100%)
chemical heat pump	化学热泵(100%)
chemical heat pumps	化学热泵(100%)
conventional heat pumps	常规热泵(100%)

Table 1: Multiple Chinese renditions of *Heat Pump*.

2.1 "Heat Pump"

Of the four possible renditions: "热泵" (heat-pump), "加热泵" (add-heat-pump), "供热泵" (supply-heat-pump) and "受热泵" (receive heat pump), it is noteworthy that some of these Chinese renditions are more informative than the English term. For example, heat pump in English has been rendered as "加热泵" (add-heat-pump) which is a better rendition as it indicates one function of the heat pump in Table 2 below.

No.	IPC[1]	English	Chinese
1	C09	While the primary purpose of refrigeration is to remove energy at low temperature, the primary purpose of a **heat pump** is to add energy at higher temperature.	致冷的首要目的是在低温时除去能量，而**热泵**的首要目的是在高温时增加能量。
2	H02	The potential benefits include one or more of reduced air noise, better dehumidification, warmer air in **heat pump** mode, or the like.	其潜在益处包括下列的一种或几种，即减小的噪音、更好的除湿、**加热泵**模式中温热的空气或类似情况。

Table 2: Authentic examples.

The advantages of these optional details are two-fold: they provide a rudimentary semantic network of associated concepts of the original target terms, and they also alert the translators that the search term may have other possible renditions when considered in a larger context.

2.2 "Wafer"

In the Table 3 below, a comparison is made between the provisions made by a well-known Chinese language resource: HOWNET (http://dict.cnki.net/dict_result.aspx), and by PatentLex. HOWNET's source data is not limited to technical documents, and their bilingual search engine also provides different renditions with information on relative frequencies, though not according to domains.

---

[1] IPC: International Patent Classification.

PatentLex	HOWNET
1. 晶片(95.29%)	1. 晶片（32.65%）
2. 硅片(2.9%)	2. 硅片（58.73%）
3. 圆片(1.53%)	3. 干胶片（0%）
4. 晶圆(0.13%)	4. 圆片（8.63%）
5. 糯米纸(0.07%)	
6. 薄脆饼(0.06%)	

Table 3: Alternate renditions of *Wafer* in Chinese and English.

It can be seen that both HOWNET and PatentLex offer alternate renditions of this technical term. However, PatentLex offers 2 more renditions than HOWNET. Furthermore, HOWNET's third rendition shows "干胶片" with 0% of usage, whereas it is not found in PatentLex's technical literature. PatentLex's "晶片"(95.29%) is the top choice in Patentlex whereas the top choice item from HOWNET "硅片"(58.73%) has only 2.9% usage in the technical texts represented by PatentLex. The broader search results of the term *Wafer* are as follows.

Matched Term （English）	Renditions (Chinese)
1.wafer	1. 晶片(95.29%) 2. 硅片(2.9%) 3. 圆片(1.53%) 4. 晶圆(0.13%) 5. 糯米纸(0.07%) 6. 薄脆饼(0.06%)
2.adjacent wafers	1. 相邻晶片(72.97%) 2. 相邻板片(27.02%)
3.bare silicon wafer	裸硅晶片(100%)
4.bonded wafers	键合的晶片(100%)
5.bottom side of the wafer	晶片底面(100%)
6.applied to the wafer	1. 施加到晶片(87.17%) 2. 应用到晶片(12.82%)
7.attached to the wafer	附着到晶片(100%)
8.backside wafer pressure	背面的晶片压力(100%)

Table 4：Fuzzy search of *Wafer*.

Some authentic examples from a wide range of alternative renditions are given in Table5.

No.	IPC[2]	English	Chinese
1	H01	Therefore, a center of rotation of the semiconductor **wafer** W can be kept in a constant position.	因此，半导体**晶片** W 的旋转中心可以被保持在恒定位置。
2	C08	The water droplet contact angle was measured within 2 or 3 seconds of placing the droplet 64 on the coated **wafer** surface.	在 2 或 3 秒内测量放置于涂布**硅片**表面上的水滴接触角。
3	A61	The implant 102 is preferably formed of relatively thin **wafer** of biologically compatible material.	植入物 102 较佳地由生物学上相容的材料做成的相当薄的**圆片**形成。
4	C07	The compound of Formula (I) can also be incorporated into a candy, a **wafer**, and/or tongue tape formulation for administration as a "quick-dissolve" medicament.	还可以将式（I）的化合物掺入到糖果、**糯米纸**和 / 或舌粘带制剂以 " 速溶 " 药物的形式给药。
5	A21	The present invention therefore addresses the problem of how to provide an approximately circular **wafer** which also has the desired crispness.	因此，本发明致力于如何提供一种大体上为圆形的、同时又具备理想的松脆度的**薄脆饼**制品的问题。

Table 5: Authentic examples of alternate renditions.

It may be noted that 糯米纸 "glutinous rice paper" (No.5 Table4) and 薄脆饼 "thin crisp cake"(No.6 Table4) are generally not technical but culinary terms. Nonetheless they can be found in the

---

2 IPC: International Patent Classification.

technical database of PatentLex under medical sciences (C07, Table5) and food industry (A21, Table5) respectively rather than just in a general language resource database.

3 Lexi Scanning

Prior to being able to access alternate renditions of a given technical term, the translator is confronted by the related and practical problem of encountering words which are altogether out of his/her vocabulary. Thus, a platform through which a translator may submit a text he/she has to work on and which could provide indications of all the embedded terms in the database through highlighting would be very much welcome. Such a provision is made by PatentLex with 1 million entries of preloaded bilingual MWE's (Tian et al., 2014; Tsou et al., 2018, 2019). The process of derivation also produced parallel sentences useful for MT research and MT evaluation (Goto et al., 2012, 2013).

4. Mining Knowledge Graph

We can construct a knowledge graph based on the bilingual term database, together with the details of the distribution of the alternate renditions. This makes use of dynamic information drawn from authentic patent documents and compiled statistics, rather than static information as found in ordinary dictionaries or handcrafted web of semantic terms. This reflects real world usage and also enables knowledge map navigation through the links between different terms and concepts.

For example, from "channel", we can obtain a list of possible related renditions in both languages with their relative frequencies, as illustrated in the chart below. If we click on a target English word "channel"(1), we will be led to 6 Chinese renditions (a) 通道(10.92%); (b) 途徑(0.02%); (c) 頻道(3.06%); (d) 路線(0.01%); (e) 槽(2.55%); (f) 信道(30.89%), each with its frequency of usage indicated. If we then choose one of the Chinese nodes, for example, (a)通道(10.92%), we are led to 5 other English terms besides the original relevant "channel" such as (2) aisle (0.04%); (3)passageway (0.49%); (4) access tunnel (0.4%); (5) conduit (6.86%); (6) passage (17.22%). We could proceed further by clicking on one of term such as (5) conduit(6.86%), and three Chinese actual renditions will be indicated: (g)導 管(5.88%); (h)管 線

(2.72%); (i)管道(41.36%). This dynamic thesaurus would facilitate the work of the protocol user. If we choose to search more deeply by following one of the renditions, such as "通道", we will obtain another set of renditions and percentages. Likewise, we can drill deeper and navigate along the rendition "conduit" and uncover another set of 3 renditions "導管", "管線" and "管道". The flowchart below illustrates the paths of navigation.

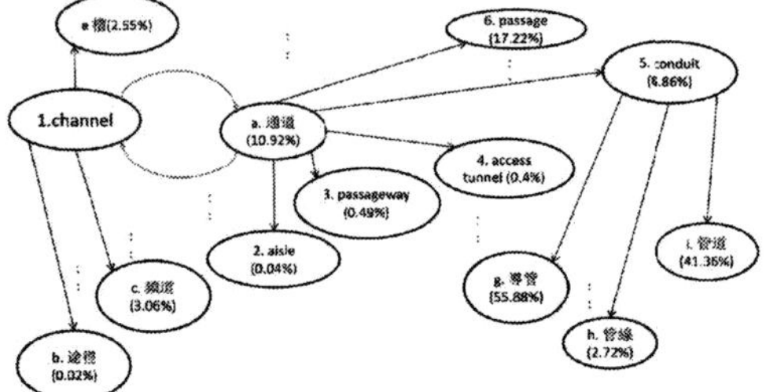

Figure 1: Flow chart: "Channel" vs "通道" bilingual knowledge graph navigation.

The provision of bilingual-knowledge graphs such as represented by the above flow chart would be useful for multilingual as well as monolingual searches.

5. Concluding Remarks

In the Age of Big Data, there is easy availability of data for developing resources and tools for translators and cross-language mediation (Tsou, 2018, 2019; Tsou et al., 2018). Four key stages in the workflow of translators have been identified with four overlapping areas in mature and developing languages technology. On the basis of an expanding database of more than one million entries of highly valued bilingual multi-word expressions in the technical fields we have developed a bilingual MWE platform, which shows how an articulated protocol could be organized proactively for translators with purposeful utilization of NLP results and tools. (Tsou et al, 2019) While some of the features are found in existing tools such as Trados (https://www.sdl.com/software-and-services/translation-software/terminology-management/sdl-multiterm/) and HOWNET, for example, Patentlex has attempted to incorporate all of them into a single platform. It is hoped that the welcomed coordinated approach underlying the PatentLex platform will allow similar efforts to be attempted for other language pairs.

References

Guihong Cao, Jianfeng Gao and Jianyun Nie. 2007. A System to Mine Large-scale Bilingual Dictionaries from Monolingual Web Pages. In Proceedings of MT Summit, pages 57-64.

Chiang, David. 2007. *Hierarchical phrase-based translation. Computational Linguistics*, 33(2), pages 201–228.

Fujii, Atsushi, Masao Utiyama, Mikio Yamamoto, and Takehito Utsuro. 2008. Overview of the patent translation task at the NTCIR-7 workshop. In Proceedings of the NTCIR-7 Workshop, pages 389-400. Tokyo, Japan.

Fujii, Atsushi, Masao Utiyama, Mikio Yamamoto, Takehito Utsuro, Terumasa Ehara, Hiroshi Echizen-ya and Sayori Shimohata. 2010. Overview of the patent translation task at the NTCIR-8 workshop. In Proceedings of the NTCIR-8 Workshop. Tokyo, Japan.

Isao Goto, Bin Lu, Ka Po Chow, Sumita Eiichiro, and Benjamin Tsou. 2012. "Overview of the Patent Translation Task at the NTCIR-9 Workshop". In Proceedings of the NTCIR-9 Workshop, pages 559-578. Tokyo.

Isao Goto, Bin Lu, Ka Po Chow, Sumita Eiichiro, and Benjamin Tsou. 2013. Overview of the patent machine translation task at the NTCIR-10 workshop. Proceedings of NTCIR-10 Workshop Meeting.

Bin Lu, Benjamin Tsou, Tao Jiang, Jingbo Zhu, and Olivia Kwong. 2011. "Mining parallel knowledge from comparable patents". In Ontology Learning and Knowledge Discovery Using the Web: Challenges and Recent Advances, pages 247-271. IGI Global.

Ruslan, Mitkov. 2016. "Computational Phraseology light: automatic translation of multiword expressions without translation resources." Yearbook of Phraseology 7.1 pages 149-166.

Ruslan, Mitkov. 2017. "Computational and Corpus-Based Phraseology: Second International Conference", Europhras 2017, London, UK, November 13-14, Proceedings. Vol. 10596. Springer.

Liang Tian, Fai Wong, and Sam Chao. 2011. *Phrase Oriented Word Alignment Method.* In Wang, Hai Feng (Ed.), Proceedings of the 7th China Workshop on Machine Translation, pages 237–250. Xiamen, China.

Liang Tian, Derek F. Wong, Lidia S. Chao, and Francisco Oliveira. 2014. *A Relationship: Word Alignment, Phrase Table, and Translation Quality. The Scientific World Journal*, pages 1–13.

Benjamin K. Tsou. 2018. Patent Translation and Text Analysis: Opportunities and Challenges in the Age of Big Data. 9TH CHINA PATENT ANNUAL CONFERENCE. Beijing.

Benjamin K. Tsou, Derek Wong, and Kapo Chow. 2017 Successful Generation of Bilingual Chinese-English Multi-word Expressions from Large Scale Parallel Corpora: An Experimental Approach, paper presented at EUROPHRAS. London.

Benjamin K. Tsou, Min-yu Zhao, Bi-wei Pan, and Ka-po Chow. 2018. The Age of Big Data and AI: Challenges and Opportunities for Technical Translation 4.0 and Relevant Training. Translators Association of China (TAC) Conference. Beijing.

Benjamin K. Tsou and Kapo Chow. 2019. From the cultivation of comparable corpora to harvesting from them: A quantitative and qualitative exploration. Proceedings of the 12th Workshop on Building and Using Comparable Corpora. Varna, Bulgaria.

Benjamin K. Tsou and Olivia Kwong. 2015. LIVAC as a Monitoring Corpus for Tracking Trends beyond Linguistics. In Tsou, Benjamin, and Kwong, Olivia., (eds.), Linguistic Corpus and Corpus Linguistics in the Chinese Context (Journal of Chinese Linguistics Monograph Series No.25). Hong Kong: The Chinese University Press, pages 447-471.

Dekai Wu, and Xuanyin Xia. 1994. Learning an English-Chinese lexicon from a parallel corpus, In Proceedings of the First Conference of the Association for Machine Translation in the Americas.

Anna Zaretskaya, Gloria Corpas Pastor and Miriam Seghiri. 2015. "Translators' requirements for translation technologies: A user survey." New Horizons in Translation and Interpreting Studies, pages 133-134.

Lynne Bowker and Gloria Corpas Pastor. 2015. "Translation technology." *The Oxford Handbook of Computational Linguistics 2nd edition.*

Exploring Adequacy Errors in Neural Machine Translation with the Help of Cross-Language Aligned Word Embeddings

Michael Ustaszewski

University of Innsbruck, Department of Translation Studies

`michael.ustaszewski@uibk.ac.at`

Abstract

Neural machine translation (NMT) was shown to produce more fluent output than phrase-based statistical (PBMT) and rule-based machine translation (RBMT). However, improved fluency makes it more difficult for post editors to identify and correct adequacy errors, because unlike RBMT and SMT, in NMT adequacy errors are frequently not anticipated by fluency errors. Omissions and additions of content in otherwise flawlessly fluent NMT output are the most prominent types of such adequacy errors, which can only be detected with reference to source texts. This contribution explores the degree of semantic similarity between source texts, NMT output and post edited output. In this way, computational semantic similarity scores (cosine similarity) are related to human quality judgments. The analyses are based on publicly available NMT post editing data annotated for errors in three language pairs (EN-DE, EN-LV, EN-HR) with the Multidimensional Quality Metrics (MQM). Methodologically, this contribution tests whether cross-language aligned word embeddings as the sole source of semantic information mirrors human error annotation.

1 Introduction

The most recent advances in artificial intelligence have brought substantial improvements to machine translation (MT). Systems based on artificial neural networks are able to produce more fluent and readable translations than most state-of-the-art phrase-based statistical (PBMT) and rule-based (RBMT) systems. The significant and highly promising advances notwithstanding, neural machine translation (NMT) still suffers from important shortcomings. Several lines of research address these shortcomings, most notably research on post-editing (PE) effort, on the evaluation and error annotation of NMT output and on (semi-)automated approaches to translation quality estimation.

Numerous studies in various language pairs and subject domains (see Section 2) have shown that NMT outperforms other types of MT in terms of fluency, while at the same time being more prone to adequacy errors such as omissions, additions or mistranslations. Adequacy errors are problematic from the perspective of the integration of NMT into translation workflows, because the identification and correction of adequacy errors is possible only by comparing NMT output to source segments, which arguably entails a higher cognitive load for post editors. Thus, participants in PE studies reported that NMT errors are more difficult to identify as compared other types of MT (Castilho et al. 2017). A phenomenon that is particularly difficult to handle for post editors and end users of NMT systems are *invisible* adequacy errors, first and foremost omissions in flawlessly fluent output that contains no traces of missing content, which means that they cannot be identified without the source text (van Brussel et al., 2018).

In view of these difficulties, the evaluation of semantic adequacy in NMT output and PE is indispensable to further advance the development of cutting-edge translation technology. Traditionally, the evaluation of MT output is performed by human annotators or post editors, but automated approaches have gained momentum as well (e.g. Moorkens et al., 2018; Specia et al., 2018). Semantic vector space models have become a cornerstone of present-day natural language processing (NLP) and as such, they play an important role in translation quality estimation, too. Cross-language embeddings trained in an unsupervised fashion (Artetxe, Labaka and Agirre, 2018; Joulin et al., 2018) are one of the most recent developments in distri-

Temnikova, I, Orăsan, C., Corpas Pastor, G., and Mitkov, R. (eds.) (2019) *Proceedings of the 2nd Workshop on Human-Informed Translation and Interpreting Technology (HiT-IT 2019)*, Varna, Bulgaria, September 5 - 6, pages 122–128.

https://doi.org/10.26615/issn.2683-0078.2019_015

butional semantics, holding the potential to improve the performance of numerous multilingual NLP tasks.

Against this background, the present paper explores to what extent cross-language aligned word embeddings can be used to inform semantic analysis in NMT output evaluation. More specifically, the correspondence between human adequacy judgments and automatically generated semantic similarity scores is assessed. The main goal is to investigate whether publicly available, pre-trained cross-language embeddings as the sole source of semantic information (i.e. used in isolation without any other resources or features that capture the semantic relation between source and target segments) are reliable estimators of translation adequacy. The analyses are performed at the sentence level for three language pairs: English-German (EN-DE), English-Latvian (EN-LV), and English-Croatian (EN-HR), using publicly available error-annotated NMT and PE datasets.

2 Related Work

A number of error analysis studies have shown that NMT is prone to adequacy errors, i.e. deficiencies with regard to the semantic transfer of content from the source to the target language. Castilho et al. (2017) compared NMT to statistical MT and observed increases in fluency but at the same time there were more errors of omission, addition and mistranslation. For instance, in NMT omission errors accounted for 37% of all errors found in 100 Chinese-to-English translation segments from the patent domain, thus being the most frequent of seven error types, while for PBMT omission errors accounted only for 8% of all errors. Similar results were observed for four other language pairs in the domain of MOOC translations. Van Brussel et al. (2018) also observed numerous omission errors (13.1% of all adequacy errors) in a comparative evaluation of 665 English sentences translated by NMT, PBMT and RBMT into Dutch. The majority of omissions in NMT (85.5%) were due to missing content words, while for PBMT and RBMT these ratios were 70.0% and 0.1% respectively. As a consequence, most omission errors in NMT (69%) are invisible, i.e. not indicated by flawed fluency, whereas in the other two MT types, annotators deemed only 23% and 7% of omissions to be invisible without source text comparisons. The study concludes that due to their frequency and often in-

visible nature, adequacy errors are a major challenge to NMT and its users. Finally, Klubička, Toral and Sánchez-Cartagena make similar observations for the EN-HR pair, concluding that "NMT tends to sacrifice completeness of translation in order to increase overall fluency" (2018, 209). All these reviewed studies employ manual human error annotation to assess the quality of MT output. From a more technical perspective, Tu et al. (2016) argue that NMT's tendency to produce over- or under-translation is because conventional systems do not maintain a coverage vector.

A complementary line of research is concerned with the automated estimation of MT output quality at run-time without the use of reference translations (Specia et al., 2018). Translation quality estimation usually requires (a certain amount) of supervision and thus human-annotated training data. Given this interdependence of human and automated approaches to quality estimation, the present contribution sets out to relate automatically generated semantic similarity scores at the sentence level with human error annotation.

3 Materials and Methods

3.1 Datasets

The analyses are based on three publicly available datasets that provide fine-grained error annotation of NMT output according to the Multidimensional Quality Metrics (MQM) framework (Lommel et al., 2014). For EN-DE and EN-LV, two datasets developed within the QT21 project (Specia et al., 2017) were used, each containing 1800 source sentences paired with the corresponding error-annotated NMT outputs and post-edited versions, 200 of which were annotated by two annotators. For EN-HR, the dataset by Klubička, Toral and Sánchez-Cartagena (2018) was used; it contains 100 source sentences together with error annotations of NMT output performed by two evaluators. Instead of post-edited target language versions, it contains human reference translations for 93 out of 100 source sentences.

From the original datasets, the raw text as well as error counts per sentence for each error type were extracted. Since the EN-HR dataset employs a customized, slightly extended version of the MQM error typology, the union of both typologies was used in this study. The two typologies are described in detail in Specia et al. (2017) and Klubička, Toral and Sánchez-Cartagena (2018).

For each dataset, only the annotations of the first evaluator were considered; however, to assess the quality of annotation, Cohen's kappa scores for inter-rater agreement on the annotation of omission errors were computed, indicating weak to moderate agreement. Summary statistics of the extracted data are shown in Table 1.

Pair	N	Tok	Errors			Kappa
			Tot	Flu	Acc	
EN-DE	1800	18.7	1.9	0.7	1.1	0.60
EN-LV	1800	22.2	1.9	0.9	1.0	0.52
EN-HR	93	20.5	1.4	0.8	0.4	0.39
Overall	3693	20.5	1.9	0.80	1.0	-

Table 1: Summary of datasets. Means are given for number of tokens and of total/fluency/adequacy errors per sentence. Cohen's kappa for agreement on omission annotation.

3.2 Cross-Language Aligned Word Embeddings

All sentences under investigation were represented as 300-dimensional word embedding vectors. To enable semantic analyses across source and target languages, pre-trained cross-language aligned *fastText*[1] word embeddings based on Wikipedia (Joulin et al., 2018) were used. In addition, for the EN-DE pair, custom cross-language aligned *fastText* embeddings we trained by aligning monolingual *fastText* Wikipedia embeddings[2] with the help of the *VecMap* toolkit[3] for cross-language word embedding mapping (Artetxe, Labaka and Agirre, 2018). For the mapping, the supervised mode of *VecMap* was used, based on the 5000-word EN-DE training dictionary from Artetxe, Labaka and Agirre (2018). Since both the pre-trained and custom embeddings are based on 300-dimensional *fastText* embeddings trained on Wikipedia, they are comparable irrespective of different mapping algorithms.

For each sentence in the dataset, the mean of the embeddings of each token in the sentence was calculated. The vector representations of the sentences in the datasets were built with the *flair* NLP library[4] implemented in Python (Akbik, Blythe and Vollgraf, 2018).

Subsequently, cosine similarity was computed between each source sentence and the following sentences:

(1) the corresponding NMT output;

(2) the corresponding PE target sentence (in the case of EN-DE and EN-LV) or the human reference translation (for EN-HR);

(3) a truncated copy of the NMT output, obtained by randomly removing 15% of its tokens;

(4) a truncated copy of the PE/reference translation sentence, obtained by randomly removing 15% of its tokens;

(5) two different sentences from the set of target sentences, randomly selected among the remaining target sentences in the given language (post-edited sentences for DE and LV, reference translation for HR);

(6) two different target language sentences, sampled from completely unrelated text collections: for DE and HR, sentences were sampled from the Universal Dependencies corpus (Nivre et al, 2016) included in the *flair* library, whereas for Latvian the *W2C* corpus[5] (Majliš and Žabokrtský, 2012) was taken as a source.

The inclusion of the sentences (3) to (6) was motivated by the need to test whether the combination of aligned word embeddings and cosine similarity adequately captures cross-linguistic similarity between sentences of varying degrees of semantic relatedness.

4 Results and Discussion

4.1 Similarity between Related vs. Unrelated Sentences

The comparison of similarity scores between source sentences and their machine-translated or post-edited equivalents on the one hand and randomly selected unrelated target sentences on the other provides insights into the general validity of the tested approach. The assumption is that the similarity between sentences in a translation relation – no matter whether machine-translated or post-edited – is higher than between unrelated pairs of source and target language sentences. What is more, it can be expected that among non-translated cross-lingual sentence pairs the similarity is higher when data is sampled from the same text collection,

---

[1] https://fasttext.cc/docs/en/aligned-vectors.html
[2] https://fasttext.cc/docs/en/pretrained-vectors.html
[3] https://github.com/artetxem/vecmap
[4] https://github.com/zalandoresearch/flair
[5] https://ufal.mff.cuni.cz/w2c

as opposed to data taken from a completely different corpus. Indeed, the results in Table 2 confirm this assumption, showing that the mean cosine similarity scores for translated source-target pairs (NMT and PE) are higher than for randomly aligned text pairs from the same dataset (MQM1, MQM2). The latter, in turn, are more similar to the source language sentences than sentence pairs obtained by assigning random sentences from unrelated corpora (X1, X2). The results are very similar for all three language pairs, suggesting the stability of cross-lingual word embeddings. It can also be seen that for EN-DE, the pre-trained and custom embeddings behave the same way, although the *VecMap*-aligned custom embeddings yield higher similarity scores. Both embedding types capture the differences between the semantically diverging sentences to the same extent.

Emb		NMT	PE	MQM1	MQM2	X1	X2
DE	pre	0.22	0.22	0.16	0.16	0.07	0.07
DE	cust	0.84	0.84	0.74	0.74	0.61	0.61
LV	pre	0.30	0.31	0.25	0.25	0.17	0.17
HR	pre	0.15	0.14	0.06	0.06	0.04	0.03

Table 3: Mean cosine similarity between source language sentences and the respective NMT and PE output, as well as randomly chosen target language sentences from the same corpus (MQM) and from different corpora (X). For DE, similarity scores were obtained from pre-trained (pre) and custom (cust) *fastText* embeddings.

4.2 Similarity between Closely-Related Sentences

To test whether the method is capable of detecting minor differences in meaning, NMT and PE outputs were juxtaposed with artificially truncated copies of these sentences by randomly removing 15% of tokens from the target sentences, not controlling for parts of speech, which means that punctuation may have been among the removed tokens. The truncation procedure is to simulate omissions in NMT output by creating semantically closely related sentences.

As shown in Table 3, the similarity scores between full vs. truncated sentences are almost identical, indicating that the method in isolation is not capable of capturing subtle semantic differences. Unlike the pre-trained embeddings, the *VecMap*-

Emb		NMT	NMT_Short	PE	PE_Short
DE	pre	0.22	0.22	0.22	0.22
DE	cust	0.84	0.82	0.84	0.82
LV	pre	0.30	0.30	0.31	0.30
HR	pre	0.15	0.14	0.14	0.14

Table 2: Mean cosine similarity between source language sentences and the respective NMT and PE output, as well as copies of target sentences randomly truncated by 15% of tokens (NMT_Short, PE_Short). Scores provided for pre-trained (pre) and custom (cust) *fastText* embeddings.

aligned embeddings do capture differences between full and truncated sentences, but the scores differ only marginally.

As shown in Table 3, the similarity scores between full vs. truncated sentences are almost identical, indicating that the method in isolation is not capable of capturing subtle semantic differences. Unlike the pre-trained embeddings, the *VecMap*-aligned embeddings do capture differences between full and truncated sentences, but the scores differ only marginally.

It would be insightful to test whether truncations by more than 15% yield different results, and whether the removal of content words has a different impact on similarity and adequacy than the removal of function words or punctuation tokens. Preliminary exploration suggested that truncations by 30% do result in lower similarity scores, albeit only to a moderate extent. This might be due to the part-of-speech-insensitive nature of the employed truncation procedure, as well as to the use of context-insensitive word embeddings, as opposed to contextualized embeddings, such as *ELMo* (Peters et al., 2018), *BERT* (Devlin et al., 2019) or *flair* (Akbik, Blythe and Vollgraf, 2018) embeddings. Systematic analyses of the impact of truncation on similarity scores are left for future work.

The (almost) nonexistent differences between full and truncated sentences further suggest limitations as to the detection of omissions or additions as one of the most relevant types of NMT adequacy errors. Table 3 also shows that no tangible differences between NMT and PE were detected by either embedding type. This issue is discussed in more detail in the following subsection.

4.3 Correspondence between Cosine Similarity Scores and Human Error Annotation

Any valid computational metric should mirror human ratings, irrespective the fact that agreement between human raters is not always unanimous, especially in cognitively and intellectually demanding tasks. In the context of MT evaluation, it can be assumed that output containing adequacy errors, as assessed by human annotators or post-editors, exhibits lower degrees of semantic similarity according to vector space models. However, this observation was not made in this study.

Table 4 relates cosine similarity to the presence or absence of certain errors in NMT output: the first group compares machine-translated sentences that, according to human annotators, are free of adequacy errors (the left column of each block, designated with F for 'false') with sentences that contain at least one adequacy error (the second column of each block, designated with T for 'true'). The mean cosine scores for this group do not reveal any differences for NMT sentences that do and do not contain adequacy errors. Similar results were obtained for NMT output with and without omission errors (second group), for NMT output that does and does not contain only adequacy errors (third group), as well as for output that does and does not contain only fluency errors (fourth group). This lack of observed differences holds for both types of cross-language aligned embeddings used in the analyses, as shown in Table 4.

It was also tested whether the absence or presence of other error types and combinations thereof (e.g. output that contains mistranslations but no fluency errors) have an influence on cosine similarity scores, but no important differences were observed. In sum, the results clearly show that when used in isolation without any other resources or features, aligned cross-language word embeddings are hardly helpful to inform cross-linguistic similarity judgments in cases of subtle adequacy deviations typical of NMT.

5 Conclusion

The measurement of cross-linguistic similarity is a highly complex problem with relevance not only to translation, but also, among other things, to semantic textual similarity (Agirre et al., 2016) or comparable and parallel corpus building (Sharoff, Rapp

Emb	Adq Err		Omission		Only Adq		Only Flu	
	F	T	F	T	F	T	F	T
DE pre	0.22	0.22	0.22	0.22	0.22	0.22	0.22	0.22
DE cust	0.84	0.84	0.84	0.84	0.84	0.83	0.84	0.84
LV pre	0.30	0.31	0.30	0.31	0.31	0.30	0.30	0.30
HR cust	0.16	0.14	0.15	0.14	0.15	0.15	0.15	0.14

Table 4: Mean cosine similarity between source language sentences and the respective NMT output, grouped according to the absence and presence of four error types. Scores shown for pre-trained (pre) and custom (cust) *fastText* embeddings.

and Zweigenbaum, 2013). Recent advances in embeddings-based vector space representations have brought significant advances to cross-linguistic semantic problems, which can be useful in the context of translation quality estimation and MT evaluation.

The present study attempted to explore the usefulness of cross-language aligned word embeddings in isolation, i.e. without further resources or features. In doing so, the correspondence of cosine similarity scores has been related to human similarity judgments of NMT output and PE. It was observed that cross-language embeddings used in isolation are only able to differentiate between sentences related by translation on the one hand and unrelated in-domain and out-of-domain sentences on the other, which means that the analysis of subtle adequacy issues frequently observed in NMT, such as omissions or additions, requires more elaborate approaches. The results from the EN-DE language pair suggest that it makes no difference whether pre-trained *fastText* or custom *VecMap*-aligned cross-language embeddings are used, because both types do not capture subtle semantic differences. Analogous comparisons for other language pairs may yield more insights into the comparability of different types of cross-language word embeddings.

The methodology employed in this study could be improved in several ways. On the one hand, the embeddings in this study were used without any parameter tuning. On the other hand, contextualized word embeddings, such as *ELMo* (Peters et al., 2018), *BERT* (Devlin et al., 2019) or *flair* (Akbik, Blythe and Vollgraf, 2018), which were shown to yield state-of-the-art results in several NLP tasks, could be used as an alternative to the context-insensitive embeddings used in this study. However, since the cross-language alignment of contextualized embeddings is a very recent and therefore still relatively unexplored line of research (e.g. Aldarmaki and Diab, 2019; Schuster et al., 2019), the use of contextualized cross-language aligned embeddings for the detection of subtle adequacy deviations is left for future work. A further potential improvement of the present methodology relates to the fact that in this study, sentences were represented as means of the embeddings of all words in the sentences. There are other approaches to compute sentence- or document-level embeddings from individual word embeddings (Chen, Ling and Zhu, 2018), and the *flair* library, for instance, implements various methods, such as minimum and maximum pooling or recurrent neural networks[6]. Similarly, there are alternatives to the traditionally used cosine similarity, for instance the word mover's distance (Kusner et al., 2015).

Given that monolingual embeddings are already being successfully employed in translation quality estimation (Specia et al., 2018), the unsupervised nature of cross-language embeddings may further promote this line of research. Yet, its application to translation quality estimation and error analysis requires more thorough benchmarking. This also means that human evaluation is still to be seen as pivotal to research into adequacy errors in NMT. Datasets that focus explicitly on omissions and additions might become an asset in this regard, since the datasets used in the present study are much wider in scope. While they do contain useful information about adequacy, complementary and more focused datasets might contribute to the development of new approaches to the automated detection of adequacy errors, including the problematic invisible omissions and additions.

Acknowledgments

I thank the four anonymous reviewers for their helpful comments.

References

Eneko Agirre, Carmen Banea, Daniel Cer, Mona Diab, Aitor Gonzalez-Agirre, Rada Mihalcea, German Rigau, and Janyce Wiebe. 2016. SemEval-2016 Task 1: Semantic Textual Similarity, Monolingual and Cross-Lingual Evaluation. In *Proceedings of SemEval 2016*. Association for Computational Linguistics, pages 497-511. http://dx.doi.org/10.18653/v1/S16-1081.

Alan Akbik, Duncan Blythe, and Roland Vollgraf. 2018. Contextual String Embeddings for Sequence Labeling. In *Proceedings of the 27th International Conference on Computational Linguistics*. Association for Computational Linguistics, pages 1638-1649. https://www.aclweb.org/anthology/C18-1139.

Hanan Aldarmaki and Mona Diab. 2019. Context-Aware Cross-Lingual Mapping. In *Proceedings of the 2019 Conference of the North American Chapter of the Association for Computational Linguistics: Human Language Technologies, Volume 1 (Long and Short Papers)*. Association for Computational Linguistics, pages 3906-3911. http://dx.doi.org/10.18653/v1/N19-1391.

Mikel Artetxe, Gorka Labaka, and Eneko Agirre. 2018. A robust self-learning method for fully unsupervised cross-lingual mappings of word embeddings. In *Proceedings of the 56th Annual Meeting of the Association for Computational Linguistics (Volume 1: Long Papers)*. Association for Computational Linguistics, pages 789–798. http://dx.doi.org/10.18653/v1/P18-1073.

Sheila Castilho, Joss Moorkens, Federico Gaspari, Iacer Calixto, John Tinsley, and Andy Way. 2017. Is Neural Machine Translation the New State of the Art? In *The Prague Bulletin of Mathematical Linguistics*, 108, pages 109–120. https://doi.org/10.1515/pralin-2017-0013.

Qian Chen, Zhen-Hua Ling, and Xiaodan Zhu. 2018. Enhancing Sentence Embedding with Generalized Pooling. In *Proceedings of the 27th International Conference on Computational Linguistics*. Association for Computational Linguistics, pages 1815-1826. https://www.aclweb.org/anthology/C18-1154.

Jacob Devlin, Ming-Wei Chang, Kenton Lee, and Kristina Toutanova. 2019. BERT: Pre-training of Deep Bidirectional Transformers for Language Understanding. In *Proceedings of the 2019 Conference of the North American Chapter of the Association for Computational Linguistics: Human Language Technologies, Volume 1 (Long and Short Papers)*. Association for Computational Linguistics, pages 4171-4186. http://dx.doi.org/10.18653/v1/N19-1423.

Armand Joulin, Piotr Bojanowski, Tomas Mikolov, Hervé Jégou, and Edouard Grave. 2018. Loss in Translation: Learning Bilingual Word Mapping with a Retrieval Criterion. In *Proceedings of the 2018

---

[6] https://github.com/zalandoresearch/flair/blob/master/resources/docs/TUTORIAL_5_DOCUMENT_EMBEDDINGS.md

Conference on Empirical Methods in Natural Language Processing. Association for Computational Linguistics, pages 2979-2984. http://dx.doi.org/10.18653/v1/D18-1330.

Filip Klubička, Antonio Toral, and Víctor M. Sánchez-Cartagena. 2018. Quantitative fine-grained human evaluation of machine translation systems: a case study on English to Croatian. In *Machine Translation,* 32, pages 195-2015. https://doi.org/10.1007/s10590-018-9214-x.

Matt J. Kusner, Yu Sun, Nicholas I. Kolkin, and Kilian Q. Weinberger. 2015. From Word Embeddings To Document Distances. In *Proceedings of the 32nd International Conference on Machine Learning. Lille, France, 2015. JMLR: W&CP volume 37.*

Arle Lommel, Hans Uszkoreit, and Aljoscha Burchardt. 2014. Multidimensional Quality Metrics (MQM): A Framework for Declaring and Describing Translation Quality Metrics. In *Revista Tradumàtica,* 12, pages 455-463. https://doi.org/10.5565/rev/tradumatica.77.

Martin Majliš and Zdeněk Žabokrtský. 2012. Language Richness of the Web. In *Proceedings of the Eighth International Conference on Language Resources and Evaluation (LREC-2012).* European Languages Resources Association (ELRA), pages 2927-2934. https://aclweb.org/anthology/papers/L/L12/L12-1110/.

Joss Moorkens, Sheila Castilho, Federico Gaspari, and Stephen Doherty (eds.). 2019. *Translation Quality Assessment. From Principles to Practice.* Cham: Springer. https://doi.org/10.1007/978-3-319-91241-7.

Joakim Nivre, Marie-Catherine de Marneffe, Filip Ginter, Yoav Goldberg, Jan Hajič, Christopher D. Manning, Ryan McDonald, Slav Petrov, Sampo Pyysalo, Natalia Silveira, Reut Tsarfaty, and Daniel Zeman. 2016. Universal Dependencies v1: A Multilingual Treebank Collection. In *Proceedings of the Tenth International Conference on Language Resources and Evaluation (LREC 2016).* European Language Resources Association (ELRA), pages 1659-1666. https://www.aclweb.org/anthology/L16-1262.

Matthew Peters, Mark Neumann, Mohit Iyyer, Matt Gardner, Christopher Clark, Kenton Lee, and Luke Zettlemoyer. 2018. Deep contextualized word representations. In *Proceedings of the 2018 Conference of the North American Chapter of the Association for Computational Linguistics: Human Language Technologies, Volume 1 (Long Papers).* Association for Computational Linguistics, pages 2227-2237. http://dx.doi.org/10.18653/v1/N18-1202.

Tal Schuster, Ori Ram, Regina Barzilay, and Amir Globerson. 2019. Cross-Lingual Alignment of Contextual Word Embeddings, with Applications to Zero-shot Dependency Parsing. In *Proceedings of the 2019 Conference of the North American Chapter of the Association for Computational Linguistics: Human Language Technologies, Volume 1 (Long and Short Papers).* Association for Computational Linguistics, pages 1599-1613. http://dx.doi.org/10.18653/v1/N19-1162.

Serge Sharoff, Reinhard Rapp, and Pierre Zweigenbaum. 2013. Overviewing Important Aspects of the Last Twenty Years of Research in Comparable Corpora. In S. Sharoff, R- Rapp, P. Zweigenbaum and P. Fung (eds.). *Building and Using Comparable Corpora.* Berlin, Heidelberg: Springer, pages 1-17. https://doi.org/10.1007/978-3-642-20128-8_1.

Lucia Specia, Kim Harris, Frédéric Blain, Aljoscha Burchardt, Vivien Macketanz, Inguna Skadiņa, Matteo Negri, and Marcho Turchi. 2017. Translation Quality and Productivity: A Study on Rich Morphology Languages. In *Proceedings of the 16th Machine Translation Summit (Volume 1: Research Track),* pages 55- 71.

Lucia Specia, Frédéric Blain, Varvara Logacheva, Ramón F. Astudillo, and André Martins. 2018. Findings of the WMT 2018 Shared Task on Quality Estimation. In *Proceedings of the Third Conference on Machine Translation (WMT), Volume 2: Shared Task Papers.* Association for Computational Linguistics, pages 689–709. http://dx.doi.org/10.18653/v1/W18-6451.

Zhaopeng Tu, Zhengdong Lu, Yang Liu, Xiaohua Liu, and Hang Li. 2016. Modeling Coverage for Neural Machine Translation. In *Proceedings of the 54th Annual Meeting of the Association for Computational Linguistics (Volume 1: Long Papers).* Association for Computational Linguistics, pages 76-85. http://dx.doi.org/10.18653/v1/P16-1008.

Laura Van Brussel, Arda Tezcan, and Lieve Macken. 2018. A Fine-grained Error Analysis of NMT, PBMT and RBMT Output for English-to-Dutch. In *Proceedings of the 11th International Conference on Language Resources and Evaluation, Miyazaki, Japan.* European Language Resources Association, pages 3799–3804. https://www.aclweb.org/anthology/L18-1600.

THE SUCCESS STORY OF MITRA TRANSLATIONS

Mina Ilieva[1], Mariya Kancheva[2]

[1] CEO at Mitra Translations,
[2] Lead Linguist at Mitra Translations,
[1]mki@mitra-bg.com
[2] mariya_kancheva@abv.bg

Mitra Translations was found back in 1989 as a small local translations business in Shumen, Bulgaria. The founder, Teodora Todorova, was then a teacher in Bulgarian language and literature and Russian as well. Her strong ambition about literature and languages motivated for establishing a business to serve people in their efforts to communicate and exchange knowledge in different languages. That time was historical for Eastern European countries and started to blow the so called "wind of change". That decade resulted in a huge migration, respectively it lead to the need of translation services. That was the first wave to the successful steps to go ahead. We remember the times of the hegemony of the typewriter and the revolution that came with computer popularization. Now, we are contemporaries of the software innovations, machine translation and the AI era, and we are eager to find out about what else the future has to offer.

Technologies and their constant updates and innovative nature drastically and irreversibly transformed this small business into a leading brand on the translation market, along with just few other LSPs integrating translation software solutions. Now, we are constantly following the new developments in software updates and online platforms and we are successfully keeping up with any new trend in the field of translation, localization, transcreation, revision, post-editing, etc. Nowadays, in Bulgaria 95% of the translation agencies have never heard of or integrated any CAT and MT tools, that is why we managed to get within the TOP 3 translation brands on the national market, because we choose to go the "hard" way. I am saying hard as there are still lots of colleagues and translators who believe that the use of technology is quite complicated and not so useful, also time and cost effective.

Introducing technologies into our everyday work brought a lot of benefits but it also made us face certain challenges. One of them was that the majority of the translators we worked with were not capable to operate or were not very confident in using the new platforms, software and web-based solutions. This was a crucial moment, a milestone which we realized would in fact give us a great advantage. This was the point when we started training our own in-house translators how to use the CAT tools and new software. We knew it from the beginning that if we wanted to succeed in the industry, we had to be ready to invest in technology and in our staff knowledge and skills. The strategy paid back really well. At the end we managed to both meet the expectations of our

Temnikova, I, Orăsan, C., Corpas Pastor, G., and Mitkov, R. (eds.) (2019) *Proceedings of the 2nd Workshop on Human-Informed Translation and Interpreting Technology (HiT-IT 2019)*, Varna, Bulgaria, September 5 - 6, pages 129–133.

https://doi.org/10.26615/issn.2683-0078.2019_016

international clients and build a competent bank of translation professionals. Basically, we provide training for our in-house translators in using CAT tools by introducing simulations and real time projects. In addition translators find webinars a useful and easy way to maintain their CAT and MT tools knowledge. They have also shared with us that while following innovations they felt well-qualified and competitive among their fellow professionals. Later on, when our trained in-house resource started working for us on a freelance base, it was easier than ever to engage competent vendors for our increasing number of projects. Today, we rely on 10 qualified in-house translators and 200+ freelance translators which add up for covering the total demand regarding all EU and Asian languages. Furthermore, we did presentations at universities in Bulgaria to make students familiar with the idea of "contemporary profession of translator" focusing on technologies and how to make use of them. It felt almost like a mission. This encouraged us to eventually devote further efforts into a training programme. In 2016 we participated in the EU Operative Programme for Human Resource Development. As part of that project we trained quite a lot of students from a few universities in Bulgaria and received positive feedback for our endeavors to bridge the gap between university and business. Students showed immediate progress and passion for new technologies. We would say that along with universities, today, we are more than certain that young professional who choose the translator's career need our support as well in bringing their work to the next level.

On the one hand we experience the problem with the shortage of qualified translators ready to work with translation technologies and on the other hand there is the problem with the shortage of qualified trainers as part of the reality in Bulgaria. The only authorized reseller of SDL Trados offers a "getting started" version of training after paying for a license. Evidently there are not enough trainers, either in practice or theory, to prepare qualified translators to use translation tools and software; and SDL Trados surely is not the only CAT tool the industry happens to require. Many believe that getting the hack of SDL Studio will be enough to use the other tools and platforms. This could be somewhat true due to the fact that the operation logic of two or more types of translation software can be similar. However we have heard some translators say that apart from Trados they were not able to "understand" or be confident with using other CAT tools. Yet another problem is that in general freelancers are not eager to pay license fees, they would not invest their time in additional training, and quite naturally they are reluctant to pay for more than one software.

The translation industry in Bulgaria lacks trained professionals in the field of DTP as well. We faced this problem in 2012 while working for a large translation project regarding huge power plant instructions for use. The translated files were ready, however the only two DTP service providers, who just to mention worked at advertising companies, offered a relatively high price for the pace of 4 pages per day. Deadline was pressuring us and we were forced to seek DTP providers based in China who luckily managed to do the task cheaper, for 10% of the price quoted in Bulgaria, and more efficiently, processing 4 pages per hour. We believe that training in the translation industry should be thought as intended industry strategy rather than existing as individual instances among companies.

Our experience at a global level confirmed that professionalism speaks a universal language. Deadlines, budget and quality are equally important to stand out from business competitors. Once again technology helps fulfill these pre-conditions and presents greater opportunities for expanding our client network. Usually each project requires the use of different tools as well as certain clients prefer project delivery in a given platform, software or format. Diversification of CAT and MT tools and web-based solutions for translation and QA is yet another demand for the business. The specialized software and programme mainly used within the company are SDL Trados Studio 2019, SDL Trados GroupShare 2015, MemoQ (cloud based server option), xtm, Translation Workspace, Wordfast, Memsource, etc. As seen from the pie chart below, SDL Trados Studio has the largest share among the four most used softwares at our company. The tendency has remained unchanged during the years with prevalence of SDL Studio, followed by MemoQ, and Wordfast and Translation Workspace with an almost equal share.

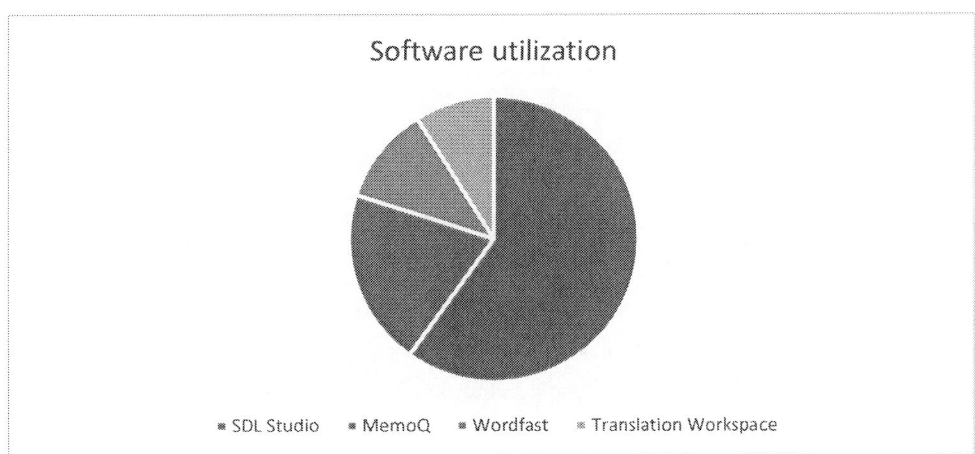

Fig. 1. Types of software utilization at Mitra Translations

Our analysis leads to the conclusion that this spread is due primarily to clients' preferences and requirements. Popularity of SDL Trados Studio among vendors might also come from the good promotion of the software in Bulgaria and the user-friendly interface. Updates are readily available almost every year and new features are added to accelerate and ease translators' work. However, since time is of great significance we must be ready to operate with any software/ online tool in advance.

Project management is another aspect of our workflow which benefits from technology implementation. File analysis and project management were also assisted by web-based TMS and CAT tools we use. The entire project workflow became more clear and structured, while time was reduced to a minimum. Figure 2 shows a breakdown of one of our projects which includes 101 files. As evident from the figure, 48.2% from the total wordcount (86,453) are repetitions, and 13.5% represent cross-file repetitions. Back in the days with no CAT tools utilization it would have taken much more time to complete this job, and consistency would probably suffer. However, again, project managers get trained internally at our company.

21	Totals							
22	Total	Type	Segments	Words	Characters	Percent	Recognized Tokens	Tags
23	Files:101	PerfectMatch	0	0	0	0.00%	0	0
24	Chars/Word:4.61	Context Match	0	0	0	0.00%	0	0
25		Repetitions	7967	41683	179009	48.21%	8379	0
26		Cross-file Repetitions	4906	11700	48249	13.53%	2902	0
27		100%	0	0	0	0.00%	0	0
28		95% - 99%	0	0	0	0.00%	0	0
29		85% - 94%	0	0	0	0.00%	0	0
30		75% - 84%	0	0	0	0.00%	0	0
31		50% - 74%	0	0	0	0.00%	0	0
32		New	9110	33070	171393	38.25%	5098	0
33		Total	21983	86453	398651	100%	16379	0

Fig. 2. File analysis, SDL Trados Studio 2017

Eventually our business analyses show that after integrating CAT tools in our translation and project management process our productivity increased to more than 50%. Mitra's experiences show that CAT tools cut the time devoted to the whole output and made translation up to 50% faster and therefore more time-efficient, moved translators' work from typing to actual translating which accelerated the translation process. The cost for the end client decreased because now we can use file analyses and automatically and precisely count repetitions, fuzzy matches and no match entries which are paid at different rates. These benefits along with the fact that international LSPs seek company vendors who are able to meet their requirements in terms of translation technology utilization, they all logically lead to better business results with Mitra increasing with 10% sales growth every year for the past few years.

As far as quality is concerned we try to incorporate any relevant QA check feature of the translation tools at our company. It saves hours of review time and boosts productivity. However, we could not help but notice that sometimes more than one QA tool should be used to eliminate certain errors. If for an identical bilingual translation file an LTB report and an SDL QA check are run, the user may find stunning discrepancies in the number and nature of reported errors and mistakes. It often helps to run for example two QA tools, however this is extremely time consuming for large texts and means extra work which goes beyond client's expectations, requirements and expenses.

Training translators and project managers, the variety of programmes which we had to introduce into our work due to business demand, and the need of applying multiple QA tools in order to get a "clean" QA report have so far been some of the challenging points related to technology implementation in our success story.

Ultimately, we are positive that proper implementation of technology (with focus on quality, cost and time) and hard work are the stepping stones in the way to become a trusted language service provider.

The four stages of machine translation acceptance in a freelancer's life

Maria Sgourou (m.sgourou@hotmail.com)

At the beginning of my career some 20 years ago, the reality of a translator was that having too many translation projects delivered per month would earn them a good living. That was true then and it is true now. The only difference is that back then one would have to translate copiously, word after word, to get the job done, while now the job is done with the help of technology which can speed up and streamline the process.

The first step to the "technologization" of the profession was the emergence of Computer Assisted Tools (CATs). I clearly remember that I did not like much the new development because I thought it would disrupt my routine and take me out of my comfort zone. It's thus fair to say that I was not very fond of technology back then. Little did I know that CATs would become my best friends. Luckily, a colleague introduced me to CATs early on and I did not miss the opportunity to take my job to the next level at a time when most translators got stuck in the translation vs technology debate. Ever since then, I never looked back; in fact, I became a technology "follower" since I could clearly see that it was helping me become more productive and thus earn more, but also have a better work-life balance.

When Machine Translation (MT) came along, I remember having the same reaction as I had with CATs. Probably even worse. I really saw an enemy there and for quite some time I refused to take it seriously.

Once again, though, I was lucky, because I met some extraordinary people who had been long involved in language technology and who helped me understand its power and the innumerable opportunities that it brought about. I thus became an early adopter.

Nowadays, I regularly use MT in my everyday work; my output is doubled and in many cases tripled, and I feel exactly as I used to after I regularly used CATs in the past.

Unfortunately, most translators are not like me. On the contrary, they still approach language technology with caution or even fear. Mainly because they don't understand it. I came to this conclusion following several surveys that I carried out on different occasions about the relationship between translators and technology. More specifically, a survey aiming to understand the use of CATs and MT by translators was carried out in Greece in 2018 and the responses revealed that age is definitely an issue when it comes to the use of technology. Neither younger colleagues nor the most experienced ones seem to use technology. The most striking feature that came out from those surveys, however, is that it is extremely difficult to establish a "freelance translator persona" due to different academic backgrounds, fields of study, experience in other sectors as well as mere demographics.

Surveys have served as a basis to observe the behavior of translators towards technology and led me to identify four stages to the acceptance of translation technology:

Stage 1

Nescience: I don't know about it therefore it does not exist

Stage 2

Contempt: I loathe it and/or make fun of it; machine translation is stealing my job

Temnikova, I, Orăsan, C., Corpas Pastor, G., and Mitkov, R. (eds.) (2019) *Proceedings of the 2nd Workshop on Human-Informed Translation and Interpreting Technology (HiT-IT 2019)*, Varna, Bulgaria, September 5 - 6, pages 134–135.

https://doi.org/10.26615/issn.2683-0078.2019_017

Stage 3

Reluctant adoption and shame: I secretly use it

Stage 4

Acceptance: I get to know it and use it; it changes my professional perspective I wonder why it took me so long.

This conclusion is particularly important for several reasons. If MT developers wish to render their products marketable and widely accepted not only by LSPs, but also by the greater translation community, they need to take these stages into account and help translators move from one stage to the next more quickly and more smoothly. In addition, knowledge of these stages is particularly important for the training of translators and their continuous professional development.

Optimising the Machine Translation Post-editing Workflow

Anna Zaretskaya

TransPerfect

As most large LSPs today, TransPerfect offers a variety of services based on machine translation (MT), including raw MT for casual low-cost translation, and different levels of MT post-editing (MTPE). The volume of translations performed with MTPE in the company has been growing since 2016 and continues to grow to this date (Figure 1, the numbers on the Y axis have been omitted as commercially sensitive information), which means tens of millions of words post-edited each month. In order to implement MT at such a large scale, the process has to be as easy as possible for the users (Project Managers and translators), with minimal or no additional steps in the

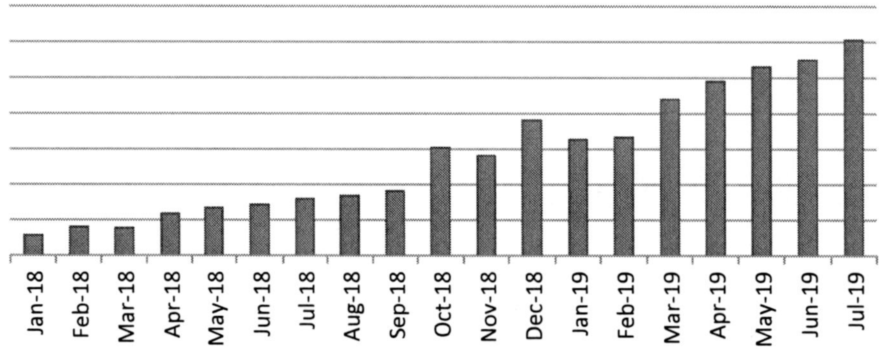

workflow.

Figure 1. Volume of MT post-editing TransPerfect

In our case, MT is integrated in our translation management system, which makes it very easy to make the switch from purely human translation workflow to the post-editing workflow (Figure 2). In this article we will share the methods we used to optimise the workflows when implementing MT, covering both the technical aspects and the processes involved.

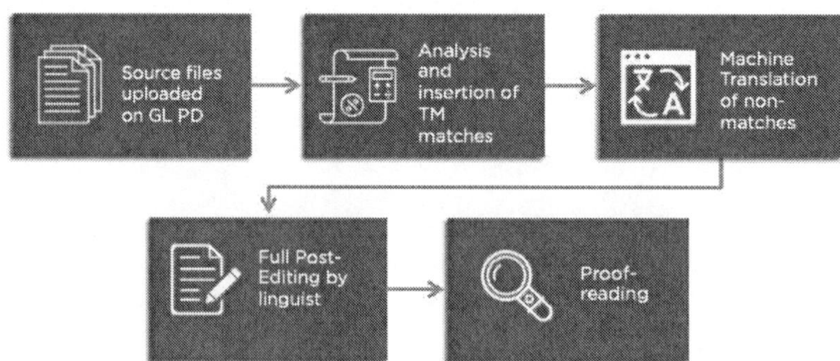

Figure 2. Standard MTPE workflow.

Temnikova, I, Orăsan, C., Corpas Pastor, G., and Mitkov, R. (eds.) (2019) *Proceedings of the 2nd Workshop on Human-Informed Translation and Interpreting Technology (HiT-IT 2019)*, Varna, Bulgaria, September 5 - 6, pages 136–139.
https://doi.org/10.26615/issn.2683-0078.2019_018

1. Machine Translation Systems

TransPerfect's MT systems use state-of-the-art neural technology and include a variety of off-the-shelf trained MT engines that we can choose from for any given project, including both generic systems and domain-specific ones. We also have access to a number of third-party MT services via APIs. Our approach consists in choosing the best possible solution and we are not limited only to proprietary systems.

Apart from generic and domain-specific MT engines we recommend customising the systems with the data specific to the content that will be translated. A typical use case is customisation for a specific client, where a generic model is *incrementally trained* using the client's Translation Memory. Engine customisation can yield improvement in the output quality of more than 20% compared to the baseline, but this is conditioned by the amount of data and the quality of this data. We have conducted several case studies, in which we explored how MT quality increases when adding more volume to the customisation data set (results of one of of these studies are summarized in Figure 3). We have found that, on average, a noticeable difference in quality is observed with incremental training with additional 50 000 translation units (TUs) in the data set, but it can differ based on the initial quality of the engine and the quality of the data. This number seems to be independent of the initial training data size of the base model, but rather to depend on the initial quality, however, this has to be confirmed by conducting more experiments.

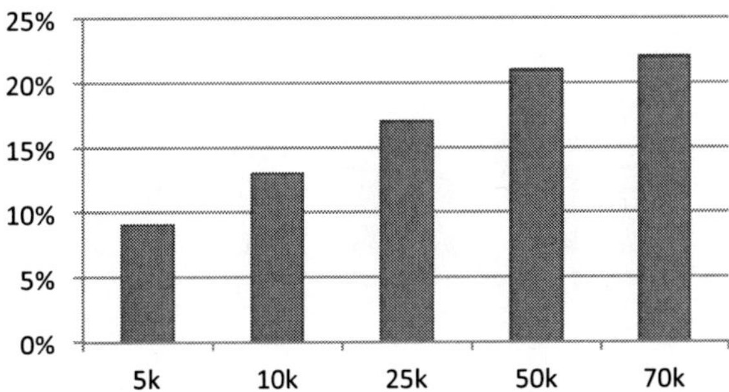

Figure 3. Case study: improvement over baseline MT quality with incremental training depending on the size of the training data set (in TUs).

After our MT systems are deployed in production they are improved over time. First of all, we collect feedback from the linguists who work on post-editing. They use a simple web interface to report frequent MT errors, which are then fixed using glossary enforcement techniques or pre- and post-processing rules. In addition, all the edits to the MT output are registered and used for engine improvement.

2. Linguist Experts

Providing training and support to our linguists is at least as important as the MT technology itself. We consider MTPE as a separate service, along with translation, subtitling, interpreting, and others, and we have established a special certification process for this service. In this process, linguists go through a training programme, which includes theoretical and practical aspects of post-editing. The training should prepare the linguists to perform post-editing efficiently while providing the quality expected by our clients. It includes practical tips on how to quickly decide whether a segment is eligible for post-editing, identify MT errors that are specifically difficult to see (these include missing negation, wrong numbers, mistranslations, among others), how to take advantage of their translation environment to be faster during post-editing, and how to make sure to deliver the desired quality of the final translation. This way we make sure that our linguists are comfortable with the task and have the right knowledge to use MTPE to their own benefit. Currently we have about 3500 linguists in our database who are certified for MTPE, which is more than a half of all our active linguists.

3. MT Evaluation

Evaluation of MT quality is performed on different stages of the workflow, it is necessary to decide where MT is suitable for a specific type of documents, and which MT engine is the best to use in each case. In MTPE projects, we use the post-editing distance (PED) as the main method of evaluation, as it measures the editing effort required. Tracking and storing the PED on a project level allows us know the amount of changes made in a specific job and confirm that we have paid the linguist accordingly. In addition, it allows us to track the performance of a specific MT engine over time, compare the PED in different languages, compare how much editing different post-editors do in the same project, and estimate how well a specific engine will perform on a specific content type by looking at the relevant historical data. Currently, the average PED of all projects is 22.21% and in one year it has decreased by almost 6%, which means that the overall quality of our MT systems is improving over time (Figure 4).

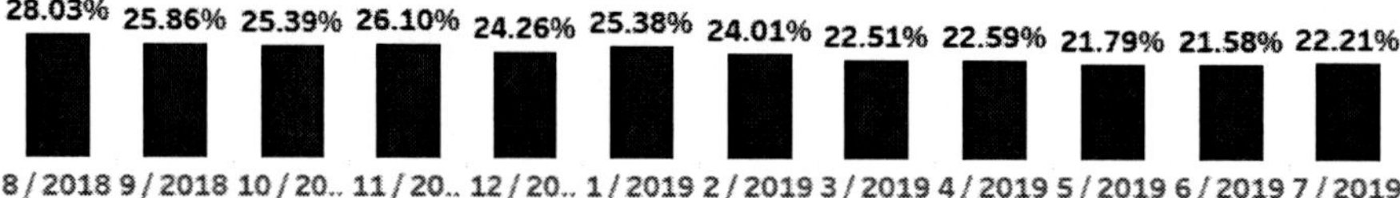

Figure 4. Average PED in the last 12 months.

4. Combining TM Matches with MT

The MT performance is crucial to the success of MT implementation but it is not the only requirement. It has to be used in combination with other tools and resources in the most efficient way. Typically, MT is applied on "low fuzzies", i.e. segments where the translation memory (TM) leverage score is lower than 75%. With the progressive improvement of the MT quality, however, the 75% threshold is being reconsidered, i.e. in many cases MT output is better than fuzzy matches. Our solution consists in comparing the average PED for MT suggestions with the average PED for TM matches and adjust the threshold as needed on an account level.

We have conducted multiple case studies on this topic, and one of the studies showed that for the specific account and language in question, MT requires less editing then almost any type of TM matches (including even 95%-99% matches). Table 1 shows the different TM match ranges and how the PED compares for MT and TM.

TM range	PED-MT	PED-TM
75-97%	15%	40%
80-84%	18%	35%
85-89%	17%	31%
90-94%	23%	21%
95-99%	*7%*	*16%*

Table 1. Comparison between the editing effort (PED) from machine translation (PED-MT) and TM matches (PED-TM) in a case study with English into Chinese translations.

5. What Have We Learnt?

One of the biggest lessons we have learnt is that MT is not a solution to all problems. On its own, it will make little difference in optimizing the translation workflow if it involves complex manual steps. It can help translators increase their productivity, but this is only one step in the workflow. Our goal to provide the best translation services to our clients in the most efficient way drives the need for automation of all the steps in the process that can be optimized. Automating certain processes can save as much time or more as an excellent machine translation system.

Another important component of success is training and support for all the people involved. Even at this advanced stage of implementing MT, it implies a change for many of our linguists and project managers, so we have to make sure that they are fully aware of all the processed and have all the knowledge needed to perform their task. We constantly work with all the roles involved (linguists, project managers, account managers, etc) by providing proactive training, answering requests, updating materials and making them easily accessible. Technology is only a tool to be used by people, and without the people its full potential will not be used.

Finally, properly using and collecting data is essential. By collecting information on how MT is used we can optimise many aspects of the process. Data on the PED and the time linguists take to post-edit can help us with MT quality evaluation, estimation of the translation budget, selection of the best MT engine, adjusting the TM match threshold any many more.

6. What next?

Our current work in progress includes automatic MT quality estimation (QE) on a document and on a segment level. On a document level, it will allow us to easily decide if the content in question is suitable for MT, and choose the best MT engine. On a segment level, it will allow us show the post-editor only the most useful segments, show the estimated quality score and know exactly where it is better to use the MT suggestion, the TM match, or start translating the segment from scratch.

Another development we are working on is Predictive MT, a predictive typing tool integrated with neural MT technology, which will allow the post-editors to see the MT suggestions that are being adjusted as they type.

Author Index

Association for Computational Linguistics
209 N. Eighth Street
Stroudsburg, Pennsylvania 18360

ISBN 978-1-7138-0299-0